T0333964

International Entrepreneurship

This book explores the importance of entrepreneurs in driving economic growth as the world economy grows and becomes more integrated and more challenging. It examines the situation in both advanced and developing countries and shows how the entrepreneurial orientation of the founders of small and medium sized enterprises has resulted in phenomenal growth, often fuelled by innovation and new technology. It contrasts the experiences of Chinese family business in China and among the overseas Chinese with the experiences of family businesses in the United States and Europe. One important conclusion is that there has been a noticeable fall in entrepreneurial proclivity in the advanced economies, in contrast to the position in emerging economies.

Susan Freeman is Professor of International Business at the University of South Australia Business School, Adelaide, Australia.

Ying Zhu is Associate Director of the Australia Centre for Asian Business at the University of South Australia, Adelaide, Australia.

Malcolm Warner was Professor and Fellow Emeritus of Wolfson College and the Cambridge Judge Business School, University of Cambridge, Cambridge, UK.

Routledge Studies in the Growth Economies of Asia

International Entrepreneurship

A Comparative Analysis

**Susan Freeman, Zhu Ying
and Malcolm Warner**

Routledge
Taylor & Francis Group

LONDON AND NEW YORK

First published 2020
by Routledge
2 Park Square, Milton Park, Abingdon, Oxon OX14 4RN

and by Routledge
605 Third Avenue, New York, NY 10017

First issued in paperback 2022

Routledge is an imprint of the Taylor & Francis Group, an informa business

British Library Cataloguing-in-Publication Data
A catalogue record for this book is available from the British Library

Library of Congress Cataloging-in-Publication Data
A catalog record has been requested for this book

ISBN: 978-0-367-49155-0 (pbk)
ISBN: 978-0-815-36337-8 (hbk)
ISBN: 978-1-351-10967-3 (ebk)

DOI: 10.4324/9781351109673

Typeset in Times New Roman
by Wearset Ltd, Boldon, Tyne and Wear

This book is dedicated to our dear colleague, mentor and friend who sadly passed away during the writing of our book. Malcolm Warner

Contents

1 Introduction

The origins of entrepreneurship and internationalization

Introduction

In this book, we make a quantum leap from the past to the present in considering entrepreneurship. Doing so is rather an act of faith, since we can never be certain there is a linear connection between two points in time. Entrepreneurship is a rather slippery notion, as it has very many dimensions and has been converted across time and space, and between different cultures. Early achievers may have had some characteristics in common with those of today but the connection is very tenuous. Proto-entrepreneurs acted in an early, simple and straightforward way but their counterparts today in the Silicon Valley or in the Chinese Zhongguancun, Haidian, area in Beijing are a very different creation.

The self-dependent entrepreneur usually is a one-man band or operates in a small company. The survival rate is very poor and even today one in three American small businesses fail within a few years. The emergence of early multinationals, such as the East India Company, are said by some to be a model for the modern Multinational Corporation (MNC). In terms of multinationals, size matters, particularly for international trade. The economies of scale also dominate the economies of entrepreneurship. Today, scale is everything as a new technological innovation needs substantial capital investment. The new unicorn billion dollar firms are the order of the day. The Stone Age entrepreneur was a very different person from the promoter and chief executive of say, Google or Baidu. It is rather remarkable that we had to wait until the end of the eighteenth century to have a precise conceptualization and definition of what is an 'entrepreneur'. Even today, pinpointing the definition of an entrepreneur, entrepreneurship and an entrepreneurial organization remains problematic. What we include within a Venn diagram clearly rests on so-called family resemblances and, indeed, fuzzy categories.

In order to resolve some of the above issues, we need to have a general contingency theory that can encapsulate these differences in time, space and culture. The extensive literature on the subject today is rather repetitive and unoriginal. Hence, this book offers new research and thoughts on the direction for the all-important aspects of International Entrepreneurship as well as the important characteristics and nature of the immigrant entrepreneur from *these* markets. By tackling the key questions related to '*what, who and why' regarding the causes, patterns/models, and processes of internationalisation of entrepreneurship* among different entrepreneurial groups with different cultural and ethnical backgrounds, we expect that there will be new findings that show distinct differences among emerging and advanced markets and between entrepreneurs across selected emerging markets given their socio-political backgrounds and historic pathways.

The origins of entrepreneurship

The origins of entrepreneurship are as diverse as they are as ancient. We continue to know very little about entrepreneurs despite the remarkable interest and numerous publications on the topic (Cunningham & Lischeron, 1991). Some suggest that the first entrepreneurs go far back in time and can be traced back to around 20,000 years ago. The first known trading between humans took place in New Guinea and Australasia around 17000 BC, where people would exchange obsidian (a volcanic glass valuable in hunting weapons) for other goods they needed, such as tools, skins and food. This early proto-entrepreneurship continued for millennia. Hunter-gatherer tribes traded goods from different parts of their regions to offer overall benefits for their tribes. Even in the Bible, there are several passages in which the term 'Canaanite' is employed interchangeably with the words for 'trader' and 'merchant,' suggestive of the idea of entrepreneur (Davies, 1994; Briard, 2001; Demoule, 2007).

A major development in entrepreneurship took place during the Agricultural Revolution, about 12,000 years ago. This was a time where there were no borders for traders and trade brought the possibility of great material wealth and new knowledge. A number of script systems emerged, such as 'foreign' languages (e.g. such as names of exotic artefacts), and expertise in technologies was also developed by traders, bringing with them many new ideas. Concepts, ideas and languages travelled as ballast embodied in traded items, or "in the minds of envoys, merchants, and craftsmen – as an intellectual stowaway" (Wedde, 1997: 45). While raw materials began to travel through Europe during the Upper Palaeolithic period (35000–10000 BC), the first known evidence for trade and barter appeared later in the Neolithic period (8000–2200 BC) and onwards (Davies, 1994; Briard, 2001; Demoule, 2007).

The birth of agriculture during the Neolithic period drove bartering practices. Initially, people exchanged mainly livestock, grain and pottery. The use of money as a common practice was to develop later. In Europe, the Neolithic period saw the introduction of tools that were designed essentially for exchange, such as the Grand Pressigny flint blades in France, some of which were found as far as 800 km away from their place of origin. A similar phenomenon was observed in the thousands of polished-axes made in Plussulien (France) and traded hundreds of kilometres away, some reaching England (Demoule, 2007). In China, cowrie shells were used as an early form of currency in the equivalent Neolithic area. The rarity of the shells ensured their value, with imitations found in many archaeological sites made from jade, stone, bone, earthenware, gold, tin and bronze. Interestingly, this type of shell was also used in Oceania, Africa and in the Middle and Far East. Its value varied depending on the distance travelled to find it. Extraordinarily, it is still used today as a currency in Ethiopia and other remote regions in Africa (Davies, 1994).

The importance of the 'entrepreneur' in early economic discourse

Remarkably, the word 'entrepreneur' was not part of the English language until it drifted from its French origins into various writings, treatises and letters within the English and American communities of economics scholars in the mid-1770s to 1870s. The word was entirely silent during the first century of the classical era until *The Wealth of Nations* by Adam Smith in 1776 but has had considerable impact on economic concepts that have been formulated since. This silence suggests that the factors of production, namely, the inputs used to produce goods and services, were seen as limited to three important elements – land, labour and capital, which Mankiw (1997) eloquently describes in his *Principles of Economics*. The term 'entrepreneur' is also not included or mentioned in the first edition of Samuelson's *Economics* published in 1948. While no doubt, both authors would have considered the importance of entrepreneurial activities, that role was simply not mentioned in the discourse on economic theory at the time. It was not until the 1930s that the word was used by Schumpeter (1934). Today it is in common usage and linked to the idea of innovation. Is it not curious, that the notion of an entrepreneur, the very factor that organizes a business and is responsible for its success or otherwise, lacks a common term in the English language to encapsulate this important risk-taking function in which an individual makes a living by making a profit through the running of a business? (Kates, 2015).

In conducting our own initial analysis, we look first at the occurrence of terms relating to 'entrepreneur' in a number of search engines [in March 2018], such as Google and Google Scholar. We then study the frequency of the term's appearance in Google Books. The methodology used in this analysis of the role of entrepreneurs in Google Books is highly novel, we would argue, at least as applied to Economic Ideas. We look at how often key terms relating to entrepreneurs appear in books in English and are graphically depicted in Google Books regarding these terms being used over the last three centuries, which we discuss and present as comparative charts below. We also suggest that Google Books may achieve wider diffusion through translations into many languages but this is rarer for journal articles.

Google Search and Google Scholar

In Table 1.1, we set out the respective scores in Google Search and Google Scholar for the words entrepreneur, entrepreneurial and entrepreneurship. We can see these occur in English in very large numbers.

Table 1.1 Google Search analysis of key terms, entrepreneur, entrepreneurship and entrepreneurial, number of entries [16 March 2018]

	Google Search	*Google Scholar*
Entrepreneur	70,000,000	890,000
Entrepreneurship	68,500,000	1,430,000
Entrepreneurial	42,900,000	1,330,000

Table 1.2 Google Search analysis of key terms, entrepreneur, inventor and innovator, number of entries [16 March 2018]

	Google Search	*Google Scholar*
Entrepreneur	70,000,000	890,000
Inventor	22,000,000	2,860,000
Innovator	11,600,000	192,000

Table 1.3 Google Search analysis of key terms, entrepreneur, international business and multinationals, number of entries [16 March 2018]

	Google Search	*Google Scholar*
Entrepreneur	70,000,000	890,000
Intl Business	15,000,000	3,040,000
Multinationals	42,800,000	256,000

In Table 1.2, we set out the scores in Google Search and Google Scholar for the terms, entrepreneur, inventor and innovator, to show their relative numbers.

In Table 1.3, we look at the respective scores in Google Search and Google Scholar for the terms entrepreneur, international business and multinationals.

Google Books

The Google Books results are derived from the field of Computational Linguistics and are based on the Google Books N-gram Corpus of terms in its initial phase of over five million books, apparently involving around 6 per cent of all those ever published from 1500-onwards; as presented here, these range from 1700 to 2000 only. The original pioneering paper by J. B. Michel et al. (2011) was to launch this new field, which researchers dubbed Culturomics (see Michel et al., 2011).

Google initially digitalized the contents of this set of published books employing optical character-recognition (OCR) technology. The contents was then compiled into a dataset that could be searched at the level of single words/ characters, with the search results plotted on a chart, year by year, a technique we apply later. When a search enters key examples of these topics into the free online search engine, namely, the Google Books N-gram Viewer, which is a text-visualization tool, a graph is shown presenting how frequently those terms or N-grams have occurred over a timeline in a given corpus of books (for example, from English, British–English, American–English and so on) over the selected years.

To use the Viewer, the researcher picks (1) a time period (the study presented here chose 1700–2000); (2) a language (we selected English as a catch-all; (3) a smoothing curve (we used factor-10 because this presented the curve more vividly than a lower one); and, then (4) enters one or more terms sought (we selected entrepreneur, for example). The vertical y-axis on the graph produced shows the relative frequency in percentage, of the terms being researched, over the time-period examined, which is indicated on the horizontal x-axis in terms of years. As a result of this mapping, one can find the percentage of all published works in the corpus of books digitalized in which the phrase sought appears for the period concerned.

Using the data from the Google project, we have concentrated on data derived from influential Google Books as the focus of the study, since these may be seen as the main iconic vehicles for the spread of new ideas, from the Enlightenment onwards, with a higher symbolic status than others. Google Books on economic, management and sociological ideas may be said to have played an especially privileged role in the creation of global intellectual reputations in this particular field of study for the authors we studied, as opposed to articles. The search encompassed the entire corpus of books digitalized by Google Books and was not just restricted to books on entrepreneurs.

In Figure 1.1 below, we create the N-gram graphic for the terms entrepreneur, entrepreneurial and entrepreneurship, as they have occurred in books over the last three centuries. The first term starts to take off in the late nineteenth century and continues rising in the twentieth century. The second starts to rise very rapidly after 1920 and the third ascends at the same time but more slowly, both reaching their peak in the year 2000.

In Figure 1.2 below, we present the N-gram graphic for the terms entrepreneur, inventor and innovator and here we can see how the term inventor overperforms most of the time *vis á vis* entrepreneur, whilst innovator underperforms. Inventor reaches a peak in the year 1940, entrepreneur in the year 2000 and innovator around 1970.

In Figure 1.3 below, we look the N-gram graphic for the terms entrepreneur, capitalist and trader. Entrepreneur reaches a peak in the year 2000, capitalist in 1980 and trader in 1930. Capitalist appears to be a more generic term.

In Figure 1.4 below, we show the N-gram graphic for the terms capitalist, entrepreneur and manager. Each of the terms has a lineage going back to 1700. Entrepreneur reaches a peak in the year 2000, capitalist in 1980 and manager in 2000. Entrepreneur is relatively subordinate to the other two in the graph.

In Figure 1.5 below, we look at the N-gram graphic for entrepreneur and IB, as well as E + IB. The curves start to take off around 1860. All curves peak around the year 2000.

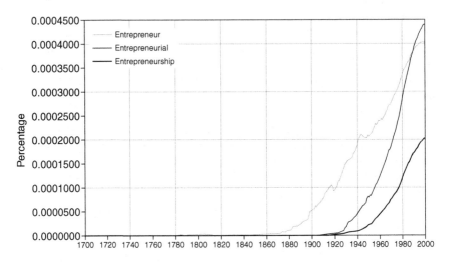

Figure 1.1 N-gram graphic for entrepreneur, entrepreneurial and entrepreneurship.

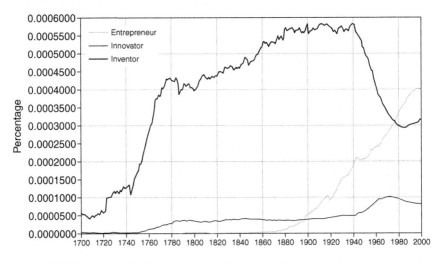

Figure 1.2 N-gram graphic for entrepreneur, inventor and innovator.

In Figure 1.6 below, we look at the N-gram graphic for entrepreneur, IB and multinationals. The first two terms take off around 1860 and the last peak much later around 1960. Entrepreneur peaks in the year 2000, IB also in 2000 and multinationals around 1990.

Returning to our discussion, the word 'entrepreneur' is French in origin, and dates back to its use by Cantillion, in an article published in 1734. Jean-Baptiste Say used the term at the time in his definitive *Traité* (essay), published in 1803 and considered to be the moment the word was incorporated into the discipline

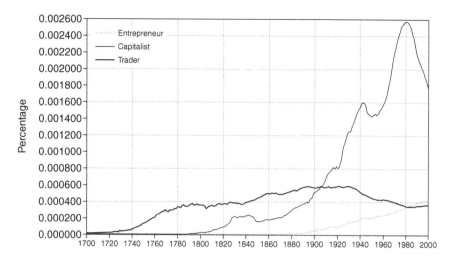

Figure 1.3 N-gram graphic for the terms entrepreneur, capitalist and trader.

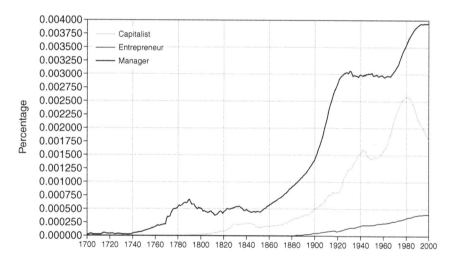

Figure 1.4 N-gram graphic for capitalist, entrepreneur and manager.

of economics in French (see Kao 1993 in Table 1; Source: McMullan & Long, 1990). Yet the concept is much older and was used in the English language by Adam Smith (1776) when he used the term, 'undertaker', as a precise translation of the French word 'entrepreneur' ([Cannan, 1976] in Kates 2015). However, as in any direct translation, the meanings are not exactly the same. The Library of Economics and Liberty website shows no fewer than 21 uses for the term 'undertaker' by Smith. See, for example: "Traders and other undertakers may, no doubt, with great propriety, carry on a very considerable part of their projects

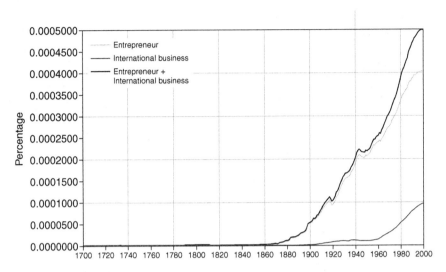

Figure 1.5 N-gram graphic for entrepreneur and IB.

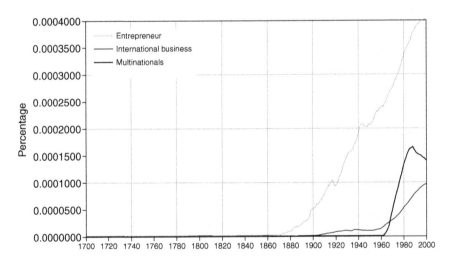

Figure 1.6 N-gram graphic for entrepreneur, IB and multinationals.

with borrowed capital" (Smith, 1776; Cannan, 1976: 326 in Kates 2015). The translation, however, uses the term as a passive noun rather than an active verb.

As an aside, in conducting our own search of the term 'entrepreneurship' in the works of Smith and Marx, we found no entries for entrepreneurship in Adam Smith's, *Wealth of Nations*. He tends to use the term, 'undertaker', which apparently was *de rigueur* in eighteenth century English (no fewer than 41 times). We then carried out a search of the three volumes of Marx's *Das Kapital* in English and found only six entries for 'entrepreneurship' in Volume 1, none in Volume 2 and again only one in Volume 3. We found that the term 'undertaker' in Smith's sense, does not appear in Marx. In Keynes' *General Theories*, there are 142 mentions of the term 'entrepreneurs' (see Kates 2015).

Various English translations of the term 'entrepreneur' from Say's *Traité* only compound the problem. For example, the American translator of the *Traité*, Prinsep (1821) says the term is difficult to translate, and 'undertaker' as a term is limited in its meaning (see Kates 2015). Prinsep explains that the term encompasses a master–manufacturer, a farmer, and a merchant – all three activities reveal an individual who takes on the "immediate responsibility, risk, and conduct of a concern of industry, whether upon his own or borrowed capital. For want of a better word, it will be rendered into English by the term adventurer" (Prinsep, editor's note in Say 1821) (see Kates 2015). Again, the above suggestion is not a completely helpful translation (Kates 2015). However, it is noted that the back translation of Adam Smith's *Wealth of Nations* (1778–1779) into French, which rendered 'undertaker' as 'entrepreneur', was hardly surprising!

Berg (2013) noted the 1811 use of the term 'entrepreneur' in *An Introduction to the Study of Political Economy* by Daniel Boileau, who states that

> the owner of stock is more particularly called a capitalist, and the individual who employs capital is denominated an undertaker (*entrepreneur*). The profit of stock must in such instances be divided in certain proportions between the capitalist and the undertaker.
>
> (Boileau, 1811: 79–80)

Berg (2013) notes the distinction between the terms 'capitalist' and 'entrepreneur' by Boileau (1811). One might ask why, indeed, 'capitalist' was used at all. Specifically, the term 'entrepreneur' is understood to be first used in John Stuart Mill's (1848) *Principles of Political Economy* (Menudo, 2013; Kates, 2015). Mill comments that it is a French term, not well translated in meaning in the English, with the term 'undertaker' a less accurate word (Kates, 2015).

Importantly, Mill addresses for the first time, the important and significant economic difference in function between an 'undertaker' and an 'entrepreneur'. Mill (1848) writes:

> The capital, or some part of it, may be borrowed: may belong to someone who does not undertake the risks or the trouble of business. In that case, the lender, or owner, is the person who practices the abstinence; and is remunerated for it by the interest paid to him, while the difference between the interest and the gross profit remunerates the exertions of risk of the undertaker.

More importantly, however, Mill then goes on to acknowledge the problematic usage of the term imported into English, which is essentially different from the

French meaning, as it "is to be regretted that this word, in this sense, is not familiar to an English ear. French political economists enjoy a great advantage in being able to speak currently of *les profits de L'entrepreneur*" (Mill [1848], 1921: 406–407). While he did not actually go on to explain the advantages that the French had in terms of the meaning of the term 'entrepreneur', the deficiency of the term in English is clearly acknowledged (Kates, 2015).

The use of the term 'entrepreneur function' is the first formal use of the word 'entrepreneur' in an English text on economics and was written by Francis Amasa Walker in *The Wages Question: A Treatise on Wages, and the Wages Class* published in 1888 (Walker, 1988). The term 'entrepreneur' is used 24 separate times and commented on as "The employing class: The entrepreneur function: The profit of business" (Walker, 1988; Kates, 2015). Walker writes: "This class comprises the modern employers of labour, men of business, 'captains of industry'." Walker goes on to add: "It is much to be regretted that we have not a single English word which exactly fits the person who performs this modern industry". He then addresses the problematic issues of using the translation of 'undertaker': "The word 'undertaker', the man who undertakes, at one time had very much this extent; but it has long since been used so exclusively devoted to funeral uses as to become an impossible term in political economy". Walker also addresses the problem of using the term 'adventurer': "The word 'adventurer', the man who makes ventures, also had this sense; but in modern parlance it has acquired a wholly sinister meaning". Finally, Walker acknowledges that the "French word 'entrepreneur' has very nearly the desired significance"; however, he then takes us back to the limitations of the English language, with the hope that over time "it may be that the exigencies of politico-economical reasoning will yet lead it to be naturalized among us" (Walker [1876], 1888: Part 11, Chapter 14, 90–91) (Kates, 2015).

Thus, the term has come into popular use and has been "naturalized", largely through the earlier efforts of Walker and Mill. It is also worth noting the discord between on the one hand, the owners of capital, and on the other hand, the actual users of this capital, the 'entrepreneurs' (Kates, 2015). This uneasiness persists today, as we reflect on Walker's comments: "In the highly complicated organization of modern industry, the employer, the *entrepreneur*, stands between the capitalist and the labourer, makes his terms with each, and directs the courses and methods of industry with almost unquestioned authority". Walker then goes on to add a politico-economic perspective that "he guarantees a reward at fixed rates" to both the labourer and capitalist, while also "taking for himself whatever his skill, enterprise, and good fortune shall secure". However, that this might be passively accepted by both the labourer and the capitalist, he refutes and finally goes on to add, that the entrepreneur too, needs to "respect his own limitations" as should the "man of wealth who has not been trained to business" (Walker [1876], 1888: Part 11, Chapter 16) (Kates, 2015).

Ely in 1891 established a further use of the term within economic discourse in the English-speaking world. In his 1891 text *Introduction to Political Economy* as "[o]ne who undertakes an enterprise; one who owns and manages a business; a person who takes the risk of profit or loss", has led to the development of a more contemporary understanding of the term 'entrepreneur' (p. 70). In his *General Theory of Employment, Interest and Money* published in 1936, John Maynard Keynes continued the use of the term in economic terminology, but yet again, did not elaborate upon the term. Not until Schumpeter in his *The Theory of Economic Development* in 1911, published in German, translated into English in 1934, does the term 'entrepreneur' become an accepted part of the English-speaking language of economics. Schumpeter elevates the entrepreneur from constituting the management of a business to also being an innovator. For the first time, we now see the link being used between the entrepreneur and innovation being acknowledged. He elaborated further in 1942 when he wrote *Capitalism, Socialism and Democracy* and introduced the concept of 'creative destruction', described as a process in which entrepreneurially led innovation takes place. This conceptualization still dominates much of the literature on entrepreneurship today, while others, such as Kirzner (1973), use the term more generally, viewing an entrepreneur as the manager of an enterprise.

Another point to note, is that being entrepreneurial does not equate to being a benefactor to society, as argued by both Baumol (2010) and Jonsson (2017). The term 'innovative entrepreneurship' is not only about creating new products and services, but also "finding creative ways" to carry out one's aims and objectives (Baumol, 2010: 155). This process can entail unproductive as well as destructive actions. Indeed, creative ways to increase one's status, wealth or power can be undertaken that actually produce no value or benefit to others or society in general, such as the furious trading in Bitcoin and other crypto-currencies (i.e. altcurrencies) throughout 2017 and into 2018. Following blockchain-supported crypto-currencies

> running non-stop for eight years, with almost no financial loss on the chain itself, we now have important ways the most reliable and secure financial network in the world claims legal scholar and computer scientist, Nick Szabo in December 2017. While Bitcoin is arguably creative, Szabo's words of wisdom on imputed value to others seem highly questionable with the recent spectacular Bitcoin and other crypto-currencies crashes of February 2018.
>
> (Ridley, 2017)

Innovative entrepreneurs will create tradable new goods and services where there are incentives, including engaging in criminal activities. Jonsson (2009) supports this with the claim that the rise of Internet-based crimes is caused by highly talented and creative people being involved. The reliable and secure financial network created through blockchain technology and crypto-currencies, according to Jonsson (2009), "is likely to be a more enduring legacy than any burst bubbles or scandals over the use of crypto-currencies by drug dealers. Blockchains may change more than money". The issues of value and beneficiaries lie at the heart of this recent rise in creative, and, some might argue, entrepreneurial activity. However, the entrepreneur here, is viewed as a funda-mental and absolutely essential part of the market process. While this example illustrates dubious displays of self-interest and even illicit behaviours harmful and pernicious to society in general, raising questions of social order that require initiatives around governance, planning and addressing criminal behaviour, there is always another perspective. Economies are able to benefit through stronger and more productive outcomes, driven by those willing to take risks "through entrepreneurially-driven market activity within a legal environment" (Kates, 2015: 6), that is set up with appropriate governance mechanisms, sanctioned by national governments and society at large.

Different approaches towards entrepreneurship, management and innovation

In the classical economic sense, the factors of production are the resources that enable man to produce goods and services, perceived as the building blocks of any industrialized or industrializing economy (Eyiyere, 1989). These factors are considered to be the key resources that enable production and are limited to three – land, labour and capital. This was supported by the main classical econo-mists, including Adam Smith (1723–1790), David Ricardo (1772–1823), John Stuart Mill (1806–1873), and successor and challenger, Karl Marx (1818–1883). Curiously, management was not included as a factor of production. However, Francis Fourier (1772–1837), Comte de Saint-Simon (1760–1825) and Alexan-der Hamilton (1757–1804) did include management as a factor of production (Drucker, 1974). As we know, the French classical economist, J. B. Say (1767–1832), adopted a very different approach and included entrepreneurship as a factor of production. Yet, some thinkers, including recent scholars (Chigbo, 2014), argue that entrepreneurship differs from management, and herein has been the continual struggle as to how we define the two, how entrepreneurship differs from management and where innovation might enter into this discussion. One's point of view is very much dependent upon the competing approaches for describing entrepreneurship. There are six commonly accepted entrepreneurial models and schools of thought, namely, Great Person School, Psychological Characteristics School, Classical School, Management School, Leadership School and Intrapreneurship School (Cunningham & Lischeron, 1991) and we add another four later in Chapter 2, namely, Transnational Entrepreneurship School, Women/Gender Entrepreneurship School, the Family Entrepreneurship School and the Entrepreneurship Ecosystems School.

From a Classical School perspective, the central characteristic of entrepre-neurial behaviour is innovation. However, from the Management School per-spective, entrepreneurs are perceived as organizers of an economic venture; they are the people who organize, own, manage and assume the risk. What lies behind these two approaches appears to be competing assumptions. From the Classical School perspective, the critical aspect of entrepreneurship is the 'process' of doing rather than owning, while the Management School approach assumes that entrepreneurs can be developed or trained in the 'technical functions' of management (Cunningham & Lischeron, 1991). From the Transnational Entrepreneurship School, Women/Gender Entrepreneurship School and the Family Entrepreneurship School who performs roles and why is linked to more than the individual, but rather the context and inclusive of the social, cultural, ethnicity, diversity and institutional norms and customs in which an entrepreneur is located. Finally, the Entrepreneurship Ecosystems School adopts an holistic perspective that includes a multi-stakeholder view of how and why certain localities are inducive for entrepreneurs to create and development new ideas into business ventures – or not.

Thus, if we integrate these various approaches, we can provide a more holistic and integrated understanding of the 'process' and the 'function'. For the former, the process is linked to behaviours and skills that include innovation, creativity and discovery. For the latter, the focus is on behaviours and skills that are viewed as functions, such as production planning, people organizing, capitalization and budgeting. However, context, networks, social embeddedness and various drivers and stakeholders offer a deeper view of 'process' and the 'functions' as part of the context, and covered with the final three schools of thought. It would be more helpful to further our contemporary understanding of what is entrepreneurship, if we perceive it as an integrated process and not merely a technical function of management, by drawing from these ten schools of thought, where appropriate to our research foci. This approach is a challenge for us, especially if we, for example, rely exclusively on the classical economic school of thought that separates entrepreneurship from management. For the present, we define entrepreneurship as a process of innovative and creative discovery by entrepreneurs that organize, manage, plan, assume the risk and capitalize the venture.

We will expand our discussion on the ten approaches or schools of thought for describing entrepreneurship later in the book. For now, we will return to our earlier discussion around economic approaches to management and the separation from entrepreneurship. We address the limitations of this approach, which is still dominant within the economic discipline today. Let us see why this might be and the problems this might create in attempting to define an integrated, contemporary and workable definition of entrepreneurship. The discussion begins with how we define the concept of 'economic' and 'economic resource'. Some economists argue that 'economic' is connected to trade, industry and development of wealth in society but is not the same as an 'economic resource' (Chigbo, 2014). Rather, an 'economic resource' is the 'supply' of something that a country, organization or person has and can therefore use. On the other hand, some economists use the terms 'factors of production' and 'economic resources' interchangeably. In addition, the overall state of technology in an industry or country can be described by managers as a 'driver' of entrepreneurship or by economists as a 'factor of production'. The term entrepreneurship has been used to define a diverse array of "activities such as creation, founding, adapting, and managing a venture" (Cunningham & Lischeron, 1991: 46). There is simply no single discipline, theory or school of thought that provides the tools or an explanation for managing an entrepreneurial venture (Stevenson, 1988). Hardly surprising then, that we do not have a consensus on how to define entrepreneurship. Thus, differences in economic interpretation arise from one's theoretical purpose, empirical focus and schools of thought about entrepreneurship, as well as the schools within the discipline of economics.

Romer (1990), Aghion and Howitt (1992), and Grossman and Helpman (1994) see technological progress as an outcome of the discovery process and generation of new ideas, which not only promotes socio-economic development and growth, but helps reduce economic stagnation. The focus of these writers is very much on the outcome, development and growth, not on the antecedents, drivers and enablers. Barro (1996) draws on the neoclassical model and extends factors of production to incorporate government policies, human capital and the diffusion of technology. These factors of production, antecedents or drivers, including technology, government policy and availability of capital, support the enablers, the entrepreneurs. Those able to develop a niche and assume the risk in the marketplace or develop a strategy to satisfy a perceived or latent need are also regarded by some as entrepreneurs (Garfield, 1986; Mill, 1848). Others refer to the identification of an opportunity as entrepreneurial (Peterson, 1985). Harbison and Myers (1959), and Heizer and Render (1991) see management as a factor of production and an economic resource, and maintain that the majority of advancements in industry and society are the result of assertive, innovative entrepreneurial managers functioning in their role as productivity catalysts. However, Barro (1996) suggests that the impact on productivity improvements of entrepreneurial managers as productivity catalysts cannot be excluded from other factors, such as demographic, governmental, legal, and economic and trade regulations.

The role of management and entrepreneurship as a key factor of production

From an economic perspective, management can be regarded as the most active of the four factors of production because it assembles and integrates the others. From an efficiency perspective, the factors of land and capital depend on labour, which in turn is governed by management (Chigbo, 2014). Management has a coordinating function across manpower, methods, markets, materials, machinery and money (the other Ms) of the organization, and thus has a unique position among the other productive factors. Chigbo (2014: 164) argues that

> some people group management and entrepreneurship together, but this is misleading/false representation. This is rather due to the fact that in a small enterprise, the owner/entrepreneur may himself act as the manager. But in the large organization, there is a divorce between ownership and management.

The statement is problematic for several reasons. First, the understanding of what is an entrepreneur and what is entrepreneurship is quite limited. Kao (1993: 69) defines entrepreneurship as "the process of doing something new and something different for the purpose of creating wealth for the individual and adding value to society". This is a broad definition that goes well beyond the management function outlined by Chigbo (2014), with the added requirement of societal good. Not all entrepreneurs achieve this second outcome, let alone the first. Additionally, recent research provides evidence that subsidiary managers can be entrepreneurial in how they develop a range of levels of autonomy and thus pursue different strategies or similar objectives but from a different perspective from the parent or headquarters (Cavanagh, Freeman, Kalfadellis & Herbert 2017; Cavanagh, Freeman, Kalfadellis & Cavusgil, 2017).

Chigbo (2014) implicitly links management and efficiency as a metaphor for entrepreneurship. Chigbo argues that the efficiency of the management factor can be improved through necessary training and development of executives, thus suggesting a relationship between competence and performance of management and facilities for developing managerial resources. According to Chigbo, the importance of management increases with the pace of industrialization and globalization, a trend that has been evident since World War II, with the subsequent rapid economic and social development (Chigbo, 2014). While management could be seen "as the single most critical social activity in connection with economic progress", the argument expressed by Chigbo (2014: 164) that a

> country can have sizable natural and manpower resources including plentiful skilled labour and substantial capital but still be relatively poor because very few competent managers are available to put these resources efficiently together in the production and distribution of useful goods and services

seems limited as his view of the drivers of entrepreneurial spirit as one of a distinct characteristic, namely the 'competence' (Chigbo, 2014).

Chigbo reduces the entrepreneurial element of the process to doing something new and different for the purpose of creating wealth as an economic factor, requiring little more than effective training and skills to produce efficient outcomes such as wealth and production. Non-economic factors are not regarded as important; it is a simple matter of human resources comprising labour and managerial resources linked to competency, without having an understanding of the non-economic factors inherent in such a resource. However, it can be said that economic motives, such as profit, are not the only determinant of an entrepreneurial opportunity (Khan, Freeman, Cavusgil & Ghauir, 2018; Khelil, 2016). Entrepreneurs may value or forgo an entrepreneurial opportunity to meet their non-economic expectations such as autonomy (Lazaris, Ngasri & Freeman, 2015; Lazaris & Freeman, 2018), or their work and family life balance (Maksimov, Wang & Luo, 2017; Marlow & Martinez Dy, 2017). These factors can be captured more comprehensively through the women/gender and ethnic and immigrant entrepreneurship schools of thought, to be addressed in Chapter 2. Thus, it is reasonable to claim that entrepreneurs cannot predict the future that entrepreneurial opportunities objectively exist

(Ramoglou & Tsang, 2016), but are subjectively imagined and believed by entrepreneurs (McMullen & Warnick, 2016; Ramoglou & Tsang, 2016).

Chigbo (2014) sees management and administration as an economic resource, stating that "[c]ertain types of activities, jobs and assignments require relatively higher managerial and administration concentration than others". Chigbo perceives management as the delivery of an entrepreneurial outcome or catalyst for productive activity, but does not explain how the process ensues. This is the point where management and entrepreneurship differ, but Chigbo does not use these terms or acknowledge the difference; he simply says that "the inputs of manpower, materials, machinery and money do not by themselves ensure growth; they become productive through the catalyst of management" (Chigbo, 2014: 164). The term 'catalyst' is not defined, analysed or characterized.

The dimension described above is part of the concept of entrepreneurship, but entrepreneurship is more than a catalyst. Edith Penrose (1914–1996), an American-born British classical economist, known for her work *The Theory of the Growth of the Firm* (1959), which describes the ways which firms grow and how fast, and creates a platform for Keynesian economics, argued that "managerial capacities should be distinguished from entrepreneurial capacity" (Kao, 1993: 70). Ogbor (2000) argues that after imagining entrepreneurial opportunities, entrepreneurs develop believability about their imagined state of the entrepreneurial opportunity. The elements of opportunity belief (i.e. potential value of an entrepreneurial opportunity, knowledge related to an opportunity, window of an opportunity and number of entrepreneurial opportunities) play a critical role in the entrepreneurial opportunity recognition process (Ramoglou & Tsang, 2018, 2017, 2016). Penrose also suggests that "identifying and exploiting opportunistic ideas for expansion of smaller enterprises is the essential aspect of entrepreneurship" (Kao, 1993: 70). This role envisaged by Penrose (1959), Mitchell and Shepherd (2010) and Khan et al. (2018) is far more active than the passive notion of the 'catalyst' offered by Chigbo (2014).

Chigbo (2014) does, however, add that "contemporary ... ideas (including both management ideas/knowledge and technological ideas/knowledge cum inventions) are equally regarded as capital". Thus, he concludes that "management and administration is a factor of production and an economic resource" (p. 165). He does allude to entrepreneurship without ever stating it explicitly, by suggesting the importance of management as a mental and communicating activity. Thus, the economic perspective is limited as a discipline in addressing the fundamentals in the more complete and holistic understanding of entrepreneurship and the entrepreneur. We will elaborate more regarding the underpinnings and definitions of entrepreneurship in Chapter 2.

The structure of this book

In tackling the complex issues regarding entrepreneurship and internationalization, we have designed this book with the following structure aimed at providing underpinnings and background, as well as case studies illustrating past

and present development of entrepreneurships, in particular their internationalization process.

After the foundations established in Chapter 1, Chapter 2 will explore underpinnings of ten schools of thought on entrepreneurship, which cover a diverse
range of disciplines and thus assumptions, both explicit and implicit. Chapter 3
will then set up a basis for achieving clarity around definitions, dimensions and
processes, new understandings, as well as evidence of new theories being
brought forward from entrepreneurship, sociology, strategy, organizational
behaviour and ecology disciplines and fields of research from the international
entrepreneurship stream. Chapter 4 will develop further analysis on issues
related to international entrepreneurship research in emerging economies to
elevate the theoretical contribution and richness of the diverse and heterogeneous nature of the emerging economies with particular emphasis on the
East–West comparative analysis. The particular focus will be on (1) defining
entrepreneurship (risk taking, proclivity and pro-activeness) and its dimension;
(2) comparing this definition with international entrepreneurship and further to
international entrepreneurship and emerging economies to provide evidence of
differences given the historical and socio-political contextual backgrounds of
international entrepreneurship and immigrant entrepreneurs; and (3) proposing
new variables of international entrepreneurship as a theoretical basis for moving
the debate forward.

Chapter 5 provides an overview of entrepreneurship and ethnicity, expanding
upon concepts and dimensions related to international entrepreneurship, including family businesses and ethnicity and immigrant entrepreneurship, to provide
further foundational discussion leading to illustrative, evidence-based cases
studies. Following the theoretical foundations established in Chapters 1 to 5, we
will move to evidence-based case studies based in Australia in Chapter 6 within
the context of family-run small medium enterprises (SMEs), migrant businesses
and international entrepreneurial activity in Australia, with a key focus on trade
and investment, key sectors and new strategic approaches for ensuring SME
competitive advantage. Chapter 7 will focus on Chinese entrepreneurs in China
and overseas, Chapter 8 on immigrant entrepreneurship and the Jewish diaspora,
and Chapter 9 will provide a final conclusion.

By focusing on the Australian experience, Chapter 6 will provide the
context and describe the development of entrepreneurs belonging to born-
globals, international new ventures (INVs) and start-ups in the early 1990s.
This early body of research will be explored offering case-based illustrations
along with theoretical underpinnings to explain international entrepreneurship,
immigrant entrepreneurship, as well as insights around the nature of entrepreneurial opportunity. Our focus will then shift to business-to-business as the
primary domain as many of the born-globals in the early and current phase of
international entrepreneurship are high-tech knowledge intensive. Other industry groups such as agribusiness and alternative energies, now on the rise, will
also be included in this study. International entrepreneurs as well as the rapid
internationlizers will be explored, with comparisons provided between the East

and West that help to explain distinguishing features of these organizations, many of whom are SMEs at both the firm and entrepreneurial level that quickly as well as gradually engage overseas. The third area of focus of this book is migrants operating in Australia, to provide comparative insights around entrepreneurial proclivity, and entrepreneurial opportunity and entrepreneurial ecosystems. These evidence-based insights will be offered on the notion of international entrepreneurship and behaviour, entrepreneurial opportunity recognition and actualization of both Australian-based as well as immigrant entrepreneurs from the East–West perspective to support new theoretical development and robustness in the international entrepreneurship emerging economy stream of research.

Chapter 7 on Chinese entrepreneurs in China and overseas will compare their internationalization process and activities based on historical evolution and current practices. Old and new generation entrepreneurs may develop similar and different patterns and processes in their internationalized activities. In addition, new Chinese SMEs going overseas or young overseas-trained Chinese entrepreneurs returning to China may develop some unique international entrepreneurship concepts and perspectives.

Chapter 8 on Jewish family businesses in the US and EU will provide evidence and analysis of the Jewish diaspora's tendencies in entrepreneurial activities in these two major developed markets. Finally, Chapter 9 will offer comparative case-based evidence and new insights into diverse socio-political emerging and advanced markets from an East–West context. New insights that provide evidence for our theoretical framework and a number of propositions will be presented to support further theoretical development in the much needed international entrepreneurship emerging economy where the real growth in SME entrepreneurship is occurring. Additional insights on comparative evidence across the three case-based contexts on entrepreneurial opportunity recognition will support our framework and development of propositions for further enhancement of more robust theoretical development in the international entrepreneurship emerging economy domain. Finally, a new research framework is developed and presented that will provide more clarity around the complexity and heterogeneous context of international entrepreneurship from the perspectives of both the developed and emerging economies embracing contemporary influences.

References

Aghion, P. & Howitt, P. (1992) Endogenous growth – Aghion and Howitt model: A Schumpeterian approach. *Econometrica*, 60(2): 323–351.

Barro, R. J. (1996) Determinants of economic growth: A cross-country empirical study, *NBER Working Paper*, 5698, August: 20–22.

Baumol, W. J. (2010) *The Microtheory of Innovative Entrepreneurship*. Kauffman Foundation Series on Innovation and Entrepreneurship, Princeton: Princeton University Press.

van den Berg, R. (2013) Societies for the History of Economics (SHOE) website (September–October: 2013) https: listserv.yorku.ca/cgi-bin/wa?A2=ind1309c&L=shoe& T=O&P=542

Boileau, D. (1811) *An Introduction to the Study of Political Economy.* London: Cadell and Davies.

Briard, J. (2001) Les objets paleomonetaires de L'Europe atlantique protohistorique. In: *Revue numismatique*, 6e serie – Tome 157: 37–50.

Cavanagh, A., Freeman, S., Kalfadellis, P. & Cavusgil, S. T. (2017). How do subsidiaries assume autonomy? A refined application of agency theory with the subsidiary-headquarters context. *Global Strategy Journal*, 7(2): 172–192.

Cavanagh, A., Freeman, S., Kalfadellis, P. & Herbert, K. (2017). Assigned versus assumed: Towards a contemporary, detailed understanding of subsidiary autonomy. *International Business Review*, 26(6): 1168–1183.

Chigbo, N. (2014) Management as a factor of production and as an economic resource. *International Journal of Humanities and Social Science*, 4(6): 162–166.

Cunningham, J. B. & Lischeron, J. (1991) Defining entrepreneurship. *Journal of Small Business Management*, 29(1): 45–61.

Davies, G. (1994) *A History of Money from Ancient Times to the Present Day.* Cardiff: University of Wales.

Demoule, Jean-Paul (ed.) (2007) *La revolution neolithique en France.* Paris: La Decouverte.

Drucker, P. F. (1974) *Management: Tasks, Responsibilities, Practices.* New York: Harper and Row.

Ely, R. T. (1891) *An Introduction to Political Economy.* New York: Chautauqua Press.

Eyiyere, D. O. (1989) *Economics Made Easy.* Benin City: Doe-Sun Publishers.

Harbison, F. & Myers, C. A. (1959) *Management and Labour Problems in Economic Development.* New York: McGraw-Hill.

Heizer, J. & Render, B. (1991) *Production and Operations Management.* Boston: Allyn and Bacon.

Garfield, C. (1986) *Peak Performers: The New Heroes of American Business.* New York: Avon Books.

Grossman, G. M. & Helpman, E. (1994) Endogenous innovation in the theory of growth. *Journal of Economic Perspectives*, 8(1) Winter: 23–44.

Jonsson, P. O. (2009) The economics of spam and the context and the aftermath of the CAN-SPAM Act of 2003. *International Journal of Liability and Scientific Enquiry*, 2(1): 40–52.

Jonsson, P. O. (2017) On the term "entrepreneur" and the conceptualization of entrepreneurship in the literature of classical economics. *International Journal of English Linguistics*, 7(6): 16–29.

Kao, R. W. Y. (1993) Defining entrepreneurship: Past, present and? *Creativity and Innovation Management*, 2(1): 69–70.

Kates, S. (2015) Origin and evolution of the term "entrepreneur" in English. From the selected works of Steven Kates, Steven Kates, RMIT University, Bepress. Available at: https: works.bepress.com/stenenkates/4/. See also Wikipedia. "Entrepreneurship" (as at 31 October 2013) http://en.wikipedia.org/wiki/Entreneurship and Wikipedia. "Linguistic relativity" (as at 3 April2014) http://en.wikipedia.org/wiki/Linguistic_relativity

Keynes, J. M. (1936) *General Theory of Employment, Interest and Money.* London: Palgrave Macmillan.

Kirzner, I. (1973) *Competition and Entrepreneurship.* Indianapolis: Liberty Fund.

Lazaris, M. & Freeman, S. (2018) An examination of global mindset and international market opportunities among SMEs. *International Studies of Management & Organization*, 48(2): 181–203.

Lazaris, M., Mohamad Ngasri, N. E. & Freeman, S. (2015) Reactive and proactive international entrepreneurial behavior: Causation and effectuation, in Pervez Ghauri & V. H. Manek Kirpalani (eds), *Handbook of Research on International Entrepreneurship Strategy: Improving SME Performance Globally*. Cheltenham: Edward Elgar Publishing Ltd, pp. 22–44

McMullen, J. S. & Warnick, B. J. (2016) Should we require every new venture to be a hybrid organization? *Journal of Management Studies*, 53(4): 630–662.

McMullan, W. E. & Long, W. A. (1990) *Developing New Ventures*. San Diego: HBJ.

Maksimov, V., Wang, S. & Luo, Y. (2017) Reducing poverty in the least developed countries: The role of small and medium enterprises. *Journal of World Business*, 52(2): 244–257.

Mankiw, G. (1997) *Principles of Economics* (8th edn). Boston: Cengage Learning.

Marlow, S. & Martinez Dy, A. M. (2017) Annual review article: Is it time to rethink the gender agenda in entrepreneurship research? *International Small Business Journal: Researching Entrepreneurship*, 36(1): 3–22.

Menudo, J. M. (2013) Societies for the History of Economics (SHOE) website (September–October: 2013) https: listserv.yorku.ca/cgi-bin/wa?A2=ind1309c&L=shoe& T=O&P=1322

Michel, J.-B., Shen, Y. K., Aiden, A. P., Veres, A., Gray, M. K., Pickett, J. P., et al. (2011) Quantitative analysis of culture using millions of digitized books. *Science*, 331(1): 176–182.

Mill, J. S. (1848) *Principles of Political Economy with Some of their Applications to Social Philosophy* (1st edn). London: John W. Parker, retrieved 7 December 2012, volume 2 via Google Books [seventh edition in 1871].

Ogbor, J. O. (2000) Mythicizing and reification in entrepreneurial discourse: Ideology-critique of entrepreneurial studies. *Journal of Management Studies*, 37(5): 605–635.

Penrose, E. T. (1959) *The Theory of the Growth of the Firm*. Oxford University Press: New York.

Peterson, R. (1985) Rising risk-takers. *Metropolitan Toronto Business Journal*, 75(1): 30–34.

Ramoglou, S. & Tsang, E. (2018) Opportunities lie in the demand side: Transcending the discovery–creation debate. *The Academy of Management Review*, 43: 815–818.

Ramoglou, S. & Tsang, E. W. K. (2017) Accepting the unknowables of entrepreneurship and overcoming philosophical obstacles to scientific progress. *Journal of Business Venturing Insights*, 8: 71–77.

Ramoglou, S. & Tsang, E. W. K. (2016) A realist perspective of entrepreneurship: Opportunities as propensities. *The Academy of Management Review*, 41: 410–434.

Ridley, M. (2017) Bitcoin is only the beginning of a global blockchain revolution. *The Australian*, 12:00AM December 5 (*The Times*) [printed copy].

Romer, P. (1990) Endogenous technological change. *Journal of Political Economy*, 98(5): 71–102.

Samuelson, P. A. (1948) *Economics: An Introductory Analysis*. New York: McGraw-Hill Book Company, Inc,. First edition.

Schumpeter, J. A. (1934) *The Theory of Economic Development*. Cambridge, MA: Harvard University Press. [Published in 1911 in German and translated in English in 1934]

Schumpeter, J. A. (1942) *Capitalism, Socialism and Democracy*. London: Routledge.

Smith, A. ([1776] (1976) *Inquiry into the Nature and Causes of the Wealth of Nations.* Ed. Edwin Cannan. Chicago: University of Chicago Press. Online library of Economics and Liberty edition. http://en.wikipedia.org/wiki/Entrepreneurship.

Theocarakis, N. (2013) Societies for the History of Economics (SHOE) website (September–October: 2013) https: listserv.yorku.ca/cgi-bin/wa?A2=ind1309c&L=shoe& T=O&P=1206

Walker, F. A. (1876) *The Wages Question a Treatise' on Wages and the Wages Class* PI. New York: Henry Holt and Company.

Walker, F. A. (1888) *The Wages Question a Treatise' on Wages and the Wages Class* PII. New York: Henry Holt and Company.

Wedde, M. (1997) The intellectual stowaway: On the movement of ideas within exchange systems: A Minoan case study, in R. Laffineur & P. Betancourt (eds), *TEXNH. Craftsmen, Craftswomen in the Aegean Bronze Age*, Aegaeum 16, Liege, 67–75. www.dartmouth. edu/~prehistory/aegean/?page_id=866

2 International entrepreneurship and schools of thought

Introduction

The definition of 'entrepreneurship' offered by Kao (1993: 69) in Chapter 1 (of this book) regards entrepreneurship as a "process of doing something new and something different for the purpose of creating wealth for the individual and adding value to society". Contemporary definitions regard entrepreneurship as more than a process of wealth creation. The international business discipline places increasing emphasis on the process of proactively engaging in business exchange rather than production (Vahlne & Johanson, 2017). There is also a growing interest in "the impact of the digital context as a defining macro-level feature of our modern world, and the role of the individual as a core microfoundation" (Coviello, Kano & Liesch, 2017: 1151). However, entrepreneurship is not obvious in the classic economic literature, where management is the preferred term. Today entrepreneurship is still not regarded as a separate discipline within any academic community; some authors suggest it is a body of literature and a field of research (Zahra & Dess, 2001; Coviello, Kano & Liesch, 2017; Vahlne & Johanson, 2017; Hakanson & Kappen, 2017; Lazaris & Freeman, 2018).

The literature stream first emerged in the 1950s in the business curricula of United States and Japanese universities. It was not until the 1970s, through to the 1980s and 1990s, that entrepreneurship become an accepted profession and a "solution to stimulate and revitalize a nation's economy" (Kao, 1993: 69). It was at this point that "entrepreneurship finally earn[ed] its place in institutes of higher learning, government and the professions" (Kao 1993: 69). Today, interestingly, entrepreneurship is acknowledged in both ideological extremes – capitalism on the one hand, and socialism (including communism) on the other since entrepreneurship is perceived to be the only recognised and viable solution to provide financial gains to individuals for undertaking risk, while simultaneously providing a mechanism for allocating wealth in the market economy, which provides for limited government intervention in the process (Ramoglou & Tsang, 2018, 2017, 2016).

Defining entrepreneurship and entrepreneurs – past, present and future

Irrespective of the focus of literature on the entrepreneurial mindset, orientation and culture (Lazaris & Freeman, 2018), on the one hand, and on the wealth creation of nations (Neesham Freeman, 2016) on the other hand, we are no closer to a common definition. However, a definition is needed, not only for the sake of classification, but for study, research and governmental policy reasons (Kao, 1993). In Table 2.1 we present several definitions – seminal, historical and from practitioners.

A range of approaches has been used to define entrepreneurship and has gained momentum since the 1970s. Encompassing a definition that is broad,

Table 2.1 Historical definitions of entrepreneurship and the entrepreneur (1730–1970–2000s)

Author	Definition
Richard Cantillon (1730)	Maintained that entrepreneurship is self-employment with an uncertain return
Nicholas Baudeau (1767)	Wrote that entrepreneurship is innovative management
Jean-Baptiste Say (1810)	Described entrepreneurship as the characteristic of an extraordinarily talented manager
Carl Menger (1871)	Differentiated entrepreneurial decision-making into four sequential stages
Alfred Marshall (1890)	Hinted at a distinction between entrepreneurs and managers
Joseph Schumpeter (1910)	Described the entrepreneur as an innovator, carrying out new combinations
Frank Knight	Defined entrepreneurship as the courage to bear uncertainty
Edith Penrose (1959)	Maintained that managerial capacities should be distinguished from entrepreneurial capacity
	Maintained that identifying and exploiting opportunistic ideas for expansion of smaller enterprises is the essential aspect of entrepreneurship
Harvey Lebenstein (1970)	Emphasized the reduction of organizational inefficiency and at the same time reversal of organizational entropy
McMullen and Dimo Dimov (2013: 1481)	Saw "entrepreneurship as a process", examined the growing disconnect between the process-oriented concept of entrepreneurship taught in the classroom and theorized about in premier journals and the variance-oriented concept of entrepreneurship that characterizes empirical studies of the phenomenon.Strongly advocated a shift in inquiry from entrepreneurship as an act to entrepreneurship as a journey, which they argued would facilitate process-oriented research by initiating a dialogue about the nature of the entrepreneurial journey, when it has begun and ended, whether it might be productively subdivided into variables or events, and what if anything remains constant throughout the process.

Sources: Adapted from Kao (1993), McMullan & Long (1990) and McMullan & Dimov (2013).

practical and measurable, Stevenson (1988) suggests a three-fold process. First, entrepreneurship is the process of making changes; second, the entrepreneurial process accomplishes everything other processes achieve but to greater effect; and third, entrepreneurship is the pursuit of opportunity beyond the resources under one's current control. Researchers have debated whether entrepreneurial opportunities are discovered or created. However, they have often overlooked the importance of the contextual variables that stimulate, shape and define the entrepreneurial act. Zahra and Wright (2016) focus on entrepreneurial activities within technology-based established companies and show how and why certain contexts are more conducive to discovery, while others promote the discovery and creation of opportunities. Zahra and Wright (2016) suggest a virtuous and dynamic cycle where discovery enriches creation, which, in turn, fosters the discovery of new opportunities. The focus on the context and key features of entrepreneurial search contributes to the behavioural theory and origins of opportunities.

Recently, McMullen and Dimo Dimov (2013: 1481) wrote on "entrepreneurship as a process", examining the growing disconnect between the process-oriented concept of entrepreneurship taught and theorized, and the variance-oriented concept of entrepreneurship that characterizes empirical studies. McMullen and Dimov advocate a shift from seeing entrepreneurship as an act to viewing it as a journey, which they argue would facilitate process-oriented research by initiating a dialogue about the nature of the entrepreneurial journey, when it began and ended, whether it might be productively subdivided into variables or events, and what, if anything, remains constant throughout the process. They argue that this shift is important, in order to have a clearer understanding of the entrepreneurial journey, to distinguish the field horizontally from research on creativity and strategy, and vertically from research on more practical business functions or more abstract systems-level concepts. Thus, we can define entrepreneurship as a process and opportunity recognition as part of a process that takes place over time and in a range of locations, including home and host markets, and, of course, more recently, virtually. Thus, it is particularly important to understand the processes that precede entrepreneurial action and what types of knowledge might support and drive the imaging, belief and actualization of an entrepreneurial opportunity (Loasby, 2011).

The earlier definition by Kao (1993) is specific but also allows for various entrepreneurial attributes, such as risk-taking, proclivity and determination – all of which have been emphasized more recently (Ngasri & Freeman, 2018; Lazaris & Freeman, 2018; Lazaris, Ngasri & Freeman, 2015). Kao also draws attention to "adding value to society" (Kao, 1993: 69). This aspect is important as it precludes criminal activities with harmful effects on the "wealth of nations" and "human beings" (Kao, 1993; Neesham & Freeman, 2016). The introduction of these two concepts allows for a deeper and contemporary understanding, suggesting that his definition still holds weight today, namely: "Entrepreneurship is a process of making changes; doing something different, thus creating wealth for the individual and adding value to society" (Kao, 1993: 70).

A further challenge is defining an 'entrepreneur'. One problem with the definition of entrepreneurship as "the pursuit of opportunity by an individual beyond the resources under his/her control" (Kao, 1993: 70), is that the definition has no limits. By describing an 'entrepreneur' as "a person who undertakes a wealth-creating and value-adding process, through incubating ideas, assembling resources and making things happen" (Kao, 1993: 70), we focus on certain specific characteristics. First, emphasis can be placed on "wealth-creating and value-adding process" and "actions involved in wealth-creating and adding value to the process through venture formation and/or the undertaking of entrepreneurial endeavours" (Kao, 1993: 70). This definition has the advantage that it characterizes the entrepreneur as one who is committed to change, wealth creation and value-adding processes that embrace societal good. Second, a more contemporary definition of an entrepreneur would preclude criminal, unethical, greed-oriented and non-value adding outcomes to societies from a global and a regional perspective, that are not focused solely on self-interest, but allow for other-oriented interests.

Given the complexities around different schools of thought and disciplines, it is not surprising that we continue to have little consensus on defining 'entrepreneurs' despite the considerable interest and numerous publications on the topic. Much of the research is fragmented and definitions are somewhat controversial, not only within, but also across different schools and disciplines. Some researchers do not regard self-employed individuals and business proprietors as entrepreneurs but rather as small business owners (Cunningham & Lischeron, 1991). Others argue that the field is in its infancy (Sexton, 1982). There is no accepted definition (Churchhill & Lewis, 1986). Some have attempted to distinguish between individual and corporate entrepreneurship, and entrepreneurs and small business owners (Carland, Hoy, Boulton & Carland, 1984). These concepts cover diverse concepts including creativity, innovation and personal traits, as well as more recent concepts such as appearance and style. Models are as numerous as there are disciplines.

The term 'entrepreneur' is frequently applied to the founder of a new business or a person "who started a new business where there was none before" (Gartner, 1985). Thus, using this approach, one who inherits or buys a business, or buys an existing enterprise or manages a turnaround as an employee is not an entrepreneur. Some argue that the term applies only to the creative activity of the innovator (Schumpeter, 1934). Other scholars refer to an opportunity as entrepreneurial (Peterson, 1985). Some suggest that those who can develop a niche in the market or are able to develop a strategy to satisfy a need are indeed entrepreneurs (Garfield, 1986).

As a classical economist, Chigbo (2014) perceives entrepreneurship as merely activities, and managers as the actors in decision-making leading to production and wealth creation. However, he does not address notions around the assumption of risk. There is a difference between a founder who recognizes an opportunity and develops a new venture, an owner manager who assumes risk and develops the venture but may not have been the founder, and a manager who draws a salary (Cunningham & Lischeron, 1991). The latter is indeed a manager but not an entrepreneur as he/she faces no risk as to whether the venture succeeds or not. This manager does not lose his/her invested capital or undertakes other risks involved in running a business, such as loss of reputation, credit rating, bankruptcy (Kao, 1993) and failure (Arasti, Zandi & Bahmani, 2014; Robson et al., 2019).

The great range in viewpoints can be linked to schools of thought on entrepreneurship, which offer unique suggestions of what entrepreneurs do and the various functions and processes associated with the entrepreneurial role.

Ten schools of thought on entrepreneurship

An agreed definition of entrepreneurship is unlikely given the reach of activity across many schools of thought, each having its own underpinning set of beliefs and purpose. Each school can be categorized according to a set of personal characteristics, opportunities, management or need for adapting the existing venture (Cunningham & Lischeron, 1991; Danes et al. 2008; Smans, Freeman & Thomas, 2014; Du & O'Connor, 2017; Marlow & Martinez Dy, 2017; Audretsch, Mason, Miles & O'Connor, 2018). Each school of thought is first discussed and then categorized according to four broad themes: personal qualities, opportunities, actions and adaptions.

Assessing personal qualities
  1   The Great Person School of Entrepreneurship
  2   The Psychological Characteristics School of Entrepreneurship

Recognizing opportunities
  3   The Classical School of Entrepreneurship
  4   Transnational Entrepreneurship

Acting and managing
  5   The Management School of Entrepreneurship
  6   The Leadership School of Entrepreneurship
  7   Women/Gender Entrepreneurship School

Reassessing and adapting
  8   The Intrapreneurship School of Entrepreneurship
  9   Family Entrepreneurship School
  10   Entrepreneurship Ecosystems School

The different entrepreneurial situations can comprise phases or stages of evolution including start-up, growth and maturity of ventures, and it is commonly agreed that they require different behaviours or skills. These differing behaviours and skills of the schools of thought are presented in Table 2.2 and are then

Table 2.2 Schools of thought for categorizing entrepreneurship

Entrepreneurial model	Central focus or purpose	Assumption	Behaviours and skills	Situation/phase
Great Person School	The entrepreneur has an intuitive ability – a sixth sense – and is born with certain traits and instincts.	Without this "inborn" intuition, the individual would be like the rest of humanity who "lack what it takes".	Intuition, vigour, energy, persistence, and self-esteem.	Start-up.
Psychological Characteristics School	Entrepreneurs are driven by unique values, attitudes, and needs.	People behave in accordance with their values; behaviour results from attempts to satisfy needs.	Personal values, risk-taking, need for achievement, and others.	Start-up.
Classical School	The central characteristic of entrepreneurial behaviour is innovation.	The critical aspect of entrepreneurship is in the process of doing rather than owning.	Innovation, creativity, and discovery.	Start-up and early growth.
Management School	Entrepreneurs are organizers of an economic venture; they are people who organize, own, manage, and assume the risk.	Entrepreneurs can be developed or trained in the technical functions of management.	Production planning, people-organizing, capitalization, and budgeting.	Early growth and maturity.
Leadership School	Entrepreneurs are leaders of people; they have the ability to adapt their style to the needs of people.	An entrepreneur cannot accomplish his/her goals alone, but depends on others.	Motivating, directing, and leading.	Early growth and maturity.
Intrapreneurship School/ Corporate Entrepreneurship School	Entrepreneurial skills can be useful in complex organizations; intrapreneurship is the development of independent units to create, market, and expand services.	Organisations need to adapt to survive, entrepreneurial activity leads to organizational building and entrepreneurs becoming managers.	Alertness to opportunities, maximizing decisions.	Maturity and change.

Continued

Table 2.2 continued

Entrepreneurial model	Central focus or purpose	Assumption	Behaviours and skills	Situation/phase
Transnational Entrepreneurship School	The immigrant entrepreneur's opportunity identification draws support from the use of country of origin (COO) ethnic and kinship ties.	Social ties influence the flow of information about opportunities, and individuals not connected to the network are unable to obtain such information.	Relying on ethnic networks, with a focus on social ties to discover or create new opportunities	Start-up.
Women's Entrepreneurship School	How gender in all its iterations impacts upon all entrepreneurial activities, rather than focusing only on how gendered ascriptions position women.	Embedded masculinity within the entrepreneurial discourse, which privileges men as normative entrepreneurial actors, while not positioning women as a proxy for the gendered, yet not gender neutral.	Gendered ability to shape the availability, accrual and flow of entrepreneurial ideas, resources and competencies between those involved with, or operating, a venture is pivotal whether at the level of the family, household, team or stakeholder group.	Early growth and maturity.
Family Entrepreneurship School	Ethnic and family contexts create the culture from which entrepreneurship emerges and how ethnic businesses are owned and operated by their family members.	The family, with its own interpersonal dynamics, acts as the crucible that mixes ethnicities, and creates culture, thereby serving as the "mediating milieu" for the entrepreneurial experience.	Supporting both family and business values (systems) along with their interaction within the cultural context of their ethnic communities.	Early growth and maturity and change.
Entrepreneurship Ecosystems School	Entrepreneurial ecosystems assist understanding of the nature of places in which entrepreneurial activity flourishes.	Some geographical environments are more conducive to entrepreneurship while others inhibit it.	Roles and types of support of governments, non-profit organizations and private companies, as well as key individuals, in the emergence and growth of entrepreneurial ecosystems	Start-up, early growth, and maturity and change.

Sources: Adapted from Cunningham & Lischeron (1991), Smans & Freeman (2014), Du & O'Connor (2017), Danes et al. (2008), Marlow & Dy (2017), Audretsch, Mason, Miles & O'Connor (2017), Arasti, Zandi & Bahmani (2014), Robson et al. (2019).

expanded upon in the following discussion by including their situation or phase of development (Trudgen & Freeman, 2014).

The Great Person School of Entrepreneurship

The fundamental question posted by this approach is: are entrepreneurs (like leaders) born, or are they made? Can you teach someone to be a manager, leader or an entrepreneur? Or does entrepreneurship rely on an inborn natural capacity to perform these types of activities? While there are those in the leadership area who believe in the charismatic leader, others believe in the 'great person' as entrepreneur, suggesting that entrepreneurs have endowed traits or qualities that are unique (Garfield, 1986). Articles or biographies written in this vein tend to focus on the ability of entrepreneurs to recognize an opportunity and make the right decisions, with an inborn ability or intuition to make things happen. These entrepreneurs rely more on their instinct than market and business forecasts (Iacocca, 1984), and are decisive, where mere mortals are not! (Cunningham & Lischeron, 1991).

The entrepreneurs described above have a strong drive for independence, success, high level of vigour, strong belief in themselves and their ability, with boundless energy, perseverance, vision, single mindedness and are able to inspire and motivate those around them. Surprisingly and controversially, other traits include physically attractive, popular, sociable, intelligent, knowledgeable, judgemental, good speaker, tactful and diplomatic. As for which of these traits might be the most important, there is no evidence to support or suggest one over another. Researchers in the early stage of leadership literature development came to a similar conclusion. This theory offers the diverse concepts mentioned above, defines entrepreneurs by the concepts and traits most valued, and tends to have a common-sense focus on people (Cunningham & Lischeron, 1991).

The Psychological Characteristics School of Entrepreneurship

The basic view in this theory is that one's behaviour is broadly determined by one's values, despite variations in situations that one might face. In turn, one's behaviour is determined by the desire to satisfy needs, whether they be power, recognition, achievement, acceptance or love. The assumption is that entrepreneurs have unique values and attitudes with regard work and life. These traits, along with needs, motivate a person to behave in a particular manner. Lachman (1980) made the comment that those who possess the same characteristics as entrepreneurs, will have a higher tendency (or potential) to perform entrepreneurial acts, than people who do not possess such characteristics. The three most popular personality characteristics include, first, personal values, such as honesty, duty and responsibility; second, risk-taking propensity; and third, a need for achievement (Cunningham & Lischeron, 1991). However, whether this contributes to being successful is not clear.

The view is that entrepreneurs cannot be trained or developed, as their activity is linked to their personality and lifestyle, which develops over time through interactions with parents, friends, mentors and life experiences. Values are fostered through family, school, religious experience and even one's culture. While the values are learned they are internalized and reflected as personal values and expressed regardless of the situation (Cunningham & Lischeron, 1991). The second trait relates to risk-taking, a concept initially introduced into English economic discourse by John Stuart Mill, and relates to risk-bearing to distinguish entrepreneurs from managers. Some go further, suggesting that an entrepreneurial function essentially involves risk measurement and risk-taking (Palmer, 1971). Risks comprise uncertainties around financial success, career opportunities, family dynamics and well-being (Sarachek, 1978).

Schumpeter (1934) took a different view, arguing that risk-taking is part of ownership, and that while entrepreneurs are the combiners, they may not be the owners. More recent views, however, suggest that entrepreneurship does indeed include the notion of assuming the risk of running a business (Cunningham & Lischeron, 1991). Some argue that entrepreneurs are more likely to be known for moderate risk to maintain control, achieve a profit and avoid the extremes of high risk and uncertainty (McClelland & Winter, 1969). Risk-taking tends to dominate as the major characteristic. The Classical School distinguishes entrepreneurial activity from managerial activity arguing that once the activity or creative aspect is complete, it is no longer entrepreneurial. In the late seventeenth century, Cantillion characterized the entrepreneur as a rational decision-maker, one who "assumed the risk and provided the management of the firm" (Kilby, 1971).

The need for achievement and industriousness is regarded as values held by many people in particular cultures. Weber (1905; 1908) wrote *The Protestant Ethic and the Theory of Capitalism*, suggesting that some cultures achieve more than others because of the values imbedded in their individuals. Capitalism and entrepreneurial drive are considered dominant in particular countries, for example, traditionally democracies with the assumption of laissez faire in business and trade (Cunningham & Lischeron, 1991). However, this concept is no longer limited to such types of economies, given the high level of entrepreneurial activity and changes in the emerging and transitional markets during the last two decades, warranting research and investigation into the values that underpin them and how they might be changing (Zhu, Freeman & Cavusgil, 2018).

The view that entrepreneurs have a distinctly higher need for achievement is common, yet to argue that this driver alone is separate from other drivers that might influence one to set up or start a business seems unlikely (Hull, Bosley & Udell, 1980). According to this school of thought, possessing the need for achievement and facing blocks and frustrations in bureaucratic, larger organizations is likely to propel an individual into entrepreneurial venture creation. Thus, needs and values assumed early in life, are characterized as achievement, control, risk-taking, tolerance of ambiguity, and type A behaviour. These values are regarded as being well-established prior to adulthood, and antecedents for entrepreneurship, but are also considered very difficult to teach or train (Cunningham & Lischeron, 1991).

The Classical School of Entrepreneurship

This school separates the manager from the entrepreneur, taken from the French verb *entreprendre*, literally translated as 'to undertake', which sounds considerably more passive as a verb in English than its active French counterpart. The French word was translated from the German verb *unternehmen* also meaning 'to undertake'. In the early sixteenth century, entrepreneurs were Frenchmen that lead military expeditions, extending by the 1700s to include contractors who undertook to construct roads, harbours, bridges and forts for the military. French economists linked the word to people who took more risks and managed more uncertainty for innovation. These definitions include notions of undertaking (founding) a venture (or adventure) necessitating a level of risk and uncertainty (Cunningham & Lischeron, 1991).

Late 1800 definitions in the English language included the concept of the "contractor" acting as the intermediary between capital and labour. While this definition does recognize the notions of innovation and managing others, it does not include risk-taking by an owner. The focus seems to be on "doing" rather than "owning" a venture or business (Hebert & Link, 1982). For Schumpeter (1934) ownership is not the focus, rather the essential element of entrepreneurship is the innovativeness of people, not the ownership. Carrying out new combinations of the means of production, implies that entrepreneurs are 'combiners' and strongly suggests that they do not have to be owners. The key factors that underpin this theory are innovation, creativity or discovery. Thus, entrepreneurship is the process of creating an opportunity, or the opportunity-seeking style of management that stimulates innovation (Peterson, 1985).

Creativity is often linked to independence and individuality, even nonconformity, which is why going against the tide or antisocial behaviour can also be associated with this notion. Thus, inventors can appear to be against the established order, even eccentric, and thus perhaps isolated, until they can draw people in and around them as the invented concept gathers credence (Cunningham & Lischeron, 1991). Steve Jobs, a co-founder of Apple Computer, is viewed as largely possessing the characteristics of being innovative, energetic, able to excite and stimulate those around him. However, once the activity is achieved, does the same energy lead to destructive management and administration? (Cunningham & Lischeron, 1991)

The Management School of Entrepreneurship

Entrepreneurship draws considerably from management theory, given initial definitions were intuitively linked to management. Often drawn from the definitions initially offered by Henri Fayol, the view is that managers perform many functions, including planning, organizing, staffing, budgeting, coordinating and controlling (Fayol, 1950). The Management School views an entrepreneur as one who organizes or manages a business undertaking and assumes risk for the sake of profit. John Stuart Mills viewed the entrepreneur as essentially a risk-taker, but also carrying out additional functions of supervision, control and providing direction for the firm (Semmel, 1984; Cunningham & Lischeron, 1991). Functions can be related to the initial start-up, including strategizing, developing the business plan, getting started, and managing the development and growth of the venture (Kao, 1989; 1993).

Other views include the movement from entrepreneurial to professional management as a strategy where the functions of coordination, including delegation of responsibilities take on a more formal structure (Roberts, 1987). This greater level of formality includes the development of formal business plans, analysing opportunities systematically, acquiring resources with a focus on working hard to achieve the desired goals (Bird, 1988; Cunningham & Lischeron, 1991). The basic belief is that entrepreneurship can be taught and developed through training in a classroom, and that the high failure rate of ventures is due to poor or limited training and decision-making, as well as lack of understanding of marketing and financing decisions. Thus, entrepreneurship is about training in the essential functions to acquire the necessary skills to run the core functions of managing a business. The learning focus is on perfecting the management capability of the person by developing the rational, analytical, cause-and-effect and managerial orientation capabilities. As entrepreneurs can be trained, specific functions are identified as important that then require training to increase proficiency to existing and new entrepreneurs, specifically in finance and marketing to reduce business failure (Cunningham & Lischeron, 1991). However, the failure rate for managers of firms adopting a late, slow and cautious sequential expansion approach is significantly lower than managers of small firms adopting other paths to internationalization as well as contextual factors impacting decision-making (Arasti, Zandi & Bahmani, 2014; Cope, 2011, Robson et al., 2019).

The Leadership School of Entrepreneurship

The leadership approach to entrepreneurship suggests that entrepreneurs need to be skilled at enlisting others to 'join their cause'. Success requires that they be able to manage people and be effective leaders or mentors, who take a leading role in motivating, directing and leading others. Thus, entrepreneurs must be leaders, able to make clear to others their vision of what is possible and to attract others to transform ideas into reality (Kao, 1989; 1993). There are broadly two streams of literature within the leadership approach to entrepreneurship. The first stream is linked to the Great Person school of thought, which suggests that traits and personal characteristics are likely to be important success factors. Like the Great Person school, early leadership research adopts a similar view, namely, that key traits including adaptability to situations, cooperativeness, energy and willingness to take responsibility are key aspects to success (Bass, 1981; Cunningham & Lischeron, 1991).

The second stream of literature is more pervasive and focuses on how successful leaders can ensure tasks are accomplished (Hemphill, 1959), which is linked to two dimensions: first, getting the tasks accomplished, and second, having concern for those performing the tasks. These two dimensions are major aspects of leadership. Other research suggests that successful leaders are those able to adjust to changing situations (Fiedler, 1966). Thus, entrepreneurial leadership goes beyond the personal traits or styles of relating to others. This research sees the role as one that brings about change, bringing in new values and skills and the ability to set clear goals while creating opportunities. The skills most important to the leadership approach to entrepreneurship are therefore those that empower people, maintaining organizational intimacy, along with the development of a supportive human resource system (Kao, 1993).

On the basis of the above, a leader can be described as a 'social architect' or an expert in promoting, preserving and ensuring the 'protection of values' (Cunningham & Lischeron, 1991). These values might include 'respect for the individual'. Some research makes the fine distinction between leading and exerting managerial control over individuals. Thus, entrepreneurs exist in complex social networks that will either inhibit or enable venture development. In the right environment, a healthy social network will provide ideas, access to key resources, commitment and support to complete tasks. More effective leaders are those able to create, instil and develop commitment to the vision that becomes institutionalized (Bennis & Nanus, 1985; Cunningham & Lischeron, 1991). Another implicit assumption is that leaders must have the capability of developing and mentoring people (Levinson, Darrow, Klein, Levinson & McKee, 1978). Experienced mentors are leaders who are able to pass on critical skills through the mentoring process, implying that the entrepreneur is far more than a manager, but also a leader of others.

The Intrapreneurship/Corporate School of Entrepreneurship

This approach evolved from a perceived lack of innovativeness and competitiveness within organizations. *Intra*preneurs, with a certain extent of discretionary freedom, are able to act as entrepreneurs in organizations and implement their own ideas without having to be owners. Intrapreneurs are alert to opportunities, and this feature is regarded as one of the key dimensions of intrapreneurial activity (Cunningham & Lischeron, 1991). It is deemed important and regarded as strategic behaviour as a means of furthering the organization's activities and discovering opportunities (McMullen & Warnick, 2016). The notion of discretionary freedom can be linked to concepts such as subsidiary autonomy. This autonomy can be developed through entrepreneurial opportunity recognition by a foreign country manager as part of the process of developing centres of excellence, through innovation and new product development, appropriate to the local environment. The skills, networks and knowledge, which originate in a foreign market suitable for the local requirements, can then be directed back to the parent headquarters as *intra*organizational learning to improve not only local, but also overall headquarter effectiveness, profit and organizational sustainability (Cavanagh, Freeman, Kalfadellis & Cavusgil, 2017; Cavanagh, Freeman, Kalfadellis & Herbert, 2017). Intraorganizational entrepreneurship allows organizations to diversify their activities into other areas, learn from their divisions, and support the creation and development of independent units that can create markets and expand innovation services and products throughout the entire organization (Cunningham & Lischeron, 1991).

Questions have been raised as to why intrapreneurship should be considered a separate school. While some argue that entrepreneurship and administrative (bureaucratic) activities are mutually exclusive, others suggest otherwise. Schumpeter (1934) argued that successful entrepreneurial activity leads to organization-building and entrepreneurs having to be managers. One of the key implicit assumptions in the intrapreneurship school is that innovation can be developed in existing organisations by supporting and encouraging people to behave as entrepreneurs in semi-autonomous units (Cunningham & Lischeron, 1991). This viewpoint is similar to the arguments discussed above for developing subsidiary autonomy and intraorganizational learning advantages and sustainable centres of excellence (Cavanagh, Freeman, Kalfadellis & Cavusgil, 2017; Cavanagh, Freeman, Kalfadellis & Herbert, 2017). It can be difficult in larger organisations, for example, to establish an affective headquarter-and-subsidiary relationship, which requires the right blend of willingness, capacities and leadership of managers from both organizational levels to reap the benefits.

In situations where this entrepreneurial behaviour by managers is not valued, or is frustrated, managers will leave to begin their own entrepreneurial ventures (Knight, 1988). While some might argue that this move is a result of the inherent differences between management and entrepreneurial activity, as argued above, to make this work effectively, managers from across the organization need to empower those willing to engage in this risky behaviour, as there can be short term and long term financial and non-financial benefits to the organization (Cavanagh, Freeman, Kalfadellis & Cavusgil, 2017; Cavanagh, Freeman, Kalfadellis & Herbert, 2017). The success of the intrapreneurial model is very much dependent upon the abilities and capabilities of the various operational levels to exploit entrepreneurial opportunities.

The school does not just support a model that encourages bureaucratic activity, but rather one that uses people effectively. The school does not promote the idea of providing freedom to managers in organizations to then become entrepreneurial. One key assumption is that individuals are required to be able to work effectively with others and especially within teams. When people work in teams, they are then in a position to better recognize the importance of political needs, and in-group and out-group behaviours in order to implement their ideas (Freeman & Lindsay, 2011). For this reason, this school of thought offers a team model where individuals must work in teams and create opportunities to solve complex organizational problems. This model requires entrepreneurs to

| Strategic Redirection | Organizational Duplicaton | Product Development | Operational Efficiency |

Figure 2.1 Focus on intra-preneurial activities.

Source: Cunningham and Lischeron (1991: 55).

have highly developed team-building capabilities, be able to create the right balance in teams and allow different but complementary input from team members. Sometimes the use of professionals may be required, and in other situations support of and assistance to operational workers (Cunningham & Lischeron, 1991). Importantly, intrapreneurial activities can enhance strategic directions, organizational duplication, product development and operational efficiency presented in Figure 2.1.

Strategic intrapreneurship may need the involvement of the key professionals and managers who understand the market conditions. Existing corporate facilities can be enhanced by the discovery of new markets. Organizational intrapreneurship requires the commitment of cross sections of people within the organization, who then must take on the responsibility of introducing and supporting the new organizational tasks across the organization. A related term is product intrapreneurship, which requires a combination of people who are familiar with product development and market conditions. The goal is to build on existing corporate facilities to develop new products. Thus, operational strategies target improvements in both the quality and efficiency of the services being offered (Cunningham & Lischeron, 1991).

Transnational (immigrant and ethnic) Entrepreneurship School

Relying on two fields of internationalization process literature, namely, immigrant entrepreneur and international business (Figueira-de-Lemos, Johanson & Vahlne, 2011), this school of thought addresses the question of how immigrant entrepreneurs in the host country identify foreign market opportunities. Based primarily on the network perspective (Blankenburg, 1995), with a focus on social network theory and social ties (Patel & Conklin, 2009), some studies in the literature on immigrant entrepreneurs attempt to explore the internationalization process of entrepreneurs (Jean, Tan & Sinkovics, 2011; Mustafa & Chen, 2010). Conversely, international business scholars have spent considerable time and effort on the internationalization process, with major emphasis on the identification of foreign market opportunities, albeit without considered focus on immigrant entrepreneurs (Ellis, 2011; Johnson & Vahlne, 2009).

The school regards the identification of business opportunities in foreign markets as a process whereby an individual identifies "new, innovative solutions to the supply of already existing products and services" (Mathews & Zander, 2007: 393). This process is an important phase of the internationalization process (Hayton, Chandler & DeTienne, 2011). Drawing on network theory, Evers and Knight (2008) and Ellis (2011) examine the processes used by firms to identify foreign market opportunities. They suggest that social ties influence the flow of information about opportunities, and individuals not connected to the network are unable to obtain such information. The limited research on the immigrant entrepreneur opportunity identification process provides support for the use of country of origin ethnic and kinship ties (Iyer & Shapiro, 1999; Jean, Tan & Sinkovics, 2011). However, this is yet to be comprehensively explored as highlighted by Ellis (2011: 99): "there is little known about the methods used by entrepreneurs for opportunity recognition ... how these opportunities come to be recognized and exploited is rarely addressed". This is supported by Chandra, Styles and Wilkinson (2009: 31) as this process "is the beginning of the inter-nationalization process and deserves more systematic research attention than it has so far received because it is the trigger that starts everything off". The literature remains unclear about the ability of social and kinship ties to facilitate immigrant entrepreneur identification of foreign market opportunities. In light of the lack of research and limited understanding, this stream of research contributes to existing literature by integrating immigrant entrepreneur (Chand & Ghorbani, 2011; Mustafa & Chen, 2010) and IB research (Ellis, 2011; Kontinen & Ojala, 2011) and examines immigrant entrepreneurs' use of social ties (including ethnic and kinship ties) to identify foreign market opportunities.

Specifically, Smans, Freeman and Thomas (2014) examined how Italian immigrant entrepreneurs in Australia identify foreign market opportunities. Australia is an ideal location to examine immigrant entrepreneurs due to the long history of immigration (Australian Bureau of Statistics, 2008). Approximately one in four Australians is born overseas, with a similar number having at least one parent born overseas. Among developed countries, only Israel has a similar immigrant profile (Borooah & Mangan, 2007). The Italian community has been present in Australia for over a century, but, interestingly, the ethnic and familial ties back to the country of origin are not the major influence on where they internationalize; rather, the choice is opportunity driven (Smans, Freeman & Thomas, 2014). The extent to which the ethnic diaspora influences these locational choices is among the issues explored in this school and is still not understood.

Women/Gender Entrepreneurship School

This school has developed a critique of contemporary approaches to analysing the impact of gender upon entrepreneurial propensity and activity. Since the 1990s, increasing attention has been afforded to the influence of gender on women's entrepreneurial behaviour. Such analyses have highlighted an embedded masculinity within the entrepreneurial discourse, which privileges men as normative entrepreneurial actors. While invaluable in revealing a prevailing masculine bias within entrepreneurship, this critique is bounded by positioning women as a proxy for the gendered subject. This is a potentially limiting analysis that does not fully recognize gender as a human property with myriad articulations enacted throughout entrepreneurial activity. To progress debate, this stream of research focuses more deeply on the notion of gender as a multiplicity, exploring the implications for future studies of entrepreneurial activity.

Some time ago, Holmquist and Sundin (1989: 1) observed that entrepreneurship research was "about men, by men and for men". This prejudicial approach has been critiqued in the intervening years with a growing body of work focused on the influence of gendered ascriptions on women's entrepreneurial activity, which has developed in scope and sophistication (Ahl, 2006; McAdam, 2012; Martinez Dy & Marlow, 2017). Focusing solely on women's entrepreneurial activity, however, suggests that the gender critique is predominantly about women, while scrutiny of the literature suggests that it is also largely written by women. Thus, there is an emergent critique about women and by women that is, in turn, assumed to be for women. In effect, moving away from the perception of women as a category to avoid is a generic proxy for the gendered subject. This helps to avoid an untenable transposition where women, as a substantive category, are conflated with – or at the least, representative of – gender, a complex theoretical construct with numerous iterations and interpretations (Butler, 2004; Kelan, 2010; Linstead & Pullen, 2006; Martinez Dy et al., 2017).

Additionally, the school addresses implicit assumptions of heteronormativity (Marlow & Martinez Dy, 2017), whiteness (Ogbor, 2000) and place (Al-Dajani et al., 2015), embedding these aspects into the prevailing critique. Consequently, we have a maturing debate analysing women's entrepreneurial behaviour (Henry et al., 2015; Jennings & Brush, 2013), which, although invaluable in recognizing sexist and misogynist gender bias, assists in avoiding the danger of partiality in presenting gender as a one-dimensional property of women alone, rather than recognizing it as a multiplicity enacted by all human subjects in a diverse range of contexts.

Drawing on examples from more established disciplines within the social sciences that have developed a broad critical engagement with notions of gender, the school draws from a number of informative debates that can usefully be incorporated into current analyses of gender and entrepreneurship. Such views argue that gender is related to, but distinctly not coterminous with, biological sex (Fausto-Sterling, 2000; Oakley, 1972). For example, the historical progress of knowledge creation from disciplines such as sociology (Anthias, 2008; McDowell, 2014), law and critical race studies (Crenshaw, 1991), feminist economics (McKay, Campbell & Thompson, 2014) and gender studies (Acker, 2006), has resulted in a conceptualization of gender that is neither the property of women nor a simple male–female variable, but instead an overarching, dynamic yet durable social structure with complex dimensions and effects (Bowden & Mummery, 2014; Linstead & Pullen, 2006; Risman, 2004).

Yet, such a complex notion of gender and related implications, remains somewhat underdeveloped within explorations of entrepreneurial activity where the gender critique still tends to dwell on the generic 'female entrepreneur'. This not only limits our understanding of gender in all its diverse forms (Linstead & Pullen, 2006; Risman, 2004) but also ensures that when gender is considered, the symbolic category of women and their activities becomes the focus, thus shepherding all things related to women into specialist, separate categories. Siphoning off women, and issues related to them in this way, then ensures that alleged 'mainstream' debates regarding 'core' entrepreneurial activities and processes (opportunity recognition, start-up, effectuation, growth and exit processes) are positioned as gender neutral, whereas in fact, they are gender blind (Jones, 2014). Creating a separate women–gender niche facilitates the persistence of such assumptions; it is not disputed that creating separate spaces that position women and their priorities, views and needs as central is invaluable to generate voice and visibility. If such spaces are used to sideline and corral challenging ideas and uncomfortable arguments that disrupt normative analyses, we risk channelling critical voices inwards to confirm the views of the converted. Rather, similar to somewhat more mature disciplines, the school is exposing more recent research streams that are more confronting and thereby disrupt assumptions regarding the role and position of gender into mainstream entrepreneurship debate. This research is finding pathways to explore how gender in all its iterations impacts upon all entrepreneurial activities, rather than focusing only on how gendered ascriptions position women in this debate.

The tendency to consider women entrepreneurs (either as a discrete category or as individuals) as typical gendered research subjects is also potentially problematic in that it may generate a reified, fictive construct of the female entrepreneur, with empirical examples removed from context. Examining the motivations, activities and accomplishments of female entrepreneurs, absented from the relations within which they 'do' and enact gender (Bruni, Gherardi & Poggio, 2004), unduly limits the scope of any analysis. Evidence indicates that most entrepreneurial activity occurs within families and households (Carter et al., 2017; Klotz, Hmieleski, Bradley, 2014); team-led ventures are common while even sole proprietors cannot create and operate ventures in a vacuum (Yang & Aldrich, 2014). Thus, how gendered ascriptions shape the availability, accrual and flow of entrepreneurial ideas, resources and competencies between those involved with or operating a venture is pivotal whether at the level of the family, household, team or stakeholder group. Within current debate, however, the dominant focus tends to remain on a mythologized female entrepreneur – isolated by her sex and defined by her gender.

Accordingly, the purpose of this school of entrepreneurship is to pursue the arguments regarding how we study the influence of gender on entrepreneurial activity. Hence, the school is categorically not a literature review of extant work, but rather, more recent discourse aims to offer a constructive critique of current debate by recognizing that as a social ascription, gender is a fundamental characterization of all human actors, whether men, women (cis and trans), intersex or gender non-conforming. As such, how gender influences behaviours, including entrepreneurial activity, will influence the way it is applied by the subject under consideration. In addition, the value of privileging gender as an isolated analytical tool is questioned. Ignoring the influence of other critical social characteristics (e.g. class, race/ethnicity and age) and how these intersect with gender, a notion captured by the black feminist construct of intersectionality (Crenshaw, 1991; Hill Collins, 2000[1990]) risks a partial explanation for social positionality and its effects (Anthias, 2001; Essers & Benschop, 2009). The school promulgates the core argument that a more sophisticated engagement with gender within the context of entrepreneurship is necessary and can be accomplished by studying how other disciplines have addressed gender biased gaps in theorizing over time.

Family Entrepreneurship School

Entrepreneurs have been traditionally epitomized as rugged individuals garnering creative forces of innovation and technology. Applying this traditional, limited and narrow view of entrepreneurship to ethnic firm creation and growth is to ignore or discount core cultural values of the ethnic contexts in which these firms operate. It is no longer possible to depend solely on human capital theory and household characteristic descriptions to understand the complex and interdependent relationships between the ethnic-owning family, its firm and the community context in which the firm operates. This school addresses the complex dynamic of ethnic firms with three purposes: first, to provide a cultural context for the ethnic groups composing the national minority business owner; second, to extend the Sustainable Family Business Theory (Stafford, Duncan, Danes & Winter, 1999; Danes et al., 2008), a dynamic, behaviourally based, multi-dimensional family firm theory, by clarifying how it accommodates ethnic firm complexities within their cultural context.

To ignore ethnic and family contexts that create the culture from which entrepreneurship emerges is to forge a myopic view of ethnic businesses owned and operated by their family members. Yet, to date, most of the research has been based on this limited view. In fact, family appears to be more important in ethnic-family businesses than in others because of the collective orientation that characterizes cultures other than, for example, Euro-American (Landau, 2007). Although ethnicity is an individual attribute, it contributes to a larger culture as individuals of the same or different ethnicities interact in families, social groups and societies (Coleman, 1988; Gollnick & Chinn, 1990). Indeed, the family, with its own interpersonal dynamics, acts as the crucible that mixes ethnicities and creates culture, thereby serving as the "mediating milieu" for the entrepreneurial experience (Rogoff & Heck, 2003; Stafford et al., 1999).

Rogoff and Heck (2003) argue that increasing research highlights fundamentally entrepreneurship cannot be understood without acknowledging the importance of the family firm and the mobilization of the family. While the traditional portrayal of the entrepreneur as a rugged individual garnering the creative forces of innovation and technology has permeated entrepreneurship research (Dimov, 2007), views are changing. Cramton (1993) identified a firm creation paradox in that creating firms followed the traditional mantra of rugged individualism publicly, but in private accounts, the firm creation was described as a collaborative entity determined mainly by changes in family relationships, rather than a desire for individual achievement or acknowledgement of economic opportunity. Some years later, Dimov (2007) recognized entrepreneurship as a dynamic, iterative social process that develops opportunities through discussion and interpretation, and accounts for the context in which these opportunities emerge.

More recently, the school has sought to avoid the narrow view of entrepreneurship limited to ethnic and family-run firms that ignores or discounts core cultural values of the community in which these firms operate (Owen & Rowe, 1995).

Yet, regardless of this desire, most literature on ethnicity and entrepreneurship has focused on traits and trends on the national level and on explanations for the differences among ethnic groups (Owen & Rowe, 1995). Theories of ethnic entrepreneurship have concentrated on ethnic and class resources affecting business development, primarily because of the nature of available data (Fairlie, 2004), which has been derived from government sources with large samples and little data on business management or from small samples of family-run firms with limited geographic or ethnic diversity and more in-depth data (Menzies, Filion, Brenner & Elgie, 2007). Within this literature stream, Bohon (2001) states that it is no longer possible to depend solely on human capital theory and household characteristic descriptions to understand the complex and interdependent relationships between the ethnic-owning family, its firm and the community context in which the firm operates.

With the emergence of national minority business owner surveys (Puryear et al., 2008), however, in-depth information is now available from random, national samples of African-American, Korean-American and Mexican-American family business owners, inclusive of owning families and their firms. Considering both the current definition of opportunity creation in the literature and the focus of most ethnic entrepreneurship literature, the study of these ethnic-owning families and their firms requires new theoretical lenses that accommodate both family and business systems along with their interaction within the cultural context of their ethnic communities. The school of entrepreneurship has several objectives, among others, to provide a cultural context for different ethnic groups composing a deeper reflection with national minority business owner studies. Furthermore, the school aims to extend theoretical frameworks, such as the Sustainable Family Business Theory, to accommodate the complexities of ethnic firms and their cultural context. Finally, the school seeks to derive implications for research, education and public policy to inform government and society about such global issues as globalization and migration, and the impact on ethnic family-run firms.

Entrepreneurship Ecosystems School

According to the Entrepreneurship Ecosystems School, entrepreneurial activity exhibits significant geographical variations within and across countries, both in terms of start-ups and scale-ups. Entrepreneurs typically establish their businesses in the localities in which they are already living and working, and businesses rarely move to distant locations once they have started trading; this suggests that some geographical environments are more conducive to entrepreneurship while others inhibit it. The concept of entrepreneurial ecosystems (EEs) has emerged in recent years as a framework to understand the nature of places in which entrepreneurial activity flourishes. Spigel (2015, 2017) defines entrepreneurial ecosystems as combinations of social, political, economic and cultural elements. These elements coexist within a region and support the development and growth of innovative start-ups, and inspire emerging entrepreneurs and other actors to take the risk of starting, funding and otherwise supporting high-risk ventures.

However, the existing literature has several failings. Despite some progress (Acs et al., 2014, 2017), the concept of entrepreneurship ecosystems is undertheorized. It remains unclear how entrepreneurial ecosystems are distinct from other concepts that seek to explain the geographical concentration of entrepreneurial activity (e.g. clusters, learning regions and regional innovation systems). Much of the literature stream encompasses limited and "superficial generalizations … rather than [on] rigorous social science research" (Acs et al., 2017: 2). More precisely, empirical studies have a tendency towards static rather than dynamic explanations which do not capture the origin, development and evolution of entrepreneurship ecosystems (Mason & Brown, 2014; Mack & Mayer, 2016; Alvedalen & Boschma, 2017). Diminutive consideration is given to the context in which entrepreneurial ecosystems emerge (Mack & Mayer, 2016). The network of interactions of individual elements in the entrepreneurship ecosystems has not been sufficiently explored (Motoyama & Watkins, 2014). Specifically, the causal mechanisms are weak and it remains unclear how the various elements in entrepreneurial ecosystems enhance entrepreneurship (Alvedalen & Boschma, 2017; Acs et al., 2017; Stam, 2015).

Increasingly, the school focus is on individuals within the entrepreneurial ecosystem, investigating how people work within and interact with firms and institutions in an entrepreneurial ecosystem to bring about the outputs and outcomes that result from entrepreneurial behaviour. Similarly, the research focus is on how the different elements in an entrepreneurial ecosystem interact with one another and how these interactions develop over time. Questions of path dependency within the system are being explored. Research that focuses on the role of networks in the entrepreneurial ecosystem context is similarly being examined to see whether these interactions can be mapped and analysed. In addition, research that adopts a "pipelines" perspective (Bathelt, Malmberg & Maskell, 2004), examining the extent, role and significance of the external networks of entrepreneurial ecosystems, is emerging. This stream of research also considers network tipping points, critical densities and vitality that assist to explain entrepreneurship ecosystems behaviour which remains underexplored.

Other scholars are examining the temporal dynamics of entrepreneurial ecosystems. Questions include: How do the systems develop over time? What are the causal relationships? What are the processes by which entrepreneurial ecosystems develop and change over time? Why do some emerging entrepreneurial ecosystems fail to develop? Why do some go into decline? Some of this work draws on recent work on resilience (e.g. Simmie & Martin, 2010; Martin, 2011; Williams & Vorley, 2014; Boschma, 2015), and the processes that result in the revitalization of entrepreneurial ecosystems that are in decline or moribund.

Increasingly, research that addresses governmental policy issues is increasing as policymakers continually search for instruments that can be implemented to stimulate entrepreneurial activity and as governments have become active in promoting entrepreneurial ecosystems not only within the developed economies, but more so in the emerging and transitional economies. Research that investigates the roles governments, non-profit organizations and private companies, as well as key individuals, play in the emergence and growth of entrepreneurial ecosystems and what types of support are in evidence is a growing research stream. Likewise, research that seeks to provide an evidence-based rationale for intervention initiatives is increasing, as are questions regarding the effect of the intervention in the short-term and over the longer term. Further research streams that seek to explore how various policies might specifically influence elements of an entrepreneurship ecosystems and conversely how elements of entrepreneurship ecosystems influence policy are increasingly popular in this school of thought.

Finally, research that takes into account industry specific entrepreneurship ecosystems and how these develop individually or integrate more broadly into regional or city-based entrepreneurship ecosystems is an extension of this stream of research, which explores and identifies the layered effects of entrepreneurship ecosystems and interactions between supra and sub entrepreneurial ecosystems. This research stream also explores how cognitive and geographic distance influences the relationships within and between entrepreneurship ecosystems and the potential effect of global relationships on local and/or industry entrepreneurship ecosystems dynamics.

An appropriate entrepreneurial model

One way of approaching the various schools of entrepreneurship is to recognize that each has an important contribution to make to our overall understanding and that each provides different insights into the complexity that shapes any study into entrepreneurship (Cooper, Woo & Dunkelberg, 1988). Furthermore, these schools are not uniquely distinct or exclusive. With the ever-expanding interest in the study of entrepreneurship there is a need for better theoretically derived frameworks, models and concepts that delineate the field, identify the building-blocks, assumptions, foci, concepts and dimensions. Some argue that differentiating the entrepreneurship field from other social sciences, especially strategic management, would be beneficial (Zahra & Dess, 2001). This view has been predicated based on the argument that entrepreneurship has become a broad label for which there is no logic or clarity. However, how the field would benefit from being separated from strategic management is debatable considering certain obvious links of the strategic management school of thought to entrepreneurship. After all, strategic management itself draws on many social science disciplines (Barney, 1991) and derives strength from its eclectic nature (Zahra & Dess, 2001).

Like entrepreneurship, strategic management is interested in the exploitation of profitable opportunities. One of the principle underlying assumptions of the Austrian School in strategic management (Schumpeter, 1934) is the temporary nature of advantage, which some might argue is a dynamic capability. Weerawardena, Sullivan Mort and Liesch (2017: 1) suggest that "Founders [entrepreneurs] transform the operational capabilities they endow to the firm, develop dynamic capabilities for use in opportunity exploitation, and deploy these to develop knowledge intensive products that they take to chosen niche markets". The role of strategic management and capability development is inseparable from the process of opportunity recognition and exploitation. To focus on the recognition of performance advantage is valuable but not enough to understand the process. Understanding the external environment is an essential requirement to understanding the entrepreneurial process (Zahra & Dess, 2001).

Recent integration of real options literature into the strategic management literature to address recognition of opportunities and the costs and uncertainties around decisions to delay full investment until more information about the environment is known, are critical to our understanding of the iterative process of entrepreneurship (Dixit & Pindyck, 1994; Zahra & Dess, 2001). Additionally, concepts of opportunity recognition, premiums for time, capital and uncertainty, equally apply to entrepreneurship as they do to strategic management if we focus on start-up or venture creation. The initial venture phases are emphasized in the approaches of both the Great Person and Psychological Characteristics schools as well as the Transnational and Entrepreneurship Ecosystems schools in describing entrepreneurship. We know that these concepts are likely to also apply to larger organizations, irrespective of their level of innovation and value creating activities if they are focused on change and survival (Zahra & Dess, 2001), where questions of early growth and maturity emerge, such as the Classical, Management, Leadership and Women/Gender schools. The focus of maturity and change is captured more acutely in the Intrapreneurship, Family and Entrepreneurship Ecosystems schools of thought on entrepreneurship.

The definition of entrepreneurship would benefit from a more holistic approach. Shane and Venkataraman (2000) highlight three areas of importance including the identification of entrepreneurial ideas: who, when and by whom are these discovered, and how are these opportunities exploited. Zahra and

Dess (2001) add a fourth area, suggesting the "outcomes" of exploiting entrepreneurial opportunities should also be included. We need to note, that not all ventures succeed and typically many fail suggesting that the learning from "entrepreneurial failure" by entrepreneurs is in need of more investigation (Sui & Baum, 2014; Sultan & Wong, 2011; Cope, 2011). Therefore, a definition of entrepreneurship as a field of scholarly enquiry would benefit from recognizing "the outcomes of the process, whether these outcomes are positive or negative, immediate or long term, or tangible or intangible" (Zahra & Dess, 2001: 9).

Another reason for the study of entrepreneurship is the development in our understanding of the role of human capital and the improvement of intellectual capital. Given entrepreneurship focuses on developing and exploiting opportunities, we need to know far more about how this "contributes to the development and growth of individuals who take part in this process" (Zahra and Dess, 2001: 9). The schools of Management, Leadership, Intrapreneurship, Women/ Gender, Transnational and Family offer valuable approaches for exploring these aspects of entrepreneurship, which are important to note because it is not a coincidence that countries and companies that promote entrepreneurial activities are also among the most proactive in developing and nurturing their human capital (CIA World Factbook, 2018). The relationship between entrepreneurship and human and intellectual capital is dynamic, with each impacting the other over time. We therefore need more research that can assist our understanding of the "major source of differences between countries and companies – that is, their ability to create and inculcate new knowledge that fosters the development of future entrepreneurial opportunities in turn" (Zahra & Dess, 2001: 9).

While Shane and Venkataraman (2000) emphasize the importance in strategic management of focusing more on individuals and opportunities and less on the environmental antecedents and consequences, Ramoglou and Tsang (2018) argue that this view is baffling, given the importance of the environmental factors as antecedents in understanding the process of entrepreneurial activities. Entrepreneurs combine various key resources in response to perceived changes in the external environment, creating new forms. The same can be said of established organisations, who similarly support and foster entrepreneurial activities in response to environmental changes (Cavanagh, Freeman, Kalfadellis & Cavusgil, 2017). Research tells us that recognizing environmental forces will improve theory-building and testing of the impact of various entrepreneurial activities on value creation in both new and established organizations. By contextualizing our research, we can better understand the moderating effects and improve prescriptive theory (Piekkari, Welch & Paavilainen, 2009). These aspects of focus are addressed through the Management, Leadership and Intrapreneurship schools as well as the of Transnational, Family, Women/ Gender and Entrepreneurship Ecosystems schools of thought on entrepreneurship. Thus, separating strategic management from entrepreneurship to address the perceived crisis in its identity suggested by Shane and Venkataraman (2000) seems debatable. There are numerous opportunities for integrating and synthe-sizing the attributes of strategic management and international entrepreneurship (Nambisan & Zahra, 2016) and drawing on one or some of the ten schools of thought to provide philosophical and theoretical underpinnings given the con-textual environment.

The important factors range from the personal qualities or values of man-agers, while others focus on being able to anticipate the future, creating as well as recognizing opportunities, to generate new ventures in a range of economies – advanced, emerging and transitional. Success of entrepreneurs can also be related to technical and non-technical managerial skills such as marketing and financial. Another factor relates to the need to change the direction of the venture, which can also be achieved within existing larger organizations, to enable the necessary change for continued organizational survival (Cavanagh, Freeman, Kalfadellis & Cavusgil, 2017). Phases of entrepreneurial venture development or evolution include start-up and early growth, maturity and change (Trudgen & Freeman, 2014), made more difficult across challenging international contexts and influences of the digital-age and e-commerce.

Each school of thought is built on certain assumptions or premises about entrepreneurial behaviour that relate to past events, traits, personal principles and values, and characteristics. This will lead to different research foci and insights. Thus, success of entrepreneurs relates to their history, their principles formed early in life, ways of managing people, how they go about planning and the management procedures they adopt, their ethnicity, gender and the totality of their experiences. The essential point to make here is that building an argument that one school is better than another is meaningless. The various schools offer different insights into a complex multidimensional concept, namely, entrepreneurship. The different definitions and criteria of each school discussed above rest on frameworks and models that have distinct traditions, assumptions and implications for research, training and value of education. Definitions of entrepreneurship vary considerably, and involve many factors, such as imagining, believing, creating, discovering, managing, controlling and change (Ramoglou & Tsang, 2018, 2017, 2016).

The ten schools discussed here provide a different platform for the type of research design and direction, and emphasis with the intended research foci. The Classical school emphasizes creativity and decision-making as its criteria and focuses on seeing opportunities and creating the venture. Histories of suc-cessful entrepreneurs provide valuable insights, potentially even personal guid-ance. The Psychology school emphasizes research and training, predicated on values and behaviours, such as risk-taking and the need for achievement. The technical emphasis of the Management and Entrepreneurship Ecosystems schools underpins key tools for managing, planning and organizing. Emphasis on the importance of leading and motivating is important to the Leadership, Transnational, Family and Women/Gender schools, and the focus is working with people as this is central, along with a clear statement of the vision. Finally, the encouragement of entrepreneurial activity within established, often larger organizations is emphasized in the Intrapreneurial school, with focus on team-building that supports creative problem-solving, autonomy and risk-taking and change. Each of the ten schools offers various avenues for a more process-oriented approach to researching entrepreneurship in recognition of opportunities, acting and managing the process, processing the need for change and, finally, for evaluating the self, that integrates the external and internal processes of entrepreneurship – as a journey.

The conceptualization for moving forward on research in entrepreneurship does not suggest a mixture of assumptions and philosophical underpinnings of the various schools. Instead, what is offered and suggested is that entrepreneurship should be conceived as an iterative process. This implies a process of personal reflection to evaluate values and drivers, planning, acting out scenarios and re-evaluating, which will then motivate people, managers and entrepreneurs to willingly embrace risk-taking and responsibility for creating and innovating (Shane & Venkataraman, 2000; Barney, 1991). The implication is also that whatever is created is of value to those within the organization as their contribution is valued as part of the process of producing services and products that are of value to the firm and multiple stakeholders, including society at large. This concept is referred to as 'systems thinking' and focuses on contributing value to the system from which the firm draws its resources, locally and globally, and not just at the level of an individual or a firm (Neesham & Freeman, 2016).

Thus, organizational behaviour, macro-organizational theory, and human resource management have benefited from adopting and maintaining an eclectic view of the domains and theory, and similarly, economics has increased its rigour by introducing theories and research questions drawn from other disciplines. Further iterative consideration to the schools of thought, and integration rather than separation, is likely to be the key to more fruitful research in the future. This is especially important given the need to understand the many changes happening in the external environment, especially from the emerging and transitional economies as a source of new learning to reduce poverty through small venture creation (Maksimov, Wang & Luo, 2017) and building uncertainty management capability (Cuervo-Cazurra, Ciravegna, Melgarejo & Lopez, 2018). The environment is a critical focus for the strategic management field, including related concepts, such as risk and uncertainty. These concepts are central to strategic management and entrepreneurship. The essential underpinnings or assumption of this iterative entrepreneurial process include creating the idea or opportunity, assessment of an individual's abilities and undertaking actions now as well as in the future. A related assumption is that managers take responsibility for the venture or share the risks with others, and are rewarded appropriately for doing so, and finally, create value for society at large – recognizing the enormous diversity in economies and the shift to the emerging and transitional.

Finally, whether opportunities are discovered or created is constantly discussed in the field of entrepreneurship (Ramoglou & Tsang, 2016). While authors sympathetic to the discovery, creation and/or the actualization approaches concur that recognition of potential opportunities is focal, their approaches to exploring the nature and process of opportunity recognition vary considerably (Ramoglou & Tsang, 2018). Entrepreneurship researchers have long called for a more process-oriented approach to researching the phenomena, however defined. Arguing that entrepreneurship is an organizational creation, Gartner (1985) pointed out that the process through which new ventures are created is an essential part of our understanding of this phenomenon. Wiklund, Davidsson, Audretsch and Karlsson (2011) arrived at a similar conclusion while disagreeing with Gartner about the nature of the phenomenon. Instead, they posited that the central focus of entrepreneurship research should be on the emergence of new economic activity. Regardless of how the phenomenon is conceptualized, entrepreneurship is a process that transpires over time. In this chapter, we have sought to explore what the above would mean to the field by explicitly equating international entrepreneurship with a journey that consists of a set of conditions that must be met, but not in any particular order – e.g. motive, means, opportunity and goal – and a series of events that may proceed in a more or less chronological order – e.g. innocence, the call, initiation, allies, break-through and celebration – requiring more flexible research designs, ideally suited to qualitative case-based approaches to better understand international business *in situ* (Pikkari, Welch & Paavilainen, 2009). In our discussion, we hope to have shown why process is essential not only to the study of the entre-preneurial phenomenon but also for distinguishing the field of entrepreneurship as well as acknowledge its strong links to creativity and strategy research, which overlap the process at the front and back ends. We have also attempted to distin-guish the field of entrepreneurship from more abstract concepts (variation) of which it is a particular manifestation and more concrete concepts (negotiation) of which it is comprised.

References

Acker, J. (2006) Inequality regimes: Gender, class, and race in organizations. *Gender and Society*, 20(4): 441–464.

Acs, Z. J., Estrin, S., Mickiewicz, T. & Szerb, L. (2014) *The Continued Search for the Solow Residual: The Role of National Entrepreneurial Ecosystem*. Bonn, Germany: The Institute for the Study of Labor (ZA).

Acs, Z., Stam, E., Audretsch, D. & O'Connor, A. (2017) The lineages of the entrepre-neurial ecosystem approach. *Small Business Economics: An Entrepreneurship Journal* 49(1): 1–10.

Ahl, H. (2006) Why research on women entrepreneurs needs new directions. *Gender and Society*, 20(4): 441–464.

Al-Dajani, H., Carter, S. & Marlow, S. et al. (2015) Entrepreneurship among the dis-placed and disposed: Exploring the limits of emancipatory entrepreneuring. *British Journal of Management*, 26(4): 713–730.

Anthias, F. (2001) *Inclusive Masculinities: The Changing Face of Masculinity*. London: Routledge.

Anthias, F. (2008) Thinking through the lens of translocational positionality: An intersec-tionality frame for understanding identity and belonging. *Translocations: Migration and Social Change*, 4(1): 5–19.

Arasti, Z., Zandi, F. & Bahmani, N. (2014). Business failure factors in Iranian SMEs: Do successful and unsuccessful entrepreneurs have different viewpoints? *Journal of Global Entrepreneurship Research*, 4(1): 1–14.

Audretsch, D., Mason, C., Miles, M. P. & O'Connor, A. (2018) The dynamics of entrepreneurial ecosystems. *Entrepreneurship and Regional Development*, 30(3–4): 471–474.

Bass, B. M. (1981) *Stogdill's Handbook of Leadership*. New York: Free Press.

Bennis, W. & Nanus, B. (1985) *Leaders: The Strategies for Taking Charge*. New York: Harper and Row.

Alvedalen, J. & Boschma, R. (2017) A critical review of entrepreneurial ecosystems research: Towards a future research agenda. *European Planning Studies*, 25(6): 887–903.

Australian Bureau of Statistics 2008, *Social Participation of Migrants*, cat no. 4102.0, Australian Bureau of Statistics, viewed 1 May 2010, www.abs.gov.au/AUSSTATS/abs@.nsf/Lookup/4102.0Chapter4202008.

Barney, J. (1991) Firm resources and sustained competitive advantage. *Journal of Management*, 17(1): 99–120.

Bates, T. (1997) Financing small business creation: The case of Chinese and Korean immigrant entrepreneurs. *Journal of Business Venturing*, 12(2): 109–124.

Bathelt, H., Malmberg, A. & Maskell, P. (2004) Clusters and knowledge: Local buzz, global pipelines and the process of knowledge creation. *Progress in Human Geography*, 28 (1): 31–56.

Bird, B. (1988) Implementing entrepreneurial ideas: The case for intention. *Academy of Management Review*, 13: 442–453.

Blankenburg, D. (1995) A network approach to foreign market entry, in K. Moller & D. Wilson (eds), *Business Marketing: An Interaction and Network Perspective*, Boston: Kluwer Academic Publishers, pp. 375–405.

Bohon, S. (2001) *Latinos in Ethnic Enclaves*. New York: Garland Publishing.

Borooah, V. & Mangan, J. (2007) Living here, born there: The economic life of Australia's immigrants. *European Journal of Political Economy*, 23(2): 486–511.

Boschma, R. (2015) Towards an evolutionary perspective on regional resilience. *Regional Studies*, 49(5): 733–751.

Bowden, P. & Mummery, J. (2014) *Understanding Feminism*. London: Routledge.

Bruni, A., Gherardi, S. & Poggio, B. (2004) Doing gender, doing entrepreneurship: An ethnographic account of intertwined practices. *Gender, Work and Organization*, 11(4): 406–429.

Butler, J. (2004) *Undoing Gender*. London: Psychology Press.

Carland, J. W., Hoy, F. Boulton, W. R. & Carland, J. C. (1984) Differentiating entrepreneurs from small business owners: A conceptualization. *Academy of Management Review*, 9(2): 354–359.

Carter, S., Kuhl, A. & Marlow, S. et al. (2017) Households as a site of entrepreneurial activity. *Foundations and Trends in Entrepreneurship*, 13: 81–190.

Cavanagh, A., Freeman, S., Kalfadellis, P. & Herbert, K. (2017). Assigned versus assumed: Towards a contemporary, detailed understanding of subsidiary autonomy. *International Business Review*, 26(6): 1168–1183.

Cavanagh, A., Freeman, S., Kalfadellis, P. & Cavusgil, S. T. (2017). How do subsidiaries assume autonomy? A refined application of agency theory with the subsidiary-headquarters context. *Global Strategy Journal*, 7(2): 72–192.

Chand, M. & Ghorbani, M. (2011) National culture, networks and ethnic entrepreneurship: A comparison of the Indian and Chinese immigrants in the US. *International Business Review*, 20(6): 593–606.

Chandra, Y., Styles, C. & Wilkinson, I. (2009) The recognition of first time international entrepreneurial opportunities: Evidence from firms in knowledge-based industries. *International Marketing Review*, 26(1): 30–61.

Chigbo, N. (2014) Management as a factor of production and as an economic resource. *International Journal of Humanities and Social Science*, 4(6): 162–166.

Churchill, N. C & Lewis, V. (1986) Entrepreneurial research: Directions and methods, in D. L. Sexton & R. W. Smilor (eds), *The Art and Science of Entrepreneurship*, Cambridge: Ballinger, pp. 333–365.

CIA World Factbook 2018, Africa: Tanzania, www.cia.gov/library/publications/the-world-factbook/geos/tz.html [accessed 15 July 2018].

Coleman, J. (1988) Social capital in the creation of human capital. *American Journal of Sociology*, 94(S): 95–120.

Cooper, A. C., Woo, C. Y. & Dunkelberg, W. C. (1988) Entrepreneurs' perceived chances for success. *Journal of Business Venturing*, 3: 97–108.

Cope, J. (2011) Entrepreneurial learning from failure: An interpretative phenomenological analysis. *Journal of Business Venturing*, 26: 604–623.

Coviello, N., Kano, L. & Liesch, P. (2017) Adapting the Uppsala model to a modern world: Macro-context and microfoundations. *Journal of International Business Studies*, 48: 1151–1164.

Cramton, C. D. (1993) Is rugged individualism the whole story?: Public and private accounts of a firm's founding. *Family Business Review*, 6(3): 56–61.

Crenshaw, K. (1991) Mapping the margins: Intersectionality, identity politics, and violence against women of colour. *Stanford Law Review*, 43(6): 1241–1299.

Cuervo-Cazurra, A., Ciravegna, L., Melgarejo, M. & Lopez, L. (2018) Home country uncertainty and the internationalization-performance relationship: Building an uncertainty management capability. *Journal of World Business*, 53(2): 209–221.

Cunningham, J. B. & Lischeron, J. (1991) Defining entrepreneurship. *Journal of Small Business Management*, 29(1): 45–61.

Danes, S. M., Lee, J., Stafford, K. & Heck, R. K. Z. (2008) The effects of ethnicity, families and culture on entrepreneurial experience: An extension of sustainable family business theory. *Journal of Developmental Entrepreneurship*, 13(3): 229–268.

Dimov, D. (2007) Beyond the single-person, single-insight attribution in understanding entrepreneurial opportunities. *Entrepreneurship, Theory and Practice*, 31(5): 713–731.

Dixit, A. & Pindyck, R. (1994) *Investment Under Uncertainty*. New Jersey: Princeton University Press.

Du, K. & O'Connor, A. (2017) Entrepreneurship and advancing national level economic efficiency. *Small Business Economics: An Entrepreneurship Journal*, 49(2): 91–111.

Ellis, P. (2011) Social ties and international entrepreneurship: Opportunities and constraints affecting firm internationalization. *Journal of International Business Studies*, 42: 99–127.

Essers, C. & Benschop, Y. (2009) Muslim businesswomen doing boundary work: The negotiation of Islam, gender and ethnicity within entrepreneurial contexts. *Human Relations*, 62(3): 403–423.

Evers, N. & Knight, J. (2008) Role of international trade shows in small firm internationalization: a network perspective. *International Marketing Review*, 25(5): 544–562.

Fairlie, R. W. (2004) Recent trends in ethnic and racial business ownership. *Small Business Economics*, 23: 203–218.

Fausto-Sterling, A. (2000) *Sexing the Body*. New York: Basic Books.

Fayol, H. (1950) *Administration Industrielle et Generale*. Paris: Dunod. (First published 1916.)

Fiedler, F. E. (1966) The contingency model: A theory of leadership effectiveness, in H. Proshansky & B. Seidenberg (eds), *Basic Studies in Psychology*, New York: Holt, Rinehart and Winston, pp. 538–551.

Figueira-de-Lemos, Johanson, J. & Vahlne, J.-E. (2013) Risk management in the internationalization process of the firm: A note on the Uppsala model. *Journal of World Business*, 46(2): 143–153.

Freeman, S. & Lindsay, S. (2011) The effect of ethnic diversity on expatriate managers in their host country. *International Business Review*, 21(2): 253–268.

Garfield, C. (1986) *Peak Performers: The New Heroes of American Business.* New York: Avon Books.

Gartner, W. B. (1985) A conceptual framework for describing the phenomena of new venture creation. *Academy of Management Review*, 10: 696–706.

Gollnick, D. M. & Chinn, P. C. (1990). *Multicultural Education in a Pluralistic Society.* Columbus, OH: Charles E Merrill.

Hakanson, L. & Kappen, P. (2017) The 'Casino Model' of internationalization: An alternative Uppsala paradigm. *Journal of International Business Studies*, 48: 1103–1113.

Hayton, J., Chandler, G. & DeTienne, D. (2011) Entrepreneurial opportunity identification and new firm development processes: A comparison of family and non-family new ventures. *International Journal of Entrepreneurship and Innovation Management*, 13(1): 12–31.

Hebert, R. F. & Link, A. N. (1982) *The Entrepreneur: Mainstream Views and Radical Critiques.* New York: Praeger.

Henry, C., Ahl, H. & Foss, L. (2015) Gender and entrepreneurship approaches: A methodological review. *International Small Business Journal*, 33: 649–666.

Hemphill, J. K. (1959) Job description for executives. *Harvard Business Review*, (Sept.): 55–67.

Hill Collins, P. (2000/[1990]) *Black Feminist Thought.* (2nd edn). New York: Routledge.

Holmquist, E. & Sundin, C. (1989) The growth of women's entrepreneurship – push or pull factors? In paper presented to the European Institute for Advanced Studies in management Conference on Small Business, University of Durham Business School. Available at: www.EIASM.be

Hull, D. L., Bosley, J. J. & Udell, G. G. (1980) Renewing the hunt for the Heffalump: Identifying potential entrepreneurs by personality characteristics. *Journal of Small Business Management*, 18(1): 11–18.

Iacocca, L. (1984) *Iacocca: An Auto-biography*, New York: Bantam Books.

Iyer, G. & Shapiro, J. (1999) Ethnic entrepreneurial and marketing systems: Implications for the global economy. *Journal of International Marketing*, 7(4): 83–110.

Jean, R.-J., Tan, D. & Sinkovics, R. (2011) Ethnic ties, location choice, and firm performance in foreign direct investment: A study of Taiwanese business groups FDI in China. *International Business Review*, 20(6): 627–635.

Jennings, J. E. & Brush, C. G. (2013) Research on women entrepreneurs: Challenges to (and from) the broader entrepreneurship literature? *The Academy of management Annals*, 7(1): 663–715.

Johanson, J. & Vahlne, J.-E. (2009) The Uppsala internationalization process model revisited: From liability of foreignness to liability of outsidership. *Journal of International Business Studies*, 40: 1411–1431.

Jones, S. (2014) Gendered discourses of entrepreneurship in UK higher education: The fictive entrepreneur and the fictive student: *International Small Business Journal*, 32(3): 237–258.

Kao, R. W. Y. (1993) Defining entrepreneurship: Past, present and? *Creativity and Innovation Management*, 2(1): 69–70.

Kao, R. W. Y. (1989) *Entrepreneurship and Enterprise Development.* Toronto: Holt, Rinehart and Winston of Canada, Ltd.

Kelan, E. R. (2010) Gender logic and (un) doing gender at work. *Gender, Work and Organization*, 17(2): 174–194.

Kilby, P. (1971) *Entrepreneurship and Economic Development.* New York: New York Press.

Klotz, A. C., Hmieleski, K. M. & Bradley, B. H. et al. (2014) New venture teams: A review of the literature and road-map for future research. *Journal of Management*, 40(1): 226–255.

Knight, R. M. (1988) Spinoff entrepreneurs: How corporations really create entrepreneurs, in Bruce A. Kirchhoff, Wayne A. Long, W. E. McMullan, Karl H. Vesper and William E. Weyzel, Jr (eds), *Frontiers of Entrepreneurial Research*, Wellesley, MA: Babson College, pp. 134–150.

Kontinen, T. & Ojala, A. (2011) Network ties in the international opportunity recognition of family SMEs. *International Business Review*, 20(4): 440–453.

Lachman, R. (1980) Towards measurement of entrepreneurial tendencies. *Management International Review*, 20(2): 108–116.

Landau, J. (2007) Enhancing resilience: Families and communities as agents of change. *Family Process*, 46(3): 351–365.

Lazaris, M. & Freeman, S. (2018) An examination of global mindset and international market opportunities among SMEs. *International Studies of Management & Organization*, 48(2): 181–203.

Lazaris, M., Mohamad Ngasri, N. E. & Freeman, S. (2015) Reactive and proactive international entrepreneurial behavior: Causation and effectuation, in Pervez Ghauri & V. H. Manek Kirpalani (eds), *Handbook of Research on International Entrepreneurship Strategy: Improving SME Performance Globally*, Cheltenham: Edward Elgar Publishing Ltd, pp. 22–44.

Levinson, D. J., Darrow, C. N., Klein, B., Levinson, M. H. & McKee, B. (1978) *The Seasons of a Man's Life.* New York: Ballantine Books.

Linstead, S. & Pullen, A. (2006) Gender as multiplicity: Desire, displacement, difference and dispersion. *Human Relations*, 59(9): 1287–1310.

Loasby, B. J. (2011) Uncertainty and imagination, illusion and order: Shackleian connections. *Cambridge Journal of Economics*, 35: 771–783.

Mack, E. & H. Mayer. (2016) The evolutionary dynamics of entrepreneurial ecosystems. *Urban Studies*, 53 (10): 2118–2133.

Maksimov, V., Wang, S. & Luo, Y. (2017) Reducing poverty in the least developed countries: The role of small and medium enterprises. *Journal of World Business*, 52(2): 244–257.

Marlow, S. & Martinez Dy, A. M. (2017) Annual review article: Is it time to rethink the gender agenda in entrepreneurship research? *International Small Business Journal: Researching Entrepreneurship*, 36(1): 3–22.

Martin, R. (2011) Regional economic resilience, hysteresis and recessionary shocks. *Journal of Economic Geography*, 12 (1): 1–32.

Martinez Dy, A. M., Marlow, S. & Martin, L. et al. (2017) A web of opportunity or the same old story? Women digital entrepreneurs and intersectionality theory. *Human Relations*, 70(3): 286–311.

Mason, C. & R. Brown. (2014) Entrepreneurial ecosystems and growth oriented entrepreneurship. Background paper prepared for the workshop organised by the *OECD LEED Programme and the Dutch Ministry of Economic Affairs*, The Hague, Netherlands.

Mathews, J. & Zander, I. (2007) The international entrepreneurship dynamics of accelerated internationalisation. *Journal of International Business Studies*, 38(3): 387–403.

McAdam, M. (2012) *Female Entrepreneurship*. London: Routledge.

McClelland, D. C. & Winter, D. G. (1969) *Motivating Economic Achievement.* New York: Free Press.

McDowell, L. (2014) Gender, work, employment and society: Feminist reflections on continuity and change. *Work, Employment and Society*, 28(5): 825–837.

McKay, A., Campbell, J. & Thompson, E. (2014) Economic recovery and recession in the UK: What's gender got to do with it? *Feminist Economics*, 19(3): 108–123.

McMullen, J. S. & Dimov, D. (2013) Time and the entrepreneurial journey: The problems and promise of studying entrepreneurship as a process. *Journal of Management Studies*, 50, 1481–1512.

McMullen, J. S. & Warnick, B. J. (2016) Should we require every new venture to be a hybrid organization? *Journal of Management Studies*, 53(4): 630–662.

McMullan, W. E. & Long, W. A. (1990) *Developing New Ventures*. San Diego: HBJ.

Menzies, T. V., Filion, L. J., Brenner, G. A. & Elgie, S. (2007) Measuring ethnic community involvement: Development and initial testing of an index. *Journal of Small Business Management*, 45(2): 267–282.

Motoyama, Y. & Watkins, K. K. (2014) Examining the connections within the startup ecosystem: A case study of St. Louis. www.kauffman.org/~/media/kauffman_org/research reportsandcovers/2014/09/examining_the_connections_within_the_startup_ecosystem.pdf.

Mustafa, M. & Chen, S. (2010) The strength of family networks in transnational immigrant entrepreneurship. *Thunderbird International Business Review*, 52(2): 97–206.

Nambisan, S. & Zahra SA. (2016) The role of demand-side narratives in opportunity formation and enactment. *Journal of Business Venturing Insights* 5: 70–75.

Ngasri, N. E. M. & Freeman, S. (2018) Conceptualizing network configurations as dynamic capabilities for emerging market born-globals", *International Studies of Management & Organization* volume 48(2), pp. 221–237.

Neesham, C. & Freeman, S. (2016) Value creation as business commitment to responsible consumption, in Dr Michael Schwartz, Dr Howard Harris and Dr Debra R. Comer (eds), *REIO: The Contribution of Love, and Hate, to Organizational Ethics*, Vol. 16, Bingley: Emerald Publishing, pp. 207–229.

Ogbor, J. O. (2000) Mythicizing and reification in entrepreneurial discourse: Ideology-critique of entrepreneurial studies. *Journal of Management Studies*, 37(5): 605–635.

Oakley, A. (1972) *Sex, Gender and Society.* Farnham: Ashgate.

Owen, A. J. & Rowe, B. R. (1995) The cultural underpinnings of running family-owned firms. *Family Business Annual*, 1(Section 1): 133–149.

Palmer, M. (1971) The application of psychological testing to entrepreneurial testing to entrepreneurial potential. *California Management Review*, 13: 32–38.

Patel, P. & Conklin, B. (2009) The balancing act: The role of transnational habitus and social networks in balancing transnational entrepreneurial activities. *Entrepreneurship, Theory and Practice*, 33(5): 1045–1078.

Peterson, R. (1985) Raising risk-takers. *Metropolitan Toronto Business Journal*, 75(7): 30–34.

Piekkari R, Welch C. & Paavilainen E (2009) The case study as disciplinary convention: Evidence from international business journals. *Organizational Research Methods*, 12(3): 567–589.

Puryear, A., Rogoff, E., Lee, M-S., Heck, R. K. Z., Gossman, Haynes, G. W. & Onochie, J. (2008) Sampling minority business owners and their families: The understudied entrepreneurial experience. *Journal of Small Business Management*, 46(3): 422–455.

Ramoglou, S. & Tsang, E. (2018) Opportunities lie in the demand side: Transcending the discovery–creation debate. *The Academy of Management Review*, 43: 815–818.

Ramoglou, S. & Tsang E. W. K. (2017) Accepting the unknowables of entrepreneurship and overcoming philosophical obstacles to scientific progress. *Journal of Business Venturing Insights*, 8: 71–77.

Ramoglou, S. & Tsang E. W. K. (2016) A realist perspective of entrepreneurship: Opportunities as propensities. *The Academy of Management Review*, 41: 410–434.

Risman, B. J. (2004). Gender as a social structure: Theory wrestling with activism. *Gender and Society*, 18(4): 429–450.

Roberts, M. (1987) Making the transition from entrepreneurial to professional management, in Neil C. Churchill, John A. Hornaday, Bruce A. Kirchhoff, O. J. Krasner and Karl H. Vesper (eds), *Frontiers of Entrepreneurship Research*, Wellesley, MA: Babson College, pp. 74–86.

Robson, M., Katsikeas, C., Schlegelmilch, B. & Pramböck, B. (2019) Alliance capabilities, interpartner attributes, and performance outcomes in international strategic alliances. *Journal of World Business*, 54(2): 137–153.

Rogoff, E. G. & Heck, R. K. Z. (2003) Evolving research in entrepreneurship and family business: Recognizing family as the oxygen that feeds the fire of entrepreneurship. *Journal of Business Venturing*, 18(5): 559–566.

Sarachek, B. (1978) American entrepreneurs and the Horatio Alger myth. *Journal of Economic History*, 38: 439–456.

Schumpeter, J. A. (1934) *The Theory of Economic Development.* Cambridge, MA: Harvard University Press.

Sexton, D. L. (1982) Research needs and issues in entrepreneurship, in Calvin A. Kent, Donald L. Sexton and Karl H. Vesper (eds), *The Encyclopedia of Entrepreneurship*, Englewood Cliffs, NJ: Prentice Hall.

Shane, S. & Venkataraman, S. (2000) The promise of entrepreneurship as a field of research. *Academy of Management Review*, 25(1): 217–226.

Simmie, J. & R. Martin. (2010) The economic resilience of regions: Towards an evolutionary approach. *Cambridge Journal of Regions, Economy and Society*, 3(1): 27–43.

Smans, M., Freeman, S. & Thomas, J. (2014) Immigrant entrepreneurs: The identification of foreign market opportunities. *International Migration*, 52(4): 144–156.

Spigel, B. (2015) The relational organization of entrepreneurial ecosystems. *Entrepreneurship Theory and Practice*, June: 7–24.

Spigel, B. (2017) The relational organization of entrepreneurial ecosystems. *Entrepreneurship: Theory and Practice*, 41(1): 49–72.

Stafford, K., Duncan, K. A., Danes, S. M. & Winter, M. (1999) A research model of sustainable family business. *Family Business Review*, 12(3): 197–208.

Stam, E. (2015) Entrepreneurial ecosystems and regional policy: A sympathetic critique. *European Planning Studies*, 23(9): 1759–1769.

Stevenson, H. H. (1988) General management and entrepreneurship, in Bruce A. Kirchhoff, Wayne A. Long. Ed McMullan, Karl H. Vesper and William E. Wetzel, Jr (eds), *Frontiers of Entrepreneurial Research*, Wellesley, MA: Babson College, pp. 667–668.

Sui, S. & Baum, M. (2014) Internationalization strategy, firm resources and the survival of SMEs in the export market. *Journal of International Business Studies*, 45(7): 821–841.

Sultan, P. & Wong, H. Y. (2011) The success of born global firms: A conceptual model. *Journal for Global Business Advancement*, 4(3): 224–241.

Trudgen, R. & Freeman, S. (2014) Measuring the performance of born-global firms throughout their development process: The roles of initial market selection and internationalisation speed. *Management International Review*, 54(4): 551–579.

Vahlne, J.-E. & Johanson, J. (2017) From internationalization to evolution: The Uppsala model at 40 years. *Journal of International Business Studies*, 48: 1087–1102.

Weber, M. (1905, 1908) *The Protestant Ethic and the Spirit of Capitalism.* Trans. T. Parsons. New York: Scriber's Sons.

Wiklund, J., Davidsson, P., Audretsch, D. B. & Karlsson, C. (2011) The future of entrepreneurship research. *Entrepreneurship, Theory and Practice*, 35(1): 1–9.

Williams, N. & T. Vorley. (2014) Economic resilience and entrepreneurship: Lessons from the Sheffield City region. *Entrepreneurship & Regional Development*, 26(3–4): 257–281.

Yang, T. & Aldrich, H. (2014) Who's the boss? Explaining gender inequality in entrepreneurial teams. *American Sociological Review*, 79(2): 303–327.

Zahra, S. A. & Dess, G. G. (2001) Entrepreneurship as a field of research: Encouraging dialogue and debate. *Academy of Management Review*, 26(1): 8–10.

Zahra, S. A. & Wright, M. (2016) Rethinking the social role of entrepreneurship. *Journal of Management Studies*, 53: 610–629.

Zhu, Y., Freeman, S. & Cavusgil, S. T. (2018) Service quality delivery in a cross-national context. *International Business Review*, 27(5): 1022–1032.

3 International entrepreneurship

Its emergence from international business and entrepreneurship

Introduction

International business activities provide opportunities for home-based entrepreneurs to discover, create and develop products and ventures in foreign (host) business environments. The foreign environment presents entrepreneurs and their ventures with many diverse factors (e.g. economic, political, social, demographic, cultural, technological, historical and geographic) that are fundamentally different from their home country markets and experiences. Nonetheless, quite apart from research extending beyond 40 years in international entrepreneurship, we still understand little about what drives entrepreneurs and their strategic behaviour in establishing and managing transnational activities and operations. This chapter provides an institutional perspective, network theory and transactional cost perspective, among others, on the links across entrepreneurship, international entrepreneurship and transnational entrepreneurship fields. In particular, drawing on institutional perspective allows us to explore significant variations among the institutional structures of home countries to offer explanations of variations in entrepreneurial endowments (see both external and internal, as highlighted and discussed in Chapter 2 under the schools of thought) of prospective transnational entrepreneurs. Transnational entrepreneurs embed themselves in foreign networks that facilitate cross-border business operations as they establish positions in foreign business networks. This discussion will allow us to move beyond the theoretical impasse in entrepreneurship and international business studies (Yeung, 2002; Teece, 2014; Forsgren, 2016; Chandra, 2017; Vahlne & Johanson, 2017).

We attempt to construct a bridge between the notion of the entrepreneur and the concept of international business. As we find in Adam Smith, the key concept is the extent of the market. The evolution of the entrepreneur is strongly influenced by the extent of the market, as is the division of labour. The classic entrepreneur operates in a limited market space, which might or might not extend beyond a frontier. The development of the entrepreneur into an international economic actor expands as he/she is dealing with a wider market. This usually, but not always, means the firm grows in terms of sales and staff.

Relatively small enterprises in certain cultures may export a high proportion of their production at an early phase in their evolution (see, for instance, born globals and international new ventures) (INVs) (Oviatt & McDougall, 1994; Freeman & Cavusgil, 2007; Chandra, 2017; Vahlne & Johanson, 2017) as is demonstrated by research in small European and Scandinavian markets, and in Asia and Africa or larger markets in Asia, and North and Latin America. The link between the entrepreneur and international business may normally be seen as described above; however, entrepreneurship can be found in the creation or sustenance of an already grown internationally operating business. Entrepreneurship can be logically independent of international business. One can study entrepreneurship without dealing with international business and indeed vice-versa. A good deal of international business does not involve entrepreneurship. Since international businesses are often large-scale organizations, they do not easily lend themselves to entrepreneurship. This is the main challenge to international business, which may be excessively centralized in its management and bureaucracy. Sometimes large international businesses attempt to grow through mergers and acquisitions with small entrepreneurial firms, or they may encourage internal entrepreneurship by so-called intrapreneurship. It is not easy to convert a practising manager into an entrepreneur, although some may think that entrepreneurs are simply born as such (see Chapter 2, schools of thought). Building a bridge between entrepreneurship and international business is thus not a particularly easy task.

Entrepreneurs and transnational enterprises

Consider the scenario of a businessperson faced with a saturated market in the home country, or one who falls upon an opportunity to expand into foreign markets. It takes great courage, exceptional qualities or "aptitudes" in the words of Joseph Schumpeter (1942: 132) to act on these situations and make things happen. The person might be an owner and/or a manager of a new or an evolving transnational enterprise. In the latter situation, the businessperson may take the business across borders by establishing another operation or several other operations abroad in order to tap into host country business opportunities. In the case of a saturated home market, an INV may be formed from inception, so that the businessperson runs an international business without undertaking the successive stages or phases of business establishment and internationalization (see Johanson & Vahlne, 1977; Buckley & Ghauri, 1993). In both scenarios, the businessperson is likely to face a myriad of challenges related to operating in a foreign land of which he/she has comparatively less information, experience and knowledge, thereby confronting a different set of institutional contexts. The challenges arising from participating in international business activities can sometimes be overcome by pure good fortune; however, it is more than likely that these challenges can be overcome only with initiatives and capabilities embedded in the social actor and his/her collection of institutional resources and relationships (networks) with various other actors (Yeung, 2002). How do we account for these exceptional phenomena arising when participating in cross-border business activities?

These phenomena are exceptional not because they are uncommon in today's global markets, but because businesspersons need to take an unfamiliar path to organize and produce economic activities in different countries and/or regions. These businesspeople are undoubtedly entrepreneurial because they have taken extraordinary risks with the intention of participating in businesses differently. Following a Schumpeterian tradition, these businesspersons create 'new combinations' in locating production facilities and/or gaining access to new markets in different country locations and/or regions. Thus, entrepreneurship is more than the initial phase where owners start business venturing (Yeung, 2002). Importantly, entrepreneurship focuses on the exceptional qualities required in processes that encompass both creating and sustaining particular business ventures, regardless of whether these ventures operate across national boundaries.

We term these businesspersons transnational entrepreneurs because they participate in entrepreneurial activities across borders. However, not all entrepreneurs become transnational entrepreneurs. Many existing entrepreneurs simply fail to participate in establishing foreign ventures during their internationalization process (Yeung, 2002). They do not manage the steps, phases and orientations necessary to internationalize. The particular challenge of international business to transnational entrepreneurship is one of the main theoretical problems to be addressed in this chapter. To achieve this systematic undertaking, we propose an institutional perspective on entrepreneurship in international business, arguing that transnational entrepreneurs are not driven simply by historical mechanisms of change. We can take a different perspective from that offered by Schumpeter (1934: 61) who perceived the entrepreneur as "merely the bearer of the mechanism of change". We conceptualize "transnational entrepreneurs as businesspersons who take specific proactive action to overcome inherent problems and difficulties associated with international business activities" (Yeung, 2002: 30). The action of these entrepreneurs is both facilitated and constrained by ongoing processes of institutional relations in two or more locations, namely home and various host country markets. These institutional relations are defined as both social ties and business networks, in which these transnational entrepreneurs are embedded, for example, political-economic structures, and prevailing organizational and cultural practices in the home and host countries. Together, these institutionalized configurations of social and organizational structuring form different business systems.

Whitley (1992: 13) defines business systems as "distinctive configurations of hierarchy-market relations which become institutionalized as relatively successful ways of organizing economic activities in different institutional environments". In this sense, different business systems are distinct and pursue ways of structuring market economies that are wide-ranging and long-term in nature. Having established in particular institutional contexts, these business systems may develop significant interconnections, thereby becoming resilient to major changes. In this way, the transnational entrepreneur is conceptualized as more than a bearer of the mechanisms of change (see Schumpeter). Rather, he/she is embedded in ongoing institutional processes that influence and shape his/her fields of action in the various countries of business activities. Thus, an institutional perspective is focused on social actors – transnational entrepreneurs themselves – and their embedded structures of institutional relations. In this sense, the perspective highlights the importance of social actors in entrepreneurship and especially in the international entrepreneurship field (Yeung, 2002).

Defining and characterizing international entrepreneurship

Since its inauguration nearly four decades ago, research in international entrepreneurship has become a fully fledged field of study, although research is never an easy process of delineating a differentiation, mobilizing concepts and principles, and building legitimacy among colleagues. What we can now comfortably and confidently say is that we can refer to international entrepreneurship as a field of research with worldwide support through various community structures, conferences, periodicals and leading journals, including its own dedicated journal – *Journal of International Entrepreneurship* – and many special issues in a range of journals across international business, management, entrepreneurship, psychology marketing and ecology since the mid-1980s (Coviello et al., 2011; Vasilchenko & Morrish, 2011; Teece, 2014; Forsgren, 2016; Chandra, 2017). Typically, new fields have emerged as a result of calls from existing disciplines which have found these new ideas to be beyond their scope. It is not uncommon for a new field to emerge from the juncture of two or more existing fields (Hagstrom, 1965) or as a result of advancing through a process of differentiation, mobilization and legitimacy building. Signals of the creation of a new field include a new name, increasing reference to it by scholars and, as mentioned above, greater visibility through community structures (Coviello et al., 2011). This is the pattern that has been followed by the emerging entrepreneurship and international business fields.

International entrepreneurship is commonly thought to have emerged initially with the seminal paper by McDougall (1989), where domestic versus INVs (i.e. businesses that rapidly internationalize, either from inception or following some external or internal factor later in their evolutionary process that drives their rapid international engagement) were compared, and a definition of international entrepreneurship was advanced, as new ventures engaged in international business. Soon after, other scholars began to write about the new phenomena as patterns and timing of new venture internationalization (e.g. Coviello & Munro, 1992; Jolly et al., 1992; Litvak, 1990; Ray, 1989; Rennie, 1993). These writings led to challenges to extant theory (see McDougall et al., 1994; Oviatt & McDougall, 1994), which signalled a new line of international entrepreneurship enquiry (Kuhn, 1996). Also featuring at this early stage, were studies assessing how entrepreneurs differed across cultures (e.g. McGrath et al., 1992a, b; McGrath & MacMillan, 1992).

Thus, this growing emergent international entrepreneurship field was moving in parallel to an increasing awareness of the real diversity of entrepreneurial activity being witnessed in an increasingly globally integrated world economy (Coviello, McDougall & Oviatt, 2011).

Zahra (1993) advanced a further definition of international entrepreneurship to capture corporate entrepreneurship and international entrepreneurship as a process, setting a firm foundation for many studies to follow. Special issues on the subject became more common, with one of the first appearing in 1996 in *Entrepreneurship Theory and Practice*, coinciding with the commencement of the McGill International Entrepreneurship Conference series initiated by Richard Wright and Hamid Etemad in 1998. Two special issues in the *Journal of International Marketing* followed in 1999 on the back of these first few conferences. Meanwhile, the *Academy of Management Journal* published a special issue on international entrepreneurship in 2000 (Coviello et al., 2011). While the concept of international entrepreneurship was now in common use in scholarly communities, it was the McDougall and Oviatt's (2000) introduction in a special issue that firmly placed international entrepreneurship within the interface of international business and entrepreneurship research. At this time, McDougall's (1989) definition of international entrepreneurship was broadened to "a combination of innovative, proactive and risk-seeking behaviour that crosses national borders and is intended to create value in organizations" (McDougall & Oviatt, 2000: 903).

Evidence of a more mainstream appeal and place for international entrepreneurship was the Best Paper of the Year Award in 2000 awarded to Zahra et al. (2000) in the *Academy of Management Journal*. Other evidence of a mounting interest in international entrepreneurship was noted in further special issues in publications including the *Journal of International Management* (2001), *Entrepreneurship Theory and Practice* (2002), *Small Business Economics* (2003) and the *Canadian Journal of Administrative Studies* (2005). A significant advancement was reflected in the inaugural release of the *Journal of International Entrepreneurship* (2003), devoted to developing the field of international entrepreneurship rather than to developing an 'international journal' of entrepreneurship – subtle but important distinction. Zahra and George (2002: 262) extended the definition of international entrepreneurship further to describe it as "the process of creatively discovering and exploiting opportunities that lie outside a firm's domestic markets in pursuit of competitive advantage". What is significant about this definition is that it focused not on international comparisons of entrepreneurial behaviour (as per McDougall & Oviatt, 2000) but rather on international entrepreneurship (Coviello et al., 2011).

In particular, 2005 was a significant year, as Oviatt and McDougall's (1994) paper in the *Journal of International Business Studies* was nominated 'Paper of the Decade' and commentaries on international entrepreneurship by Autio (2005) and Zahra (2005) were also included in the journal. A further definition of international entrepreneurship appeared in the same year offered by Oviatt and McDougall (2005: 540), and similar to Zahra and George (2002) included the concept of opportunity identification: "International entrepreneurship is the discovery, enactment, evaluation, and exploitation of opportunities – across national borders – to create future goods and services". One thing that Oviatt and McDougall (2005) stressed in their paper was that international entrepreneurship had two key foci: (1) entrepreneurship across borders, and (2) comparative studies of entrepreneurship across borders – again their reminder of this subtle but important difference (Coviello et al., 2011).

From 2005 to 2009, an increasing range of special issues appeared in high-quality journals covering a diverse range of disciplines including international business, entrepreneurship, small business and marketing. These special issues included publications such as the *Journal of International Business Studies* (2005), *Small Business Economics* (2005; 2008), *Management International Review* (2005), *International Business Review* (2005), *International Marketing Review* (2006), *Journal of World Business* (2007) and *Strategic Entrepreneurship Journal* (2009). This period was an important one for establishing international entrepreneurship studies among a range of top quality journals and 2009 also saw the launch of yet another profile-raising initiative, this time the *ie-scholars.net*, initiated by Rod McNaughton and Hamid Etemad, designed as a virtual community to integrate and support international entrepreneurship research from a global perspective. The importance of this field was reaffirmed by a significant grant of $1.95 million from the Canadian Social Sciences and Humanities Research Council (Coviello et al., 2011).

In addition to awards and special issues that now appeared regularly during this period – too numerous to mention as can also be said of the initial two decades of 1980–2010, the Han B Thorelli Award for the most significant and long-term contribution to international marketing and theory granted by the *Journal of International Marketing* was awarded to a number of international business and international entrepreneurship scholars including Knight (2000), Burgel and Murray (2000) and Chetty and Campbell-Hunt (2004). Papers by scholars of international entrepreneurship in the early to mid-2000s were also now regularly cited in various top ten cited article lists (e.g. Harzing, 2007 Publish or Perish series) including the *Journal of International Marketing*, *International Business Review* and *Management International Review*. Furthermore, the earlier international entrepreneurship works of scholars in the mid to late 1990s were now highly cited in a range of top-quality journals such as the *Journal of International Business Studies, Entrepreneurship Theory and Practice* and *Journal of Business Venturing*. As much as a decade ago, international entrepreneurship scholars such as Hambrick and Chen (2008) were clearly cited as researchers who made the international entrepreneurship position between entrepreneurship and international business more comfortable and pronounced. In addition, during this time, international entrepreneurship scholars regularly identified with each other through key journals and a number of community structures (e.g. the annual McGill Conference on international entrepreneurship, the *Journal of International Entrepreneurship*), and this was supported by an increasing and flourishing body of research in international entrepreneurship.

As indicated as recently as 2011 in the *Journal of Business Venturing*, Coviello et al. (2011: 626) stated: "After twenty-two years, the field of IE [international entrepreneurship] has managed to differentiate itself, mobilize, and gain some legitimacy".

Noticeable in the international entrepreneurship legitimacy process was the importance of literature reviews to assist with the clarity of concepts and dimensions of international entrepreneurship, which emerged decisively in the early to mid-1990s. The reviews in turn helped the process of differentiation. One of the early reviews signalled international entrepreneurship as a distinct and potential field of study (Giamartino et al., 1993; Wright & Ricks, 1994), which built upon Coviello and McAuley's (1999) review of small and new firms and their non-traditional pathways to internationalization. Sub-fields or categories also began to feature in reviews of early internationalizing firms (Rialp et al., 2005), studies on founding, inception, internationalization processes, marketing strategies and firm performance, building on the earlier foundation of INVs and born globals (Aspelund et al., 2007). A review of national culture and its impact on entrepreneurship across three levels of enquiry – namely, individual, institutional and national level characteristics – was an important development (Hayton et al., 2002). Later, a review of cross-cultural entrepreneurship studies followed, identifying major gaps in content, research design and analytical approaches (Engelen et al., 2009). At about the same time a review of the application of international entrepreneurship in the marketing discipline (Styles & Seymour, 2006) and management policy also followed (Cumming et al., 2009). While other reviews focused on a particular theoretical lens, for example, opportunity recognition (Di Gregorio et al., 2008), culture and values (Tiessen, 1997), and transactional costs (Zacharakis, 1997).

However, of potentially greater interest to this emerging field was yet another group of scholars that had raised a series of concerns and issues with research within the international entrepreneurship field and international entrepreneurship research overall. For example, Gamboa and Brouthers (2008: 555) raised concerns about the extent of the international entrepreneurship scope, suggesting international entrepreneurship research may merely be a replication of international business studies, with an emphasis on smaller and new firms with little to say about the larger MNEs. Similarly, in a review of international entrepreneurship research, Keupp and Gassmann (2009) raised concerns that while the focus of international entrepreneurship research had shifted away from just the analysis of small and new firms from inception, the international entrepreneurship major trend in research still centred mostly on SMEs. The researchers argued that this small firm dominant perspective was making it difficult to extend the field of international entrepreneurship and offer theoretical generalizability. Keupp and Gassmann also made the interesting observation that many international entrepreneurship studies were using frameworks and models not derived from international business or entrepreneurship. For this reason, the writers called for greater integration and consistency across the theories developed in international entrepreneurship research. Coombs et al. (2009)

stated the same concerns in their review of international entrepreneurship research, suggesting that the field was in a rudimentary stage of development but they did add that the field showed promise. These reviews were especially important for driving necessary change and improvement in subsequent studies.

International entrepreneurship scholars responded by suggesting that much of the criticism centres on the lens used by scholars to view international entrepreneurship research, as those above are what we might term scholars of "classical international business, innovation, management, finance or strategy" (Coviello et al., 2011: 627). International entrepreneurship scholars have argued that a sound understanding of how the international entrepreneurship field has emerged is necessary to fully appreciate the direction it has taken. Thus, small firm internationalization has been a principle element in the emergence of the international entrepreneurship research field. Scholars have argued that simply studying comparisons of small and large firms, as suggested by Gamboa and Brouthers (2008), is not the same as research that focuses on "entrepreneurial activity during internationalization, or research on entrepreneurship across international contexts" (Coviello et al., 2011: 627).

Further arguments were presented highlighting the importance of future international entrepreneurship reviews focusing on the intersection between the two fields of entrepreneurship and international business. The view taken was that failure to account for traditional SME exporters may mean that datasets would not be applicable to entrepreneurship but rather only to international business. In addition, the arguments stressed that it is important that reviews clearly stipulate whether they are simply comparing entrepreneurship across cultures, an approach which continues to be a popular focus, or whether the reviews are looking at international entrepreneurship in different cultural settings, as the former approach may not actually address international entrepreneurship research. Areas that continue to be fruitful for future international entrepreneurship research are social capital theory as a lens, institutional contexts in emerging or transitional economies, finance and institutional theory, to name a few. The Jones, Coviello and Tang (2011) review in the *Journal of World Business* provided a very comprehensive assessment of international entrepreneurship history and categories of structure as well as a map of the research field. The review also categorizes three distinct themes within the international entrepreneurship research field, namely, entrepreneurial internationalization, international comparisons of entrepreneurship, and international comparisons of entrepreneurial internationalization. These distinctions are very helpful for international entrepreneurship scholars to expand the theoretical development of the international entrepreneurship field and also provided multiple thematical lenses and operational issues for each of the three research areas, similar to those raised above.

Terminology in international entrepreneurship

One helpful clarification of labels used in international entrepreneurship, sometimes incorrectly, is the difference between born-global and INV. These terms do not have the same meaning and thus should not be used interchangeably (Jones et al., 2011). One way of addressing the issue of interchangeability is to use an historical analysis to show where the different terms originated and the reasons for the current trend towards interchangeability which makes comparisons with young and new ventures problematic. The term born global is commonly understood to have been first coined by Rennie (1993) in a consultation report on the phenomenon with attempts to operationalize early internationalizing firms as a term in international entrepreneurship research by scholars, such as Rialph et al. (2005). The other popular term, INV, was first introduced by Oviatt and McDougall (1994), offering four types of INVs including the 'global start-up', defined as a new venture active in many countries and coordinating many value chain activities across borders. These researchers have consistently used this term since the mid-1990s. However, many international business scholars have been using these terms interchangeably.

Oviatt and McDougall (1994) were very aware of the debate in the international business field on the difference between 'international' and 'global', when they developed their four-type INV classification. Commonly, 'international' is regarded as involvement in just one or a few countries, while 'global' implies involvement in many or more than one region or continent. Thus, an Australian early internationalizing SME operating in one or two countries in the immediate Asian region would not be regarded as a global SME but rather a regional early internationalizing SME. However, many mainstream studies have not clarified these issues until recently, nor have these studies acknowledged that the situation is different for firms dealing with a range of countries and regions, and scope of activities along the value chain, where greater levels of complexity exist for global companies compared to international young and new internationalizing SMEs. For example, early research in international entrepreneurship by Aspelund and Moen (2005) made a distinction between the geographically focused start-up and the truly global start-up in 'early internationals' or what Lopez at al. (2009) termed as merely 'born regionals'. Clearly, similar conceptual development was occurring with the research of a number of authors, though with slightly different but comparable terminology.

As the distinction between global and international companies was deemed relevant, and it was acknowledged that there is more than one type of INV and born global, so too were other more important delineations between terms such as 'new' and 'born' emerging. For this reason, research into INVs and born globals should focus on new and young firms; it is essential that stages of development, phases of commitment and life-cycle, and evolutionary processes are articulated clearly. Thus, defining characteristics such as age, rather than firm size or even the scope of the firm's foreign activities, needs to be made clear from the outset in international entrepreneurship research. Of course, size and scope are frequently impacted by how early and quickly a firm might grow and internationalize from inception. Based on this argument, it is important for researchers in international entrepreneurship to clarify whether they are focusing on small firms or SMEs, just as it is important to distinguish between a start-up and a young venture. This clarification is important because certain firms are small, yet well-established in their organizational experience and life-cycle, as well as potentially other characteristics; these characteristics need clarification, as does the level of the analysis, in order to make it clear whether the focus is at the level of the entrepreneur, firm or institutional level (Coviello et al., 2011).

An important research area in international entrepreneurship still in need of attention is the entrepreneurial behaviour of larger firms within both themes – internationalization and entrepreneurship, and international entrepreneurship and cross-national studies – as this would offer excellent opportunities for comparison with born globals and INVs. One potential methodological challenge in future international entrepreneurship research is the study of born globals and INVs that, having internationalized early and quickly, are now well beyond the point of internationalization, and thus well-advanced in their life-cycle. Thus, scholars need to ensure that the characteristics and nature of their studies are well-defined to avoid further confusion (Coviello et al., 2011). Another area in international entrepreneurship research requiring greater attention is multiple level analysis (Keupp & Gassmann, 2009), as this would assist greatly in our understanding of the impact and extent of entrepreneurial behaviour of the leader of a firm or team, the very nature of the firm, type and extent of networks and the context, and how each of these relationships might directly or indirectly influence each other as part of the internationalizing process. This approach would also assist investigations into how and why different entrepreneurial behaviours and internationalization pathways are impacted by firm age and experience of entrepreneurs. This kind of future investigation faces additional complexities in research design as different types of levels may have varying impacts on entrepreneurship and internationalization. This possibility could be due to particular circumstances, events or critical incidents, as well as timing related to international entrepreneurial opportunity evaluation (Chandra, 2017), which might include particular institutional factors.

Institutional factors, opportunity triggers and critical incidents in international entrepreneurship

Damoah (2018) conducted a qualitative study on the internationalization process of SMEs from Africa perceived as entrepreneurs. This study is a recent example of critical incidents being taken as a useful approach to studying institutional factors and opportunity triggers in international entrepreneurship in an especially challenging institutional context. Interestingly, this study draws upon a range of international entrepreneurship theories (e.g. the resource-based view, the stage theory, the network theory and the contingency theory) to develop an international entrepreneurship model integrated under one label – the international entrepreneurship theory. However, the study is not an analysis of international entrepreneurship in the true sense, as it focuses on exporting SMEs and not internationalizing young and new SMEs at inception or through their life-cycle. However, the context and methodology lend themselves well to questions on international entrepreneurship and international entrepreneurship in cross-cultural contexts. Importantly, while the study bases itself on an SME's export propensity lens, it explores the critical incidents that trigger the behaviour, in this case, export initiation of SMEs perceived as entrepreneurial orientation.

Damoah (2018) not only links critical incidents, episodes and events that trigger export initiation to SME export propensity (i.e. the critical events and/or incidents that trigger the likelihood of whether a small firm will initiate export) but also to entrepreneurial orientation. Unsolicited orders, winning government awards and having an international orientation are among the critical incidents that drove SMEs in the garment and textile sub-sector of Ghana to begin export-ing. This particular case represents an important deviation from the predominant Internet and high-tech based industry analyses that dominate most of the inter-national entrepreneurship studies on young and new internationalizing SMEs. Overall, six main critical incidents were identified by Damoah (2018): (1) con-tacts established through participation in trade fairs; (2) contacts established through international orientation (previous residency abroad); (3) contacts and recommendations established through friends and families abroad; (4) winning national government awards; (5) being in receipt of unsolicited orders; and (6) contacts and recommendations established through joint venture ownership. For example, from the perspective of SME firm owners, trade fairs were regarded as important opportunities that could trigger export business. The six critical incidents were categorized using dimensions offered by Leonidou et al.'s (2007) classification based on a firm's proactive internal behaviour, pro-active external behaviour, reactive internal behaviour and reactive external behaviour. Thus, international entrepreneurship literature was integrated with SME export propensity literature, and linked to critical incidents. The latter is an important methodological approach that links process to change triggers through this form of analysis.

While five theoretical frameworks were integrated to explore the critical incidents that trigger export initiation of SMEs from Ghana, contingency theory was the most dominant framework employed by Damoah, 2018). Again, drawing on earlier literature from international entrepreneurship, categoriza-tions by Leonidou et al. (2007) were used to highlight the main triggers of export initiation among SMEs largely caused by external stimuli. An analysis of the critical incidents revealed that in most cases networking contacts estab-lished played an important role. For example, contacts gained through trade shows, previous foreign residency abroad, joint venture ownership and friends and families abroad are all network-related incidents. However, placed within a critical incident analysis, we can see more clearly, how most of the incidents seemed serendipitous and episodic (e.g. receipts of unsolicited orders), yet some entrepreneurs took full advantage of the incidents and exploited them

(Damoah, 2018). The act of maximizing and/or taking advantage of episodic events and being able to initiate export business supports the concept of entrepreneurial orientation, frameworks from international entrepreneurship literature and the contingency framework. The basic assumptions of international entrepreneurship (McDougall et al., 1994) are highlighted and supported in the study by Damoah (2018).

One contribution of the paper is that, unlike previous studies that use objective quantitative measures to examine the issue from other perspectives, Damoah (2018) uses the critical incident approach, which allows one to delve deeper into the phenomenon. Another contribution is that it sheds light on the internationalization process of manufacturing SMEs from an under-researched and a less-know geographical institutional context. The diverse context and use of new methodological approaches would be helpful in more studies in entrepreneurship, internationalization and cross-cultural studies in international entrepreneurship.

Finally, the study by Damoah (2018) extends the literature examining the propensity of SMEs to export into the international entrepreneurship field. While some work is prevalent in the area (Martineau & Pastoriza, 2016), most variables are researched as quantitative objective predictors. For example, organizational level predictors (e.g. firm size, firm age, firm network capacity and innovative products) (Dana et al., 2016; Wadhwa et al., 2017), individual level predictors (e.g. owner manager's personality characteristics – age and education) (Adomako et al., 2017; Child et al., 2017), institutional level predictors (e.g. central government's export interventions) (Crick & Spence, 2005) and the structure of the domestic market (Maria-Perez & García-Alvarez, 2009; Fakih & Ghazalian, 2013; Babatunde, 2017).

Damoah (2018) also offers some novel ideas on internationalizing SMEs and entrepreneurial orientation. While Damoah's study examines similar quantitative objective factors that facilitate and/or influence the likelihood of export, it also explores the critical incidents approach, which delves deeper into the subjective factors of the issue rather than merely the facilitating factors. It provides an approach for understanding the dynamic nature of entrepreneurial orientation for internationalizing SMEs. It has been argued that the internationalization of SMEs is a complex phenomenon that cannot be understood in detail using only quantitative objective determinants (Villena, 2019). Novel approaches such as the critical incidents approach are timely and useful for studying entrepreneurship, internationalization and cross-border entrepreneurial differences. The critical incident as a trigger for export propensity according to Bell et al. (2001, 2003), Nummela et al. (2006) and Zineldin (2007) refers to a significant episode, crisis time or crucial moment that leads to the opportunity for export.

Despite the ongoing advancement of studies in the SME internationalization field, rich and robust explanations and interpretations of the critical episodes, events and incidents that propel export initiation have not been offered. It is therefore an opportune time for the research community in the international entrepreneurship field to extend studies such as those of Damoah (2018) to understand internationalizing SMEs' entrepreneurial orientation and behaviour, integrated with external factors (institutional) using a critical incidents approach. The research gap is thus represented by the lack of adequate understanding regarding the critical incidents that trigger the export initiation of SMEs, such as in the example of Damoah (2018), as well as a lack of understanding of young and new internationalizing SMEs well into their life-cycle, enabling causal relationships to be more closely observed and clearly established. The approach in Damoah's (2018) study, therefore, partially fills the gap by empirically exploring the critical incidents that trigger SME export initiation in manufacturing in lesser known regions (e.g. Ghana and South Africa). More studies are needed in the international entrepreneurship and international business field that draw from this approach to better elucidate the theoretical lens important to advancing the field conceptually (e.g. entrepreneurial orientation and opportunity triggers) at different levels of analysis (entrepreneur, firm and institutions), ecosystems in which global and internal firms operate (Teece, 2014) and in lesser known contexts (emerging and institutional country environments). Having focused thus far on SMEs, we now turn to theories in international entrepreneurship that address larger MNEs.

Internalization, entrepreneurship, capabilities and cross-border market co-creation

Teece's (2014: 9) new capabilities-based theory of the firm addresses inadequacies of the theory of the MNE and competitive advantage by looking through the lens of organizational capabilities, strategy and entrepreneurship. Teece's theoretical foundation integrates the 'internalization scholars' and the 'international management scholars'. He draws from earlier works on capabilities to incorporate the theory of the MNE (Augier & Teece, 2007, 2008; Pitelis & Teece, 2010; Teece, 2006) and international business (Rugman & Verbeke, 1992; 2003) into his capabilities/entrepreneurship framework. The goal of this theory is to integrate economic, organizational and entrepreneurial theories of the firm to demonstrate how "both governance and entrepreneurship/capabilities perspectives are needed to shed light on the nature of the MNE, and the foundations of [sustained competitive advantage] SCA" (Teece, 2014: 9).

There are two rationales or prongs to the internalization perspective, one of the most dominant literatures in the international business field for the past three decades (Dunning & Lundan, 2008). The more common and advanced school of thought promotes the view that "transaction costs/hold-up issues that are avoided by internalization" (p. 10) and is supported by Buckley and Casson (1976), Dunning (1981), Rugman (1981), Teece (1975, 1976, 1981) and Williamson (1981), to mention a few seminal authors. Contractual issues and market failure are perceived as the major reasons for internalization, with the rationale of the internalization school of thought used to identify the relative merits of various entry modes (e.g. exports, licensing and FDI).

The second lesser known rationale or prong of the internalization school of thought does not base itself in essence on transaction cost. Instead, it highlights the "common (organizational) culture of an integrated enterprise and the ease of coordination inside the firm, as compared with coordination through the market" (Teece, 2014: 10). Furthermore, integration has other positives such as "pathways to learning, and ... sharing know-how and expertise through cross-border technology and ... transfer within the MNE" (Teece, 2014: 10). Significantly in this second prong, "facilitating opportunity identification, personnel exchanges, learning, integration, and assisting in technology transfer are likely to be very important, and cannot be squeezed under the rubric of economizing on transaction costs" (Teece, 2014: 10). The focus is not on saving transaction costs but far "more about being entrepreneurial and effective in the development, transfer, and orchestration of differentiated organizational and technological capabilities (Teece, 1981)" (Teece, 2014: 10). This approach to the MNE is what we call knowledge-based, whereby the role of the MNE is to transfer knowledge and know-how across borders.

Cantwell (1989) was a scholar who recognized early on the importance of integrating contractual frameworks with a theory of capability development. However, the international business field has tended to leave the capability considerations underdeveloped, some would argue, to its detriment. Thus, the time is now appropriate to work more closely with the second prong, that is, focus on capabilities, and to strengthen this rationale with "entrepreneurial considerations, and linked to transaction-cost comparative governance perspective" (Teece, 2014: 11). In doing so, the first prong is sufficiently developed to support both. Thus, the Teece (2014) model aims to provide a "combined entrepreneurial/capabilities conceptual perspective within which transaction costs can be contained" (Teece, 2014: 11). Some of the main concerns with earlier attempts is the lack of robust conceptualization of capabilities. Earlier work by Teece (1981) explains how both transaction-cost type and capabilities-type theories are able to coexist. Some have even argued that the 'ownership' component of Dunning's ownership, location and internalization (OLI) model, can be interpreted as firm-specific advantages and national institutions, and thus a proxy for firm-level capabilities. However, the OLI model of internalization theory does not explain well the source of firm-specific assets development.

Dunning and Lundan (2008) make a considerable contribution explaining how path-dependent resources and capabilities of the firm and its institutional infrastructure support dynamic growth, emphasizing the important link between microstructure capabilities and the evolution of the (institutional) macrostructure. Nonetheless, given the global nature of technological capabilities, development of this capability inhouse is no longer tenable, and requires effectively orchestrated technologies within and beyond the firm to compete effectively and sustainably (Augier & Teece, 2007).

Both market creation and co-creation are dynamic entrepreneurial concepts, primarily ignored in the first prong of transaction-cost, and vary considerably from market-entry mode decisions that have been the major focus of colleagues from the first prong (Brouthers, 2013; Hennart, 2009). Market failure and perfect market hypotheses still dominate much of the thinking of the scholars from this first prong, despite knowing that there are inherent problems with this thinking. Market failure thinking also has little conceptual explanatory power when it comes to understanding the complexity of such entrepreneurial concepts. Indeed, from an entrepreneurial perspective, market creation and co-creation activities are not merely responses to market failure. The reality might be that the market has not yet emerged, is still in its infancy or still needs to be recognized as an opportunity by an entrepreneurially managed business, where entrepreneurial and creative problem solving is encouraged as part of the create and co-create process (Pitelis & Teece, 2010).

The main point here, is that internalizing activity to solve transactional challenges does not necessarily assist entrepreneurial MNE managers to discover, create and actualize new products, processes and ideas that may become the next new global solution to latent needs. Being able to hone their capabilities around creating, actualizing and ensuring they have readily available skilled suppliers, and not just customers to reach, requires "a market creation and co-creation view of the MNE ... obviously rather different from [market failure] contractual approaches" (Teece, 2014: 12). Research by Cavanagh, Freeman, Kalfadellis and Herbert (2017) and Cavanagh, Freeman, Kalfadellis and Cavusgil (2017) reveals how subsidiaries in some MNEs assume different types of autonomy, largely perceived as entrepreneurial acts. Drawing from agency theory within the subsidiary-headquarters context, these researchers provide evidence of intraentrepreneurship. The integration required between creation and co-creation upstream and downstream, implies working with inter and intraentrepreneurial participants, including within the MNE and outside with customers, suppliers, competitors and in international contexts, providing additional opportunities for learning and new product development. Teece (2014: 12) argues that "a prime reason why MNEs exist is that their cross-border presence, entrepreneurial capacities, [and] organizational capabilities are integral to the market creation and co-creation process, both upstream and downstream, and also laterally".

Thus, it is fundamental to recognize the importance of capabilities within MNEs and not just at the individual entrepreneurial level. MNEs play an integral role in stimulating activity between entrepreneurs and their environment by influencing markets, shaping trends and demand, and assembling the resources and complements needed to develop, support and sustain markets. What is currently missing from the theory of the MNE is the important role played by entrepreneurial MNEs to influence, shape, motivate and support new ecosystems within which global, regional, international and domestic firms must coincide, operate and compete and complement. MNEs provide other roles such as supporting new investments in complementary sectors and other necessary infrastructure to facilitate new product development and successfully launch new products. In this sense, MNEs are an essential participant in driving the vitality of specific business ecosystems.

This role is especially significant because ecosystems are partly endogenous, given they are usually co-created by global MNEs. The role of the MNE in driving entrepreneurial ecosystems is contrary to the Porter (1980, 1985) view underpinned by the industrial economics model, which places the industry as the focus for the analysis, and market structures as an exogenous outcome. In contrast, in Teece's (2014) entrepreneurial model of the growth of the firm, the impact of endogenous entrepreneurial decision-making within the MNE is the domain of analysis as it influences market structures exogenously. The concept of ecosystems is endogenous and constitutes the focus of Teece's (2014) entrepreneurial model. Therefore, the industry is not highlighted as the focus for competitive analysis in a dynamic model that captures the complexity of the important influence that MNEs have on the facilitation, vitality and sustainability of ecosystems. The entrepreneurial MNE is thus fundamental to stimulating innovation through infrastructure, investment, competition, creation and co-creation. This perception of the role of the firm is thus contrary to the Coasian firm where "there is at best a modest role for the manager, no room for the entrepreneur, and no need for the leader" (Teece, 2014: 12). We now turn to yet another theoretical lens, namely, the importance of business networks in international entrepreneurship, used in research in larger and smaller MNEs, but especially in the study of smaller, new and young internationalizing SMEs.

Business networks and international entrepreneurship

In a further iteration of the original (1977) Uppsala internationalization process model in 2009, Johanson and Vahlne offered a reformulation by including both network theory and entrepreneurship theory into their model. This process model is an important link between entrepreneurship and internationalization, as the Uppsala internationalization process model is fundamental to understanding the development process for recognizing and exploiting opportunities in a business sense under conditions of foreign risk (Johanson & Vahlne, 1977, 2009, 2011; Vahlne & Johanson, 2013, 2017). Foreign risk is an outcome of dealing with uncertainties derived from activities in foreign markets and subsequent commitments made in these foreign networks (Johanson & Vahlne, 1977, 2009, 2011; Vahlne & Johanson, 2017; Coviello, Kano & Liesch, 2017). In this section we critically examine this important model reformulation, building on recent discussion offered by Forsgren (2016). It is important that we do so, as the Uppsala process model (originally referred to as a stage model) and its many iterations (1990, 2003, 2006; Vahlne & Johanson, 2017) since 1977, continue to have a major influence on research in international business of SMEs and the link between entrepreneurship and internationalization.

While there are, of course, other process models that date back to this time, for example, Luostarinen's (1989) internationalization process model with its early emphasis on lateral rigidity as a behavioural characteristic in strategic decision-making, none has provided as much influence on current international business research and entrepreneurship as the original Uppsala model and Vahlne and Johanson's subsequent models. This is especially so for smaller firms and new and young SMEs, where internationalization is regarded "as an entrepreneurial process in a business network context" (Forsgren, 2016: 1135). Johanson and Vahlne (1977) wrote one of the most cited articles, if not the most single cited article, in the international business scholarly community on the internationalization process of firms, both small and large. Interestingly, the original 1977 model was based on four case studies of large manufacturing firms in Sweden. By raising and addressing some of these concerns, it is expected that the Uppsala model and iterations, including the most recent (Vahlne & Johanson, 2017) will continue to help develop the theoretical foundations for international entrepreneurship.

Business theory is central to the Uppsala model and the process of firm internationalization. The firm's market was modified in the original model from 'country' to a 'business network' in the 2009 iteration (Johanson & Vahlne, 1977, 2009). What is the significance of this fundamental change? If we conceive lack of market knowledge as a fundamental challenge facing firms, then the concept of "liability of foreignness" means that a firm does not have a position in the foreign network, notionally understood as "liability of outsidership" (Johanson & Vahlne, 2009: 2015). Thus, moving from an outsider to an insider in a foreign network is the key to understanding differences between how to operate in the home market compared to the host (foreign) market. The business context and not the country border become the central focus, and the foreign market is now viewed as a business network.

However, if we examine this so-called difference more closely, in simple terms, the essential "difference between a domestic network and a foreign one is the liability of foreignness" and not outsidership (Forsgren, 2016). While being an outsider is significant, being an outsider in relation to a domestic or a foreign network is essentially the same – a firm is still an outsider, albeit, more challenged in a foreign network in which it is less familiar. This view refers to the concept of psychic distance (Johanson & Vahlne, 1977), and the effect of the liability of foreignness (Johanson & Vahlne, 2009). Thus, all firms are really outsiders in business networks, trying to find a way through to a valuable insider position. Outsidership needs more development if we are to refine our understanding of foreignness and internationalization.

We can therefore argue that a firm's view of outsidership is related to the "distance between its current business and the relevant foreign network" and we can thus analyse causal relationships between outsidership and internationalization "by analysing the characteristics of the business network in which the firm is embedded and how such embeddedness influences the distance to a potential network" (Forsgren, 2016: 1137).

We certainly know that the type, level and extent of a firm's embeddedness will impact its ability to manage challenges and experience new ideas, innovate, locate new partners and create new ventures. Thus, the characteristics of the business network in which a business embeds itself does impact the possibility of becoming an insider in a foreign network and the ongoing development of the company's foreign business activities.

In terms of embeddedness, it is important to distinguish between two types: first, structural embeddedness, with the focus on "whom one knows" (Dacin et al., 1999), which relates to firm advantages derived from one's business network position. It thus includes examination of open vs. closed networks, as open networks support information diversity and access to important opportunities facilitated by brokerage contacts to connect disconnected groups across network "structural holes" (Burt, 1992; Oehme & Bort, 2015). In contrast, closed networks focus on trust building and cooperative behaviours for tacit knowledge exchange, as a result of social capital that is facilitated through close bonds and close-knit networks. Second, relational embeddedness deals with "how well one knows them" (Moran, 2005: 1130) and relates to the learning advantages from dyadic information and knowledge exchanges due to close relationships (Gulati, 1998; Nahapiet & Ghoshal, 1998). The internationalization process and liability of outsidership research can benefit from closer examination of both types of embeddedness in research into international entrepreneurship.

How does this link to entrepreneurship? Networks are both open and closed, and fundamental to opportunity recognition. From the perspective of recognizing business opportunities, firm embeddedness makes the entire process much easier, certainly for foreign market opportunities (Moran, 2005) when networks are open. The main reason behind this assumption is that new opportunities are far more likely to exist in business networks that are unrestricted and thus rich with 'structural' holes as more, new, novel and different kinds of information are likely to exist in open rather than closed networks. The above is not only conducive to recognizing new opportunities but also driving entrepreneurial innovative activities, given the nature of the competitive pressures. Foreign customers or suppliers have greater opportunities to meet others through these open networks (Walker et al., 1997), which can help stimulate entrepreneurial orientation that drives entrepreneurial recognition. Closed networks also support entrepreneurial behaviour. Closed relationships between a home-based supplier and a foreign customer, reduce risk, opportunism and tacit knowledge exchange, and thus, over time, build and support further cooperative behaviour leading to ongoing development of foreign business opportunities and commitment to foreign networks.

This assumption is entirely consistent with the 2009 Johanson and Vahlne, business network internationalization process model. However, open rather than closed networks have the additional benefit of avoiding what we call the "paradox of over embeddedness" (Uzzi, 1997), where such embeddedness leads to lack of innovation and opportunity recognition. This result arises because only a small number of known and trusted networks are relied upon, rather than a wider and more diverse reach, which provides richer, novel and potentially new information, leading to entrepreneurial opportunity recognition, new product development, new contacts and partners, for venture creation. Thus, there is a trade-off between safe and trusted contacts, compared to more diverse and information-rich contacts that enhance the flexibility and recognition opportunity process (Gargiulo & Benassi, 2000). However, it is important to note that close, trusted and committed relational embeddedness also has a positive impact on innovation (Moran, 2005). Moreover, as much of the information and knowledge required for successful innovation is tacit, only strong and close relational embedded actors are likely to achieve successful innovative entrepreneurial outcomes.

Returning to the notion that internationalization is an entrepreneurial concept (Jones & Coviello, 2005) where the "liability of newness" (Mudambi & Zahra, 2007) is the common firm experience when moving away from trusted and close ties to new practices and situations with increased risk (Moran, 2005), assessing resource quality becomes much more difficult. Thus, from an entrepreneurial, network and internationalization perspective, "deep relationships with other business actors in the firm's business network will facilitate the establishment of a position in a foreign network in order to develop a business opportunity) (Forsgren, 2016: 1138). The same principle applies to a foreign network that a new firm wishes to enter. The closer and tighter the network, the more difficult it will be for outsiders to penetrate. Alternatively, if foreign network relationships are at arm's length, it will be easier for outsiders to manage the opportunity discovery process as an outsider (Coviello, 2006). The downside, of course, is that the foreign network may be less reliable for developing opportunities because of greater potential for opportunism given the higher levels of uncertainty about commitment and cooperation, known as "defection opportunism" (Gargiulo & Benassi, 2000: 193).

Thus, we can summarize the arguments above by suggesting that when a firm's network is relatively open or the foreign local industry network is not excessively concentrated, it allows for far more possibilities for an outsider to establish linkages with the local knowledge sources that are significant for competence creation. If the foreign network is open, it reduces the firm's liability of outsidership associated with the entrepreneurial activity of discovering business opportunities. However, at the same time, this network is likely to increase the liability of outsidership related to the possibility of actually developing the identified opportunities. This outcome is evident because it is more complex to manage foreign risk and secure the quality of exchange of the required resources in an open network than is likely to be the case in a closed network, where the firm has the likelihood of forming many close relationships, ideal for tacit knowledge exchange, to support entrepreneurial creation. Finally, "the issue becomes one of how the firm can strike a balance between networks that reduce the liability of outsidership in [the] opportunity discovery phase of the internationalization process, and networks that reduce it in the opportunity development phase. This is a fascinating area for future research" (Forsgren, 2016: 1138).

Conclusion

In this chapter we have attempted to provide an institutional perspective, network theory and transactional cost perspective, as well as highlighting important theorist and academic contributors over the past four decades or more that have assisted in developing the links across entrepreneurship, international entrepreneurship and transnational entrepreneurship fields. The importance of drawing on an institutional perspective allows us to explore and challenge the significant variations among institutional structures of home countries. This discussion has then allowed us to provide a foundation on which to offer explanations of variations in entrepreneurial endowments of prospective transnational entrepreneurs. Transnational entrepreneurs embed themselves in foreign networks that facilitate cross-border business operations as they establish positions in foreign business networks. Networks can be open and closed, and while they have advantages and disadvantages, both are important to the discovery, belief, venture creation and development process. We have also discussed Teece's (2014: 9) new capabilities-based theory of the firm, which addresses inadequacies in the theory of the larger MNE and competitive advantage by drawing on the lens of organizational capabilities, strategy and entrepreneurship. This is an important step in the development of intraentrepreneurship and the type of organizational environments that invite and nurture creative and entrepreneurial activities within larger organizations. Teece's (2014) work offers a rich theoretical foundation to integrate the internalization scholars and the international management scholars. In particular, Teece draws on earlier works with regard to capabilities in the theory of the MNE (Augier & Teece, 2007, 2008; Pitelis & Teece, 2010; Teece, 2006) and international business (Rugman & Verbeke, 1992, 2003) in his capabilities/entrepreneurship framework. Teece then embarks on his primary goal, which is to go beyond this theory to integrate economic, organizational and entrepreneurial theories of the firm to demonstrate how "both governance and entrepreneurship/capabilities perspectives are needed to shed light on the nature of the MNE, and the foundations of [sustained competitive advantage] SCA" (Teece, 2014: 9). This important work has provided a foundation for discussion that allows us to move beyond the theoretical impasse in entrepreneurship and international business studies (Yeung, 2002; Teece, 2014; Forsgren, 2016; Chandra, 2017; Vahlne & Johanson, 2017).

In the next chapter, we attempt to understand the impact of the environment over the last two decades on entrepreneurship in emerging markets. During this period in particular, we have seen a staggering increase in emerging market multinational companies (EMMNCs[1]), both large and small, engaged in cross-border trade and investment, surpassing the prior dominance of developed market MNCs originating from the triad economies: North America, Western Europe and Japan. Studying emerging market MNCs is not new, with seminal studies such as Lall (1983) and Lecraw (1993). However, in-depth examination has gained momentum in the last decade (*The Economist*, 2017). Attributed to a greater emphasis placed on emerging market as emerging market MNCs embark on a path of accelerated internationalization (Bonaglia, Goldstein & Mathews, 2007; Xie, Reddy & Liang, 2017), some studies suggest that the last two decades of spectacular growth in emerging market allowed many emerging market firms to catch up with their developed market counterparts. This is no longer the case with a new "wave of inventive young [start-up] firms emerging from China" and other emerging markets springing onto the global stage (The Economist, 2017). The question of the dominance of these enterprises is no longer debateable. However, a question is still open with regard to what lies behind the manner in which emerging market MNCs are ensuring international competitiveness in their start up, growth and internationalization (establishment and consolidation) development.

Note

1 The terms EMMNCs, Emerging Multinationals and Third World Multinationals are used interchangeably in the literature (Jormanainen & Koveshnikov, 2012).

References

Adomako, S., Opoku, R. A. & Frimpong, K. (2017) The moderating influence of competitive intensity on the relationship between CEOs' regulatory foci and SME internationalization. *Critical Perspectives on International Business Journal of International Management*, 23(2): 180–193.

Aspelund, A., Madsen, T. K. & Moen, O. (2007) A review of the foundation, international marketing strategies, and performance of international new ventures. *European Journal of Marketing*, 41(11/12): 1423–1448).

Aspelund, A. & Moen, O. (2005) Small international firms: Typology, performance and implications. *Management International Review*, 45 (Special Issue 3): 37–57.

Augier, M. & Teece, D. J. (2007) Dynamic capabilities and multinational enterprise: Penrosean insights and omissions. *Management International Review*, 47(2): 175–192.

Augier, M. & Teece, D. J. (2008) Strategy as evolution with design: The foundations of dynamic capabilities and the role of the managers in the economic system. *Organizational Studies*, 29(8–9): 1187–1208.

Autio, E. (2005) Creative tension: The significance of Ben Oviatt's and Patricia McDougall's article toward a theory of international new ventures. *Journal of International Business Studies*, 36(1): 9–19.

Babatunde, M. A. (2017) Export propensity and intensity of Nigerian SMEs. *Journal of Small Business and Entrepreneurship*, 29(1): 25–55.

Bell, J., McNaugthon, R. & Young, S. (2001) Born-again global firms: An extension to the 'born global' phenomenon. *Journal of International Management*, 7(3): 173–189.

Bell, J., McNaugthon, R., Young, S. & Crick, D. (2003) Towards an integrative model of small firm internationalization. *Journal of International Entrepreneurship*, 1(4): 339–362.

Bonaglia, F., Goldstein, A. & Mathews, J. A. (2007) Accelerated internationalisation by emerging markets' multinationals: The case of the white goods sector. *Journal of World Business* 42(4): 369–383.

Brouthers, K. (2013) A retrospective on: Institutional, cultural and transaction cost influences on entry mode choice and performance. *Journal of International Business Studies*, 44(1): 14–22.

Buckley, P. J. & Ghauri, P. (eds). (1993). *The Internationalization of the Firm: A Reader*. London: Academic Press.

Buckley, P. J. & Casson, M. C. (1976) The future of the multinational enterprise. London: Palgrave Macmillan.

Burgel, O. & Murray, G. C. (2000) The international market entry choices of start-up companies in high-technology industries. *Journal of International Marketing*, 8(2): 33–62.

Burt, R. (1992) *Structural Holes: The Social Structure of Competition*. Cambridge: Harvard University Press.

Cantwell, J. A. (1989) *Technological Innovation and Multinational Corporations*. Oxford: Blackwell.

Cavanagh, A., Freeman, S., Kalfadellis, P. & Cavusgil, S. T. (2017) How do subsidiaries assume autonomy? A refined application of agency theory with the subsidiary-headquarters context. *Global Strategy Journal*, 7(2): 172–192.

Cavanagh, A., Freeman, S., Kalfadellis, P. & Herbert, K. (2017) Assigned versus assumed: Towards a contemporary, detailed understanding of subsidiary autonomy. *International Business Review*, 26 (6): 1168–1183.

Chandra, Y. (2017) A time-based process model of international entrepreneurial opportunity evaluation. *Journal of International Business Studies*, 48: 423–451.

Chetty, S. & Campbell-Hunt, C. (2004) A strategic approach to internationalization: A traditional versus a "born-global" approach. *Journal of International marketing*, 12(1): 57–81.

Child, J., Hsieh, L., Elbanna, S., Karmowska, J., Marinova, S., Puthusserry, P. & Zhang, Y. (2017) SME international business models: The role of context and experience. *Journal of World Business*, 52(5): 664–679.

Coombs, J. E., Sadrieh, F. & Annavarjula, M. (2009) Two decades of international entrepreneurship research: What have we learned – where do we go from here? *International Journal of Entrepreneurship*, 13: 23–64.

Coviello, N. E. (2006) The network dynamics of international new ventures. *Journal of International Business Studies*, 37(5): 713–731.

Coviello, N., Kano, L. & Liesch, P. W. (2017) Adapting the Uppsala model to modern world: Macro-context and micofoundations. *Journal of International Business Studies*, 48: 1151–1164.

Coviello, N. E. & McAuley, A. (1999) Internationalization and the smaller firm: A review of contemporary empirical research. *Management International Review*, 39(3): 223–256.

Coviello, N. E., McDougall, P. P. & Oviatt, B. M. (2011) The emergence, advance and future of international entrepreneurship research – An introduction to the special forum. *Journal of Business Venturing*, 26(6): 625–631.

Coviello, N. & Munro, H. (1992) Internationalizing the entrepreneurial technology-intensive firm: growth through linkage development. Paper presented at the Babson Entrepreneurship Research Conference. INSEAD, France.

Criado, A. R., Urbano, D., Josep, R. & Vaillant, Y. (2005) The born-global phenomenon: A comparative case study research. *Journal of International Entrepreneurship*, 3(2): 133–171.

Crick, D. & Spence, M. (2005) The internationalisation of 'high performing' UK high-tech SMEs: A study of planned and unplanned strategies. *International Business Review*, 14(2): 167–185.

Cumming, D., Sapienza, H., Siegel, D. S. & Wright, M. (2009) International entrepreneurship: Managerial and policy implications. *Strategic Entrepreneurship Journal*, 3(4): 283–296.

Dacin, T. M., Ventresca, M. J. & Beal, B. D. (1999) The embeddedness of organizations: Dialogue and direction. *Journal of Management*, 25(3): 317–356.

Damoah, O. B. O. (2018) A critical incident analysis of the export behaviour of SMEs: Evidence from an emerging market, *Critical Perspectives on International Business*, 14(2/3): 309–334.

Dana, L. P., Grandinetti, R. & Mason, M. C. (2016) International entrepreneurship, export planning and export performance: Evidence from a sample of winemaking SMEs. *International Journal of Entrepreneurship and Small Business*, 29(4): 602–626.

Di Gregorio, D., Musteen, M. & Thomas, D. E. (2008) International new ventures: The cross-border nexus of individuals and opportunities. *Journal of World Business*, 43(2): 186–196.

Dunning, J. H. & Lundan, S. M. (2008) *Multinational Enterprises and the Global Economy*. Cheltenham: Edward Elgar.

Dunning, J. H. (1981) Alternative channels and modes of international resource transmission, in R. W. Moxon & H. V. Perlmutter (eds), *Controlling International Technology Transfer: Issues, Perspectives and Implications*, New York: Pergamon Press, pp. 3–27.

Engelen, A., Heinemann, F. & Brettel, M. (2009) Cross-cultural entrepreneurship research: Current status and framework for future studies. *Journal of International Business Studies*, 7(3): 163–189.

Fakih, A. & Ghazalian, P. L. (2013) Why some firms export? An empirical analysis for manufacturing firms in the MENA region. IZA Discussion Paper 7172, *Institute for the Study of Labor (IZA)*, Bonn, pp. 1–31.

Forsgren, M. (2016) A note on the revisited Uppsala internationalization process model – the implications of business networks and entrepreneurship. *Journal of International Business Studies*, 47: 1135–1144.

Freeman, S. & Cavusgil, S. T. (2007) Entrepreneurial strategies for accelerated internationalization of smaller born globals. *Journal of International Marketing*, 15(4): 1–40.

Gamboa, E. C. & Brouthers, L. E W. (2008) How international is entrepreneurship? *Entrepreneurship, Theory and Practice*, 32(3): 551–558.

Gargiulo, M. & Benassi, M. (2000) Trapped in your own net? Network cohesion, structural holes, and the adaptation of social capital. *Organization Science*, 11(2): 183–196.

Giamartino, G. A., McDougall, P. P. & Bird, B. J. (1993) International entrepreneurship: The state of the field. Entrepreneurship. *Theory and Practice*, 18(1): 37–42.

Gulati, R. (1998) Alliances and networks. *Strategic Management Journal*, 19(4): 293–317.

Hagstrom, W. D. (1965) *The Scientific Community*. New York: Basic Books.

Hambrick, D. C. & Chen, M.-J. (2008) New academic fields as admittance-seeking social movements: The case of strategic management. *Academy of Management Review*, 33(1): 32–54.

Harzing, A. W. (2007) *Publish or Perish*, available from http://.harzing.com/pop/htm.

Hayton, J. C., George, G. & Zahra, S. (2002) National culture and entrepreneurship: A review of behavioural research. *Entrepreneurship Theory and Practice*, 26(4): 33–52.

Hennart, J. F. (2009) Down with MNE-centric theories! Market entry and expansion as the bundling of MNE and local assets. *Journal of International Business Studies*, 40(9): 1432–1454.

Johanson, J. & Vahlne, J.-E. (1977) The internationalization process of the firm: A model of knowledge development and increasing foreign commitments. *Journal of International Business Studies*, 8(1): 23–32.

Johanson, J. & Vahlne, J.-E. (2009) The Uppsala internationalization process model revisited: From liability of foreignness to liability of outsidership. *Journal of International Business Studies*, 40: 1411–1431.

Johanson, J. & Vahlne, J-E. (2011) Markets as networks: Implications for strategy-making. *Journal of the Academy of Marketing Science*, 39(4): 484–491.

Jones, M. V. & Coviello, N. E. (2005) Internationalization: Conceptualizing an entrepreneurial process of behavior in time. *Journal of International Business Studies*, 36(3): 284–303.

Jolly, V. K., Alahunta, M. & Jeannet, J.-P. (1992) Challenging the incumbents: How high technology start-ups compete globally. *Journal of Strategic Change*, 1(1): 71–82.

Jones, M. V., Coviello, N. E. & Tang, Y. K. (2011) International entrepreneurship research (1989–2009): A domain ontology and thematic analysis. *Journal of International Business Studies*, 26(6): 632–659.

Jormanainen, I. & Koveshnikov, A. (2012) International activities of emerging market firms. *Management International Review*, 5(5): 691–725.

Keupp, M. M. & Gassmann, O. (2009) The past and future of international entrepreneurship: A review and suggestions for developing the field. *Journal of Management*, 35(3): 600–633.

Knight, G. (2000) Entrepreneurship and marketing strategy: The SME under globalization. *Journal of International Marketing*, 8(2): 12–32.

Kuhn, T. S. (1996) *The Structure of Scientific Revolutions* (3rd edn). Chicago: The University of Chicago Press.

Lall, S. (1983) *The New Multinationals.* Wiley: New York.

Lecraw, D. (1993) Outward direct investment by Indonesian firms: Motivations and effects. *Journal of International Business Studies*, 24(3): 589–600.

Leonidou, L. C., Katsikeas, C., S., Palihawadana, H. & Spyropoulou, S. (2007) An analytical review of the factors stimulating smaller firms to export: Implications for policy makers, *International Marketing Review*, 24(6): 735–770.

Litvak, L. (1990) Instant international: Strategic reality for small high technology firms in Canada. *Multinational Business*, 2: 1–12 (Summer).

Lopez, L. E., Kundu, S. K. & Ciravegna, L. (2009) Born global or born regional? Evidence from an exploratory study in the Costa Rican software industry. *Journal of International Business Studies*, 40(7): 1228–1238.

Luostarinen, R. (1989) *Internationalization of the Firm: An Empirical Study of the Internationalization of Firms with Small and Open Domestic Markets with Special Emphasis on Lateral Rigidity as a Behavioral Characteristic in Strategic Decision-making* (3rd edn). Helsinki: The Helsinki School of Economics. ACTA Academiae Oeconomicae Helsingiensis, Series A: 30: ISSN 0356–9969; ISBN 951–699–229–3.

McDougall, P. P. (1989) International versus domestic entrepreneurship: New venture strategic behavior and industry structure. *Journal of Business Venturing*, 4(6): 387–400.

McDougall, P. P. & Oviatt, B. M. (2000) International entrepreneurship: The intersection of two research paths. *Academy of Management Journal*, 43(5): 902–906.

McDougall, P. P., Shane, S. & Oviatt, B. M. (1994) Explaining the formation of international new ventures: The limits of studies from international business research. *Journal of Business Venturing*, 9(6): 469–487.

McGrath, R. G. & MacMillan, I. C. (1992) More like each other than anyone else? A cross-cultural study of entrepreneurial perceptions. *Journal of Business Venturing*, 7(5): 419–429.

McGrath, R. G., MacMillan, I. C. & Scheinberg, S. (1992a) Elitists, risk-takers, and rugged individuals? An exploratory analysis of cultural differences between entrepreneurs and non-entrepreneurs. *Journal of Business Venturing*, 7(2): 115–135.

McGrath, R. G., MacMillan, I. C., Yang, E. A.-Y. & Tsai, W. (1992b) Does culture endure, or is it malleable? Issues for entrepreneurial economic development. *Journal of Business Venturing*, 7(6): 441–458.

Maria-Perez, R. & García-Alvarez, T. (2009) The internationalization strategy of Spanish indigenous franchised chains: A resource-based view. *Journal of Small Business Management*, 47(4): 514–530.

Martineau, C. & Pastoriza, D. (2016) International involvement of established SMEs: A review of antecedents, outcomes and moderators. *International Business Review*, 25(2): 458–470.

Moran, P. (2005) Structural vs relational embeddedness: Social capital and managerial performance. *Strategic Management Journal*, 26(12): 1129–1151.

Mudambi, R. & Zahra, S. (2007) The survival of international new ventures. *Journal of International Business Studies*, 38(2): 333–352.

Nahapiet, J. & Ghoshal, S. (1998) Social capital, intellectual capital, and organizational advantage. *Academy of Management Review*, 23(2): 242–266.

Nummela, N., Loane, S. & Bell, J. (2006) Change in SME internationalizations: An Irish perspective. *Journal of Small Business and Enterprise Development*, 13(4): 562–583.

Oehme, M. & Bort, S. (2015) SME internationalization modes in the German biotechnology industry: The influence of imitation, network position, and the international experience. *Journal of International Business Studies*, 46(6): 629–655.

Oviatt, B. M. & McDougall, P. P. (2005) Defining international entrepreneurship and modeling the speed of internationalization. *Entrepreneurship Theory and Practice*, 29(5): 537–553.

Oviatt, B. M. & McDougall, P. P. (1994) Towards a theory of international new ventures. *Journal of International Business Studies*, 25(1): 45–64.

Pitelis, C. N. & Teece, D. J. (2010) Cross-border market cocreation, dynamic capabilities and the entrepreneurial theory of the multinational enterprise. *Industrial and Corporate Change*, 19(4): 1247–1270.

Porter, M. E. (1980) *Competitive Strategy: Techniques for Analyzing Industries and Competitors*. New York: Free Press.

Porter, M. E. (1985) *Competitive Advantage: Creating and Sustaining Superior Performance*. New York: Free Press.

Ray, D. M. (1989) Entrepreneurial companies 'born' international: Four case studies. Paper presented at the Babson Entrepreneurship Research Conference, St Louis, USA.

Rennie, M. W. (1993) Global competitiveness: Born global. *The McKinsey Quarterly*, 4(4): 45–52.

Rialp, A., Rialp, J. & Knight, G. A. (2005) The phenomenon of early internationalizing firms: What do we know after a decade (1993–2003) of scientific inquiry? *International Business Review*, 14(2): 147–166.

Rugman, A. M. & Verbeke, A. (2003) Extending the theory of the multinational enterprise: Internalization and strategic management perspectives. *Journal of International Business Studies*, 34(2): 125–137.

Rugman, A. M. & Verbeke, A. (1992) A note on the transnational solution and the transaction cost theory of multinational strategic management. *Journal of International Business Studies*, 23(4): 761–771.

Rugman, A. M. (1981) *Inside the Multinationals: The Economics of Internal Markets.* New York: Columbia University Press.

Schumpeter, J. A. (1934) *The Theory of Economic Development: An Inquiry into Profits, Capital, Credit, Interest and the Business Cycle.* Harvard Economic Studies, Vol. 46, Cambridge, MA: Harvard College.

Schumpeter, J. (1942). *Capitalism, Socialism and Democracy.* New York: Harper and Brothers.

Styles, C. & Seymour, R. G. (2006) Opportunities for marketing researchers in international entrepreneurship. *International Marketing Review*, 23(2): 126–145.

Teece, D. J. (1975) *The Multinational Corporation and the Resource Cost of International Technology Transfer.* Philadelphia: Economics Department, University of Pennsylvania.

Teece, D. J. (1976) *The Multinational Corporation and the Resource Cost of International Technology Transfer.* Cambridge, MA: Ballinger Publishing.

Teece, D. J. (1981) The multinational enterprise: Market failure and market power considerations. *Sloan Management Review*, 22(3): 3–17.

Teece, D. J. (2006) Reflections on the Hymer thesis and the multinational enterprise. *International Business Review*, 15(2): 124–139.

Teece, D. J. (2014) A dynamic capabilities-based entrepreneurial theory of the multinational enterprise. *Journal of International Business Studies*, 45: 8–37.

The Economist 2017. Four BRICs don't quite make a wall. *The Economist.* www.economist.com/news/finance-and-economics/21723133-brazil-russia-india-and-china-have-done-even-better-forecastthanks-mainly [7 July 2017].

Tiessen, J. H. (1997) Individualism, collectivism, and entrepreneurship: A framework for international comparative research. *Journal of Business Venturing*, 12(5): 367–384.

Uzzi, B. (1997) Social structure and competition in interfirm networks: The paradox of embeddedness. *Administrative Science Quarterly*, 42(1): 35–67.

Vahlne, J.-E. & Johanson, J. (2013) The Uppsala model on evolution of the multinational business enterprise – from internalization to coordination of networks. *International Marketing Review*, 30(3): 189–210.

Vahlne, J.-E. & Johanson, J. (2017) From internationalization to evolution: The Uppsala model at 40 years. *Journal of International Business Studies*, 48: 1087–1102.

Vasilchenko, E. & Morrish, S. (2011) The role of entrepreneurial networks in the exploration and exploitation of internationalization opportunities by information and communication technology firms. *Journal of International Marketing*, 19(4): 88–105.

Villena, M. F. (2019) Export performance of SMEs: An empirical analysis of the mediating role of corporate image. *Journal of Small Business Management*, 57(2): 386–399.

Wadhwa, P., Wadhwa, P., McCormick, M., McCormick, M., Musteen, M. & Musteen, M. (2017) Technological innovation among internationality active SMEs in the Czech economy: Role of human and social capital of CEO. *European Business Review*, 29(2): 164–180.

Walker, G., Kogut, B. & Shan, W. (1997) Social capital, structural holes and the formation of an industry network. *Organization Science*, 8(2): 109–125.

Whitley, R. (1992) *Business Systems in East Asia: Firms, Markets and Societies.* London: Sage.

Williamson, O. E. (1981) The modern corporation: Origins, evolution, attributes. *Journal of Economic Literature*, 19(4): 1537–1568.

Wright, R. W. & Ricks, D. A. (1994) Trends in international business research: Twenty-five years later. *Journal of International Business Studies*, 25(5): 687–702.

Xie, E., Reddy, K. S. & Liang, J. (2017) Country-specific determinants of cross-border mergers and acquisitions: A comprehensive review and future research directions. *Journal of World Business*, 52(2): 127–183.

Yeung, H. W.-I. (2002) Entrepreneurship in international business: An institutional perspective. *Asia Pacific Journal of Management*, 19: 29–61.

Zacharakis, A. L. (1997) Entrepreneurial entry into foreign markets: A transactional cost perspective. *Entrepreneurship Theory and Practice*, 21(3): 23–39.

Zahra, S. A. (2005) A theory of international new ventures: A decade of research. *Journal of International Business Studies*, 36(1): 20–28.

Zahra, S. A. (1993) A conceptual model of entrepreneurship as firm-level behavior: A critique and extension. *Entrepreneurship Theory and Practice*, 17(4): 5–21.

Zahra, S. & George, G. (2002) International entrepreneurship: The current status of the field and future research agenda. In M. A. Hitt, R. D. Ireland, D. Sexton and M. Camp (eds), *Strategic Entrepreneurship: Creating an Integrated Mindset*, Malden, MA: Blackwell Publishers, pp. 255–288.

Zahra, S. A., Ireland, R. D. & Hitt, M. A. (2000) International expansion of new venture firms: International diversity, mode of market entry, technological learning, and performance. *Academy of Management Journal*, 43(5): 925–950.

Zineldin, M. (2007) International business relationships and entry modes: A case of Swedish automotive industry Scania and Volvo in Mexico. *Cross Cultural Management: An International Journal*, 14(4): 365–386.

4 International entrepreneurship in emerging and Western markets

The rising influence of China

Introduction

Over the past two decades, small to medium-sized enterprises (SMEs) in China have reached high levels of international development that can only be described as remarkable. However, because of China's unique cultural and institutional environment, there is still limited understanding of the influence of managerial determinants on internationalization. This chapter looks at this recent development and explores some of the reasons for this spectacular rise, the reasons for innovation having risen so quickly in this economy and recent examples during this period of development.

The innovation model of internationalization as well as other institutional models are explored in order to revisit and attempt to explain this dynamic development of Chinese SMEs' export operations. We discuss reasons why cultural differences might be contributing to this behaviour. We observe that exporting Chinese SMEs and the entry mode chosen by other Chinese firms are influenced by managerial perceptions, as well as a negative country-of-origin effects and strict overseas quality standards.

In addition, external and internal drivers act as 'change agents' in propelling the rapid international involvement of these SMEs. To understand the situation holistically, various stakeholders – government and export promotion agencies – are included in this study to show how a strong and directive partnership can develop and deliver needs-based supports, as well as create the right conditions to encourage non-exporters to participate in international operations. Finally, we provide recent examples of new rapidly growing Chinese SMEs, exporters and those engaged in FDI to identify the drivers, the enablers and some of the more recent concerns about the sustainability of such international activities.

Chinese culture and entrepreneurship

Studies of the characteristics of entrepreneurs from various cultures, in contrast with those of non-entrepreneurs, suggest that entrepreneurs share broadly similar characteristics, irrespective of culture. For example, an early study (McGrath, MacMillan & Scheinberg, 1992) surveyed over 700 entrepreneurs across nine countries and identified common traits, including being innovative, proactive and aggressive. However, an expanded survey of 1,217 entrepreneurs and 1,206 non-entrepreneurs in eight countries (McGrath, MacMillan & Scheinberg, 1992) showed distinct differences between the two groups, quite separate from their culture, highlighting some key attitudinal differences. This study indicated that entrepreneurs are rare and 'outliers' of a culture, and it is because of these characteristics and attitudes that they emerge and can often be truly labelled as extraordinary.

Some studies in psychology, for instance, have attempted to identify culture-neutral personality traits of entrepreneurs. A typical entrepreneur, for example, is likely to have five distinct characteristics: "initiating a life of self-determination and independence, finding new opportunities and ways of structuring and developing the enterprise (being) hard-working and persistent in goal striving, establishing a social network, and taking the risk of failure" (Brandstäter, 2011: 223). While such studies are helpful, there is a further aspect to understanding successful entrepreneurs – they must also be willing and able to participate in entrepreneurial activities. While entrepreneurs might be regarded as outliers, they still need to work in a context in common with others. For this reason, it is implausible to suggest that they might be somehow immune to cultures and the various norms and nuances that exist within a culture (Zhu, Freeman & Cavusgil, 2018). Entrepreneurs develop within a culture, which more or less shapes them, therefore they possess unique features of that culture. For this reason, the relationship between a national culture and entrepreneurship is an important one, notwithstanding the fact that it is difficult to determine national cultures since globalization has influenced the increased mobility of persons and most economies have histories of migration, somewhat clouding the notion of a single culture over a multicultural environment. There are, of course, some very typical and well cited cross-cultural entrepreneurial studies in this research stream into cross-cultural studies.

One such study is Hofstede's (1980, 2001) account of cultural dimensions that provides a well-known taxonomy to differentiate national cultures with regard to people's values and behavioural preferences and extrapolated to business organizational behaviour. For this reason, the theory of cultural dimensions is frequently used in cross-cultural research on entrepreneurship (Hayton et al., 2002). More recent studies by Hofstede have seen further updates to his theory. Assisted by his various colleagues, his studies assume the presence of six cultural dimensions – power distance, uncertainty avoidance, individualism vs. collectivism, masculinity vs. femininity, long-term vs. short-term orientation, and indulgence vs. restraint (Hofstede, Hofstede & Minkov, 2010). The first four dimensions are the most commonly studied in entrepreneurship (Hayton et al., 2002). Repeated studies continue to hypothesize that cultures facilitating entrepreneurship are most likely to score high in individualism, low in uncertainty avoidance, low in power distance and high in masculinity (Hayton et al., 2002). An early study partly supports the hypotheses, by arguing that while the degree of individualism is positively associated, power distance is negatively correlated with the rate of national innovation rate, closely associated with entrepreneurship.

Apart from Hofstede's theory, researchers have considered the relationship of entrepreneurship and cultural values and beliefs to other dimensions such as the need for achievement, autonomy and self-efficacy (Shane, Kolvereid & Westhead, 1991). The study identified four dimensions that underpin new business creation. They include recognition of achievement, independence from others, learning and development, and roles (Shane, Kolvereid & Westhead, 1991). While each varies in emphasis, these dimensions are systematically identified across countries. Research of a comparative nature has also assessed individuals from diverse countries regarding perceptions of traits supposedly commonly associated with entrepreneurial motivation. Another study investigated perceptions of entrepreneurs' four traits: innovativeness, locus of control, risk-taking propensity and energy level (Thomas & Mueller, 2000). The findings are consistent and confirm earlier studies which indicated that there are no cultural differences with regard to perceptions.

Complex relationship between Chinese culture and entrepreneurship

Apart from the aforementioned cross-cultural studies, another stream of study has focused on Chinese culture and has discussed its impact on entrepreneurship in China or overseas Chinese communities (e.g. Chan, 1997; Liao & Sohmen, 2001; Poutziouris et al., 2002; Zapalska & Edwards, 2001). Nonetheless, the studies lack specific detail with regard to Chinese cultural characteristics. For instance, three key features of traditional Chinese culture observed by overseas Chinese expatriates includes: paternalism, the unique personal system and xenophobia (Wang, 2012). Four key markers of Chinese culture include: familism, collectivism, hierarchy and emphasis on hard work. What we can observe is that culture is a flexible concept and it is arguably difficult to determine what should or should not be encompassed in the possibilities of conceptualizing culture (Wang, 2012; Yan, Wickramasekera & Tan, 2018).

As previously stated, specifically with regard to cross-cultural studies, Hofstede's (1980, 2001) model is regarded as a useful framework, despite disagreements in the literature (Baskerville, 2003; McSweeney, 2002). Yet, in terms of idiosyncratic dimensions of culture, viewpoints beyond Hofstede's model may be more appropriate. Three cultural dimensions stand out – self, interaction of self and others, and social environment (Wang, 2012). First, entrepreneurship is a process throughout which simultaneous personal striving and the supporting social network perform critical roles (Brandstäter, 2011). Therefore, 'self' in the social/cultural context is a fundamental factor influencing entrepreneurial activities. The 'self' and 'self-esteem' within Chinese culture, are demonstrability unlike those depicted by Western psychological studies. In addition, individual self-construal determines one's interaction/communication style, considered a vital cultural dimension by anthropologists (e.g. Hall, 1976). Finally, as a collectivistic society, the behaviours of the Chinese are significantly moulded by the social environment and, in this regard, entrepreneurs are not immune to their environment. The public's attitude towards business failure and the legal and ethical climate is different from the more individualistic Western cultures. A loss of face is a considerably more important and debilitating barrier for entrepreneurs from the East than for those in the West.

The above-mentioned three cultural dimensions can be further interpreted and extended to five points – self-construal, self-evaluation, communication style, public attitude toward business failure, and the legal and ethical climate – the potential positive or negative influences of which on entrepreneurship are significant (Wang, 2012). However, it must be emphasized that unlike national territories, cultures have imprecise borders, and thus most findings regarding cultural differences at the national level are susceptible to condemnations about underrepresentation or overgeneralization. Cultures are not fixed, as evidenced by recent decades of great changes in many aspects of China, and culture is not exempt. The considerable Chinese subcultural variations have not been properly investigated because of the incredible complications in doing so, which might significantly contribute to the tangible difference in entrepreneurial performance among different territories and peoples of China. Notwithstanding these limitations, identifying meaningful implications will provide for a better understanding of the relationship between culture and entrepreneurship and for the creation of appropriate policies to enhance entrepreneurship (Wang, 2012; Liu, 2017; Yan et al., 2018).

It can be said that Chinese culture has some advantages in driving entrepreneurship, including family involvement and financial support, emphasizing the engagement of social networks, and achievement-oriented education. However, the shortcomings are numerous. Studies suggest that characteristics such as suppressing proactiveness and verbalization in formal settings, over-concern with others' estimation of self-image, and over-dependence on implicit rules, theoretically confine entrepreneurial and innovative activities in China (Wang, 2012).

Nonetheless, remarkably, overseas Chinese have attained exceptional achievements in entrepreneurship as they have at home, especially in the last two decades (Yan, Wickramasekera & Tan, 2018). This aspect must be considered in future investigations if one observes the recent spectacular successes. However, studies must also be mindful of the failures, some played out dramatically on a global scale following IPOs on local and numerous foreign stock exchanges (The Economist, 2019). If we assume that Chinese culture does not advantageously influence entrepreneurship, why then do we see the sojourners (i.e. Chinese based overseas) deeply influenced by Chinese culture becoming successful entrepreneurs? If these entrepreneurs were completely acculturated into the overseas societies that apparently promoted entrepreneurship, why do indigenous residents, who have grown up in those cultures, perform worse than Chinese immigrants in general? (Wang, 2012; Yan et al., 2018). Two other features of Chinese culture must also be considered in order to understand this apparent conundrum – pragmatism and adaptiveness (Australian Department of Foreign Affairs and Trade, 1995; Redding, 1990). Studies suggest that Chinese are good at doing business in a practical manner and acclimatizing to new environments. Overseas Chinese entrepreneurs may combine the valuable elements of both their original and host cultures, conceivably contributing to positive business ventures (Yan et al., 2018).

Recent changes in Chinese SME export development

SMEs are increasingly dynamic and they make a substantial contribution to economic growth and job creation (Bianchi, Glavas & Mathews, 2017; Bose, 2016; Hånell & Ghauri, 2016; Pinho & Pinheiro, 2015). Given the importance of SMEs, their internationalization has become a central research topic in recent decades. Strikingly, exporting is the most common strategy adopted by SMEs to internationalize (Martineau & Pastoriza, 2016). In China, the rapid growth of the export sector is a key driver of its impressive economic growth in recent decades. Many SMEs have also developed as new players in international markets by exporting (Alon, Yeheskel, Lerner & Zhang, 2013). Remarkably, SMEs account for 98.9 per cent of businesses and more than 60 per cent of China's gross domestic product (GDP) (National Bureau of Statistics of the People's Republic of China [NBSC], 2014). Given the economic importance of SMEs and the benefits of exporting, there is keen interest among policymakers to inspire greater involvement of Chinese SMEs in international markets (Kahiya, Dean & Heyl, 2014).

The definition of a SME in China will vary considerably across industries.

The National Bureau of Statistics of China (NBSC) defines SMEs in the manufacturing industry as any firm with an annual turnover of less than ¥400 million or fewer than 1,000 employees (NBSC, 2011). Typically, Chinese SMEs have between 80 and 1,000 employees, and revenues ranging from ¥10 million to ¥200 million (Yan et al., 2018). While this definition varies considerably from what might be characteristic in advanced economies, it is consistent with definitions of SMEs in larger emerging markets.

Increasingly, research is exploring the problems experienced by Chinese SMEs (Alon et al., 2013; Zhang, Ma & Wang, 2012; Zhang, Ma, Wang, Li & Huo, 2016). However, with few exceptions (e.g. Jansson & Söderman, 2012), most internationalization process research in the Chinese context focuses chiefly on post-export activity using a country-based scope of foreign countries to which Chinese firms are exporting (e.g. Zhang et al., 2016). However, few studies explore the process as it evolves over time (Welch & Paavilainen-Mäntymäki, 2014). More research is now emerging to address this research gap by focusing on the pre-export phase and using a processual lens to examine how and why the internationalization process begins.

As millions of Chinese SMEs are yet to enter the international market, it is practical to understand the reasons that contribute to or inhibit managerial commitment to internationalization. For instance, as a substantial part of the Go Global policy and more recent One Belt, One Road initiative, policymakers in China want to know how best to encourage non-exporters to begin internationalization while also inspiring current exporters to increase their international involvement (Wang, 2012; Yan et al., 2018). The efficiency of export support from the government is demonstrated by successfully identifying firm needs, with export barriers and drivers as useful proxies for understanding these requirements (Kahiya & Dean, 2016). Export barriers have captured most research attention to date, but these studies tend to lack detailed understanding of the institutional context within which internationalization decisions occur (Lattemann et al., 2017). Due to China's unique cultural and institutional environments, it remains uncertain whether studies conducted in developed economies can be applied to elucidate the internationalization behaviour of Chinese firms (Alon, Child, Li & McIntyre, 2011; Alon et al., 2013; Zhang et al., 2012, 2016).

In comparison to SOEs, Chinese SMEs are perhaps influenced to a greater degree by market forces. Thus, SMEs become a suitable context in which to consider the applicability and test current internationalization frameworks developed within the Western context (Liu, Xiao & Huang, 2008). Therefore, new research streams are emerging that draw on the rich insights into Chinese SMEs aimed at increasing our knowledge of export barriers and providing degrees of analysis into the types of challenges that may prevent non-exporters from participating in international activities and the drivers that may inspire export development. Research that looks at export stages or phases is another sub-category of this research stream, namely, the study of the awareness, interest and adoption factors that test the innovation-adoption models (e.g. Lim, Sharkey & Kim, 1991). Change agents around this process are another sub-category within this stream of research (Wang, 2012; Yan et al., 2018).

For example, while earlier research found that a manager's experience and competencies (e.g. Forsgren, 2016; El Makrini, 2015) are important in decision-making and that Chinese entrepreneurs have low education levels and operate with limited capabilities in assessing foreign markets (Cardoza, Fornes, Li, Xu & Xu, 2015; Liu et al., 2008), a recent case-based study suggests contrary findings. The study found that the managers/founders of Chinese exporting SMEs were highly qualified, most with tertiary-level education. While a note of caution needs to be added to this argument since these findings do not necessarily mean that higher education levels will always ensure managerial commitment, the findings do show what is happening in China more recently to explain how rapidly things are changing in this very competitive and sophisticated market context (Yan et al., 2018). The said study provides evidence regarding the importance of education as a facilitator for foreign market research, how it mitigates psychic distance and, finally, how it impacts the decision-making process. In particular, all managers/founders surveyed pointed out that their global mind-set was very much influenced by the skills and knowledge obtained from higher education, and indicated how and why these skills assisted them to process complex information quickly and imaginatively, using social media and other internet-based tools in fast-moving dynamic international markets.

However, more recent industry-based reports and global consultancy-based projects are reporting that, on the one-hand, while Chinese SMEs are growing rapidly, using multiple entry modes including export, alliances, FDI and issuing IPOs to raise capital at start-up, a picture is slowly emerging that suggests that these strategies are not necessarily sustainable. While a large expansion in new venture creation and domestic and international expansion is being reported, there have also been several recent high-profile collapses of early stage exporters and international start-ups (*The Economist*, 2019). We now look at this trend to see how and why this is happening and possible implications for Chinese as well as foreign firms across the global economy.

The changing context of entrepreneurial activity in emerging markets

Only a few years ago, innovation by emerging market (EM) firms was still regarded as 'copycat and counterfeit'. A new breed of young Chinese and emerging markets entrepreneurs has emerged who are audacious, talented and globally minded. Interestingly, the foreign direct investment (FDI) flowing into China into these start-ups is predominantly from developed markets venture-capitalists, the majority from the US and Japan. Approximately US$77 billion in venture-capital investment were poured into Chinese companies from 2014 to 2016, up from US$12 billion between 2011 and 2013 (*The Economist*, 2017). These firms are referred to as the new 'fourth wave' smaller emerging MNCs, which aim to capture this changing context. Many begin as exporters and quickly develop other modal strategies such as alliances and joint venturing. Others embark on FDI early in their evolution to raise capital and expand quickly in their domestic market, where considerable experience can be developed before engaging in rapid expansion abroad, utilizing the latest leading-edge technologies.

Characterized as nimble new innovators, Chinese entrepreneurs of SMEs are using world-class technologies, ranging from supercomputing to gene editing. Having established themselves as start-ups in competitive home country environments such as China, they are now rapidly heading abroad (The Economist, 2017). How Chinese entrepreneurs recognize opportunities and develop new ventures, what advantages these entrepreneurs experience in their emerging market institutional context and how they evolve to ensure their international competitiveness, is important, globally and regionally. Thus, this chapter explores how emerging market SMEs compare to developed market SMEs, navigate their institutional context and develop social and institutional linkages to create wealth for the individual (entrepreneur) and pursue ventures to exploit opportunities home and abroad.

Increased interest in emerging market SMEs is thus reflective of the shift in the competitive landscape. Emerging market SMEs that influence this composition (Deng, 2012), are better able to affect the pace of change in the global competitive landscape, and are more prominent and play a larger role than in previous decades (Goldstein, 2009; *The Economist*, 2017). Given this context, the study of sustainable international competitiveness in relation to the recent and increasingly disruptive nature of the changing global competitive landscape needs closer examination (Cheng, Guo & Skousen, 2011). In their review of 1,055 foreign market entry studies, Surdu and Mellahi (2016) note that only 70 focused on emerging market MNCs. Leading authors such as Bartram, Boyle, Stanton, Burgess and McDonnell (2015: 135) highlight "the need for further studies that examine the strategic behaviour, management and industrial relations practices and their effects on MNEs from emerging countries". As emerging market MNCs gain importance and recognition, it is crucial to understand factors influencing their international competitiveness, given the periodic turbulence in large emerging markets (BEMs) as occurred in early 2014 with some emerging markets experiencing dramatic economic declines, currency problems and political instability (Cooper & Remes, 2013; *The Economist*, 2014). While ensuing recessions occurred in some BEMs such as Russia and Brazil (The Economist, 2017), other countries, such as China and India, are experiencing rising technology and e-commerce global industry sector dominance (*The Economist*, 2017), reflective of the heterogeneity of emerging markets as well as the resilience of some markets.

An example of the above can be seen in 2014 with the slowing down of emerging market currency rates, which reached their lowest in January 2014 and then regained momentum with a sudden and unpredictable volatility in most EMs (especially the BEMs), spreading to smaller emerging markets (*The Economist*, 2014). Political instability in economies such as Turkey, Venezuela, South Africa, Ukraine, Vietnam and Thailand (Arnold, 2014; *The Economist*, 2014) also contributed to the panic seen in early 2014 in emerging markets (The Economist, 2014). Despite preliminary signs of growth and recovery in 2017, the International Monetary Fund still views even the larger BEMs, such as Russia and Brazil, as being in recession in contrast to China and India (*The Economist*, 2017, 2019).

Over the last decade, Chinese SMEs and large MNCs together with strong government support and strategic focus have developed and exploited the latest technologies to dominate globally in the growth of electrical vehicles, industrial robots and microchip production (Belton, 2019). However, there are signs that China's dominance and success in the global technology sector is slowing. Despite the early success of start-ups that have become large MNCs, such as Alibaba, Tencent and search engine Baidu, employee numbers in these companies have recently been reduced dramatically. Overall, one in five Chinese tech companies plan to reduce recruitment and many entrepreneurs think that this slowing down will continue (Belton, 2019).

The US–China trade war partly explains why the above situation has developed as both nations have imposed tariffs on each other's goods since 2018.

Prior to the trade war, the Chinese economy demonstrated a staggering double-digit growth trajectory in six of the last 15 years. A slowing down of the economy to 6.3 per cent growth in 2019 is now predicted by the International Monetary Fund (Belton, 2019). While this predicted growth figure is still double the world's average, it is nonetheless troubling, as this is China's slowest growth since the 1990s. This situation is having a considerable dampening effect on "China's start-up scene", with an estimated "third of the world's 'unicorns' – start-ups worth more than $1bn (£769m)" (Belton, 2019).

However, China is currently planning a major restructuring as the economy and tech sector *cool* or slow (Belton, 2019). Internal reasons for the rapid rise and now slowing of the technology sector start-ups have also been attributed to the easy availability of finance and capital. The Shanghai-based start-up entrepreneur and managing director of technology firm Chinaccelerator, William Bao Bean, argues: "What drove things completely insane was too much money". Bean maintains that there was "real push for economic growth from the government" with "big funding from state" finance, which has now "levelled off". He explained: "*Before*, you could get $3m with two people knocking and a smile". However, Bean suggests that: "*Now* you can get $3m with two people knocking and a smile *and six weeks of meetings*". Competition has also meant a decline in earnings of some of the well-known dockless bike-sharing rivals, Mobike and Ofo, leading to falls in market share and rising debt. For example, Ofo owes approximately one billion yuan ($148m; £11m) in unpaid debts. In December 2018, Dai Wei, Chief executive of Ofo defaulted on suppliers' payments resulting in a Beijing court decision to blacklist the company. As a further example, Mobile lost 4.6 billion yuan in 2018 and it is now unlikely to make profit until 2021 (Belton, 2019).

Only two years ago, China's 6,200 online peer-to-peer lending platforms, like Weida and Yirendai, were a thriving bubble, but since then, as many as 80 per cent have closed or have encountered major difficulties in the Shanghai region alone (Belton, 2019). Another reason for slowed growth in the technology sector is the saturation of China's market. For example, "While only 56% of the population is on the internet, Tencent, Shenzhen's internet giant that last year became Asia's first $500bn-plus company ... this percentage includes most of the people who buy online" (Belton, 2019). However, greater interconnectivity is emerging within the technology sector. The saturation has meant that SME start-ups are having to align themselves with China's online giants, as costs of the dominant platforms are high for new entrants. This situation has resulted in greater integration within the technology sector, with over half the more recent unicorns aligning with the two more established and earlier examples, Tencent or Alibaba in the last year, creating a bifurcation of the market into clans. Competition and the need for innovative solutions has resulted in the technology market undergoing restructuring internally, creating strong links among SME start-ups and other older SMEs in China "wanting access to artificial intelligence models on big amounts of data" to link "with Tencent, Alibaba, or Baidu", creating substantial advantages for the industry at home and globally (Belton, 2019). Access to big data supports Chinese start-ups to build their local base and to develop competencies and knowledge around the industry to compete effectively with foreign entrants and deal with rivals in the Chinese market. There is also a growing trend in industry towards concentration and vertical integration in B2B rather than B2C with start-ups selling more to businesses instead of consumers (Belton, 2019). Up to two years ago, start-ups would target customers in, for example, the gaming industry; however, the focus has now been switched to businesses such as real estate and medical companies. The slowdown has also encouraged greater efficiencies and focus for SMEs. This efficiency is arguably exactly what many tech firms need and is likely to support the continued sustainability of the industries in China (Belton, 2019).

Recent research highlights the importance of Chinese transnational entrepreneurs who develop born-global firms (another term for start-ups that rapidly internationalize from inception to many regions of the globe) to maturity by using their technological knowledge, international connections and bicultural advantages to navigate and leverage institutional complexity (Liu, 2017). Collaborative entry mode with distributors enables start-up firms' high growth rapidly, whereas transnational entrepreneurs play a central role in building and expanding international networks. Initial public offerings in overseas stock exchanges accelerate the high growth trajectory of start-up firms by signalling their maturity (Liu, 2017). Transnational entrepreneurs migrate from one country to another and maintain business links in both their former and their current locations (Drori et al., 2009). By extension then, transnational entrepreneurial activities involve cross-national contexts and are initiated and carried out by actors who are embedded in at least two different social and economic arenas. Based on their dual (or multiple) embeddedness, the actions of such entrepreneurs are enabled and/or constrained by the institutional structures in which they operate (Saxenian, 2007). Research suggests that these particular characteristics of transnational entrepreneurs are highly relevant for the growth trajectory of start-up firms (Liu, 2017).

What is significant to the above-mentioned phenomenon is the importance of entrepreneurial knowledge in high-tech knowledge-intensive sectors. To its credit, this is something the Chinese government has focused on in the last decade or so. Evidence shows that most Chinese international start-ups are in the technology sectors and that this is fundamental to the success they have experienced so rapidly (Liu, 2017). A typical example is the prevalence of start-ups in the Chinese solar PV industry (Liu, 2017) and the related complex history. Despite Chinese firms contributing significantly to production within the solar industry, global consumption is driven by developed markets, typically, the US and Western European markets. One significant driver is the 'feed-in tariff' available in both Germany and Spain. These markets provide incentives, such as subsidies, for consumers to install solar panels on their homes (Haley & Schuler, 2011). In the last decade, China has become one the key players globally in the solar PV sector. For example, in 2009, China embarked on an ambitious target of installing 20 gigawatts of solar power by 2020. This figure represented more than the total global solar PV capacity available in 2008 (Solar Plaza, 2009). Consistent with most high-tech products within the broad renewable energy industry, solar companies are a typical example of those that produce knowledge-intensive standardized products for global markets. There is virtually no domestic Chinese PV market, and, for this reason, Chinese solar companies are a good example of start-ups, because they were developed to meet the needs of the global market and have done so from their inception (Liu, 2017).

From a theoretical perspective, the knowledge-based view has often been used to examine the internationalization process of the born-globals or start-ups (Hohenthal et al., 2014). Specifically, entrepreneurs who have the necessary technological and international knowledge play a significant role in developing a global start-up (Nordman & Melén, 2008), which highlights the influence of entrepreneurs in driving the internationalization process. Importantly, for rapid knowledge development, born-global or global start-up entrepreneurs are able to draw on both pre-existing and forming new relationships to proactively and quickly create new knowledge for the rapid commercialization of their technology products (Freeman et al., 2010).

Given the above scenario, emerging market firms will need to continually navigate their home and host country (operational) environments in order to recognize opportunities and maintain venture survival (The Economist, 2014). Given the heterogeneity among the emerging markets, recovery from the monetary crisis or market disruptions will vary considerably. This context is especially important as evidence suggests (Hennart, 2009) that emerging market firms depend greatly on their home and host country environment to internationalize and to exploit opportunities. Reports indicate that recent start-ups, such as the earlier examples of Baidu, Alibaba and Tencent, Chinese internet giant start-ups now known as BATS, and older start-ups, referred to as Unicorns, are innovating and developing new ventures initially at home; their technology is being 'pulled' rather than 'pushed' out of China through FDI by Japanese and US-based firms wanting access to the latest technology (*The Economist*, 2017). Thus, emerging markets' dominance in the high tech area in the last two decades across so many important current and future industries is likely to generate a very positive future for these markets. To date, the study of emerging market MNCs has been generally limited to 'how' and 'why' they internationalize and not on their subsequent growth, maturity and consolidation phase, with the development of sustainable international competitiveness and commitment. The latter aspects will be an important area for future research.

Theoretical explanations

In order to extend our understanding, studies that not only explain the creation of new ventures or start-ups, but go beyond this initial internationalization period and examine the factors underpinning sustainable international competitiveness of emerging market MNCs that have already internationalized successfully (Kothari, Kotabe & Murphy, 2013), will be an important area of future research in international business and internal entrepreneurship. We describe these phases as the 'creation' (inception and early growth) and 'post-internationalization' (maturity, establishment and consolidation) development (Trudgen & Freeman, 2007). This research will contribute to the existing body of knowledge by extending the application of traditional and current theories to emerging market MNCs, emphasizing the social context (that elevates the importance of business networks, social personal ties and social linkages in order to do business) (Lindstrand & Melen Hanell, 2017). The most prevalent theories are the resource-based view (RBV) (Barney, 1986a, 1986b, 1991; Penrose, 1959; Peteraf, 1993; Wernerfelt, 1984), contingency theory (Chandler, 1962; Lawrence & Lorsch, 1967) and the Linkage, Leverage and Learning (LLL) framework (Mathews, 2006), the latter specifically devised to explain how emerging MNCs internationalize through a rich social context and develop international and market-specific social capital (Lindstrand & Melen Hanell, 2017) to navigate complex institutional frameworks. These theories can be offered as platforms for the way new models might be developed in future research.

Global start-ups (born-globals) and transnational entrepreneurs

Born-globals are frequently defined as "small, technology-oriented companies that operate in international markets from the earliest days of their establishment" (Knight & Cavusgil, 1996, p. 11). Common characteristics of this type of firm are that they are young, knowledge-intensive companies that self-develop and innovate with a focus on tech-based products for global markets (Almor, 2011; Knight & Cavusgil, 2004; McDougall & Oviatt, 2000). There has been considerable research since the late 1980s, yet little progress has been made to identify the role individual entrepreneurs play in developing these firms (Karra et al., 2008). One stream of research emphasizes the primary influence of managers' past experiences, current goals and ambitions, and motivation (Madsen & Servais, 1997). As discussed earlier, the knowledge-based view is frequently drawn on to study the internationalization process of born-globals (Hohenthal et al., 2014).

Transnational entrepreneurs have an important role as bridge spanners across national boundaries that have a considerable influence on the development of local industries (Saxenian, 2002, 2007; Wadhwa et al., 2011). Studies have examined returnee entrepreneurs, but transnational entrepreneurs significantly differ from returnee entrepreneurs. For example, returnee entrepreneurs are primarily focused on their original home country markets, though some do adopt an international orientation relying on their experience and ethnic social ties in countries from which they have returned (Lin & Tao, 2012). By contrast, transnational entrepreneurs are far more likely to exploit advantages in the global market by leveraging their transnational experience, and proactively responding to perceived demand for their products or services. Importantly, the founding manager/entrepreneur's international experiences assist in mobilizing knowledge flows that stretch beyond the geographical boundaries of the home or domestic market and support global market expansion. The advantage of international experience of transnational entrepreneurs is that it helps to mitigate barriers and support a born-global's interactions and negotiations with businesses in other cultures (Kuemmerle, 2005). Also, the social capital of migration is a significant antecedent and plays a central role in prompting the international growth and development of start-ups (Prashantham & Dhanaraj, 2010). Transnational entrepreneurs with the right type of international social capital can facilitate a new firm's rapid growth on a global scale. Thus, compared with returnee entrepreneurs, transnational entrepreneurs are more likely to develop into start-ups on a global rather than national or single international market scale. Specifically, transnational entrepreneurs that possess both advanced technological know-how and an entrepreneurial orientation are in a strong position to commercialize their technological capabilities and innovations, and create further alliances with international markets to expand their scope of opportunity (Liu, 2017; Yan et al., 2018).

Collaborative entry mode and born global growth

Collaborative entry mode is a critical decision regarding organizational form for firms wishing to internationalize (Gomes et al., 2011). For example, collaborative arrangement helps firms to access the necessary resources (Speckbacher et al., 2015). In addition, knowledge protection and institutional safeguards impact foreign market entry modal choice of SMEs (Maekelburger et al., 2012). Therefore, investigation of the impact of collaborative entry mode choice on firm growth is important. Growth of a firm can be observed as a process view (Leitch et al., 2010) and comparing the process perspective with institutional context provides deeper understanding of born-globals' growth, which is combined with the transnational entrepreneur's role. During growth, collaborative entry modes play an important role for the transnational entrepreneur because, as born-globals export products overseas, collaboration can reduce resource constraints and is helpful in managing uncertainty. Significantly, born-globals generate most of their income from overseas market activities (Coviello, 2015), requiring intensive interaction with their overseas partners in managing and developing the business.

Collaborative entry modes are dynamic relationships with multiple sellers and buyers interacting with each other over time (Narayandas & Rangan, 2004). Collaborative entry modes facilitate observation and adaptation through interactive relationships with foreign partners. A recent study demonstrates that maturing technology-based born-globals can increase survival through acquisition (Almor et al., 2014). Finally, born-globals usually possess limited resources as they typically begin their global strategy at or near inception, which can considerably constrain entry mode choices. Furthermore, a recent study revealed that maturing born-globals' HRM practices evolve over time as resource constraints change (Glaister et al., 2014).

Born global and institutional complexity

The institutional context is a significant driver of entrepreneurial and born-globals' growth (Welter, 2011; Wright & Stigliani, 2013). Competing institutional demands require organizations to respond appropriately when confronting institutional complexity (Greenwood et al., 2011). One approach to exploring the interaction with institutional complexity by actors is to examine institutional logics (Lounsbury & Boxenbaum, 2013) and how individuals navigate through competing institutional logics (Pache & Santos, 2013). A study of entrepreneurs from China, Russia, France and the US identifies the impact of institutional complexity on venture growth (Batjargal et al., 2013). International networks and initial public offering (IPO) are two ways to deal with institutional complexity. For example, networking competences to create strategic alliances and collaborative partnerships with key suppliers, distributors and joint venturing partners can help born-globals to overcome resource constraints in order to realize rapid international growth (Freeman, Edwards & Schroder, 2006). Network development requires internal firm resources and a strong entrepreneurial orientation to drive the process of capturing network benefits, including new opportunities, improving competitive advantages and reducing uncertainty and risk for business-to-business (B2B) born-globals (Sepulveda & Gabrielsson, 2013). Nonetheless, export manufacturers' dilemma during international growth is that manufacturers must develop strong local market competences while simultaneously reducing the cost of distributor opportunism (Cavusgil et al., 2004; Wu et al., 2007). Leveraging experiential network knowledge to increase the value of business relationships in overseas markets is one way to manage this (Hohenthal et al., 2014). Additionally, transnational entrepreneurs have an important role to play in supporting growth by leveraging their knowledge of global markets. Strategic re-structuring by born-globals through outward (exports and strategic alliances) and inward (imports and exclusive reseller arrangements) orientations, demonstrate the fundamental role played by entrepreneurs in born-globals' strategies and growth (Freeman et al., 2013). The study by Freeman et al. explored the managerial mind-set of smaller born-globals leading to the documentation of four states of commitment to accelerated internationalization by top management.

Finally, IPO listings are another important factor in managing institutional complexity, because IPOs in foreign markets entail institutional environments that may be vastly different from a firm's home (domestic) country institutional environment. The effectiveness of born-globals in navigating different institutional contexts impact their creation, development and growth. IPO is a significant achievement for firm growth and is regarded as an indication of a firm's maturity (Almor, 2013). Firms that indicate financial, innovational and managerial resource slack send positive signals to likely investors about the quality of the IPO when these companies list (Mousa & Reed, 2013). The transnational context necessitates that transnational entrepreneurs be fully attuned to diverse institutional, structural and cultural factors, all of which significantly impact born-global growth and survival. Therefore, entrepreneurial ability to manage competing institutional demands is fundamental to the growth and maturity trajectory of born-globals (Liu, 2017). Consequently, transnational entrepreneurs can fast-track born-global growth by effectively managing institutional complexity. Firms that originate in complex markets have the added advantage of greater knowledge around the navigation process. This knowledge is what makes born-globals, especially from the Chinese technology sectors, unique compared to their Western counterparts (Yan et al., 2018; The Economist, 2019).

Conclusion

This chapter is timely and firmly linked to current international business problems requiring urgent attention, given the important role emerging market MNCs, many of whom are SMEs, are increasingly playing in global trade and investment. The preceding discussion on theories can be used to explain the largely innovation-oriented nature of export commitment by Chinese SMEs, the importance of managerial characteristics and perceptions in SME internationalization decision-making, with reference to person-driven elements. Key concepts, including home and host country environments and values, attitudes and needs which drive their commitment are fundamental to understanding the unique institutional environment and importance of change agents in the Chinese context (Wang, 2012; Liu, 2017; Yan et al., 2018). This type of research requires exploration of a combination of psychological characteristics, central to explanations of entrepreneurial behaviour, entrepreneurial leadership and the ability of entrepreneurs to adapt their style to the needs of customers, harness the latest technology and social media platforms, and the necessary finance and capital to create new ventures as well as sustain existing firms. Theoretical underpinnings were summarized to offer deeper insights into the awareness, interest and adoption stages of the I-model as innovation, the diffusion of which is and most probably will remain, a defining characteristic of the rapid growth and success of Chinese SME start-ups in exporting and FDI.

New and helpful insights are likely to be offered by research that addresses new emerging market MNCs, such as those from China and India, and the challenges these firms continue to face, as well as emphasizing the importance of social and institutional linkages in doing business in these economies and highlighting the organizational configuration strategy literature. Social and institutional linkages help to explain why entrepreneurs cannot accomplish goals alone but depend on others, and how and why people's values influence the way they behave (psychological characteristics), as discussed earlier. Further research can highlight why values, culture and entrepreneurship are closely linked and thus form a point of difference when context, values and culture are taken into account, such as the situation in China. These aspects will bring into sharper focus the importance of context and cultural differences of emerging and developing markets compared to developed markets, helping to explain how the home and host country environments drive entrepreneurial recognition and opportunity exploitation, and how smaller emerging markets MNCs ensure international competitiveness in foreign markets, in their pre and post-internationalization (early growth through to maturity and change) development.

In Chapter 2 we examined different schools of thought on entrepreneurship, and the activities of entrepreneurs, avoiding the pitfalls of arguing which school is offering a superior set of criteria. On the contrary, judgement of one model over another, rests on the nature of the research question and assessment of which issues and focuses are important to the investigation, entrepreneurial process and, most importantly, the context. Chapter 2 should be read in close conjunction with Chapter 4. This important link is predicated on the type of information or data that researchers ideally want to emphasize in focusing on different aspects of the entrepreneurial process (Cunningham & Lischeron, 1991). The psychological school of thought and the great person school of thought in entrepreneurship offer insights into personal evaluation of an entrepreneur's values, while the classical school can elicit understanding of the process for imagining, believing, creating and actualizing an opportunity (Khan, Freeman, Cavusgil & Ghauri, 2019). Management and leadership schools offer a diverse array of technical and non-technical skills, and interpersonal capabilities in order to develop organizational efficiency and settings that support and motivate risk-taking and creative opportunity development and execution. Finally, the intrapreneurship school offers insights into organizational renewal, redirection and change, emphasizing the capability of managers to build teams that are willing to take the necessary risks because they know they have managers willing to take responsibility for the operation or venture (Cunningham & Lischeron, 1991).

What is emphasized in our iterative conceptualization of entrepreneurship is personal evaluation, planning, acting and re-evaluating. A key assumption underpinning the model is that those who assume responsibility for the venture, assume some or all of the risk, and are rewarded for doing so. The various schools offer differing insights in order to understand core values, how to respond to the future, improvements in managerial skills and ways for changing and adapting to the future (Cunningham & Lischeron, 1991). A research agenda needs to be broader than drawing upon one school of thought on entrepreneurship alone. Rather, knowledge that explores and examines all facets of the entrepreneurial process, namely the entrepreneur's values, goals, approach to identifying opportunities, methods for acting and developing managerial capabilities and different mechanisms for adapting and re-evaluating, are essential to deeper clarity around this concept.

Future research endeavours will also require a greater understanding of the changes occurring in the context and why these are so, to be able to place the research effectively in the environment in which these phenomena are currently occurring. Given emerging market MNCs are the future "economic engines" (Jormanainen & Koveshnikov, 2012: 692) and the "disruptive effect that [the environment] seem[s] to have on their global industries" (Ramamurti, 2009: 8), especially with the recent BEM entrepreneurial global technology start-ups (The Economist, 2017; 2019), there is greater need to examine emerging market global start-ups and MNCs more closely. A greater understanding of how these firms can both achieve and sustain international competitiveness via strategic fit with the current vibrant, dynamic, competitive and volatile environment will allow governments, practitioners and researchers to revise established expectations for emerging market MNCs.

References

Almor, T. (2011) Dancing as fast as they can: Israeli high-tech firms and the great recession of 2008. *Thunderbird International Business Review*, 53(2): 195–208.

Almor, T. (2013) Conceptualizing paths of growth for technology-based born-global firms originating in a small-population advanced economy. *International Studies of Management and Organization*, 43(2): 56–78.

Almor, T., Tarba, S. Y. & Margalit, A. (2014) Maturing, technology-based, born-global companies: Surviving through mergers and acquisitions. *Management International Review*, 54(4): 421–444.

Alon, I., Child, J., Li, S. & McIntyre, J. R. (2011). Globalization of Chinese firms: Theoretical universalism or particularism. *Management and Organization Review*, 7(2): 191–200.

Alon, I., Yeheskel, O., Lerner, M. & Zhang, W. (2013). Internationalization of Chinese entrepreneurial firms. *Thunderbird International Business Review*, 55(5): 495–512.

Arnold, M. S. (2014) In emerging Asia, political risk is back on the agenda. *Wall Street Journal*, 16 May, viewed 28 May, http://blogs.wsj.com/economics/2014/05/16/in-emerging-asia-political-risk-is-back-on-the-agenda/.

Australian Department of Foreign Affairs and Trade, East Asia Analytic Unit. (1995) *Overseas Chinese Business Networks in Asia*. Retrieved from www.dfat.gov.au/publications/catalogue/ocbni.pdf

Barney, J. B. (1986a) Organizational culture: Can it be a source of sustained competitive advantage?. *The Academy of Management Review*, 11(3): 656–665.

Barney, J. B. (1986b) Strategic factor markets: expectations, luck, and business strategy". *Management Science*, 32(10): 1231–1241.

Barney, J. B. (1991) Firm resources and sustained competitive advantage", *Journal of Management*, 17(1): 99–120.

Bartram, T., Boyle, B., Stanton, P., Burgess, J. & McDonnell, A. (2015) Multinational enterprises and industrial relations: A research agenda for the 21st century. *Journal of Industrial Relations*, 57(2): 127–145.

Batjargal, B., Hitt, M. A., Tsui, A. S., Arregle, J., Webb, J. W. & Miller, T. L. (2013) Institutional polycentrism, entrepreneurs' social networks, and new venture growth. *Academy of Management Journal*, 56(4): 1024–1049.

Belton, P. (2019) Why is the white hot Chinese tech sector cooling down?, *Technology of Business* 7 May 2019 www.bbc.com/news/business-48146915 [search 6 August 2019]

Bianchi, C., Glavas, C. & Mathews, S. (2017) SME international performance in Latin America. *Journal of Small Business and Enterprise Development*, 24(1): 176–195.

Baskerville, R. F. (2003) Hofstede never studied culture. *Accounting, Organizations and Society*, 28: 1–14.

Bose, T. K. (2016) Critical success factors of SME internationalization. *Journal of Small Business Strategy*, 26(2): 87–109.

Brandstäter, H. (2011) Personality aspects of entrepreneurship: A look at five meta-analyses. *Personality and Individual Differences*, 51, 222–230.

Cardoza, G., Fornes, G., Li, P., Xu, N. & Xu, S. (2015) China goes global: Public policies' influence on small- and medium-sized enterprises' international expansion. *Asia Pacific Business Review*, 21(2): 188–210.

Cavusgil, S. T., Deligonul, S. & Zhang, C. (2004) Curbing foreign distributor opportunism: An examination of trust, contracts, and the legal environment in international channel relationships. *Journal of International Marketing*, 12(2): 7–27.

Chan, S. (1997). Migration, cultural identity and assimilation effects on entrepreneurship for the overseas Chinese in Britain. *Asia Pacific Business Review*, 3: 211–222.

Chandler, D. M. (1962) *Strategy and Structure*. Cambridge, MA: MIT Press.

Cheng, J. L. C., Guo, W. & Skousen, B. (2011) Advancing new theory development in the field of international management. *Management International Review*, 51(6): 787–802.

Cooper, R. & Remes, J. (2013) The still emerging markets, vol. 2014, no. 21 March, www.mckinsey.com/insights/mgi/in_the_news/the_still-emerging_markets.

Coviello, N. (2015) Re-thinking research on born globals. *Journal of International Business Studies*, 46(1): 17–26.

Cunningham, J. B. & Lischeron, J. (1991) Defining entrepreneurship. *Journal of Small Business Management*, Jan 1991: 29–45.

Deng, P. (2012) Accelerated internationalisation by MNCs from emerging economies: determinants and implications. *Organizational Dynamics*, 41(4): 318–326.

Drori, I., Honig, B. & Wright, M. (2009) Transnational entrepreneurship: An emergent field of study. *Entrepreneurship Theory and Practice*, 33(5): 1001–1022.

El Makrini, H. (2015) How does management perceive export success? An empirical study of Moroccan SMEs. *Business Process Management Journal*, 21(1): 126–151.

Forsgren, M. (2016). A note on the revisited Uppsala internationalization process model – the implications of business networks and entrepreneurship. *Journal of International Business Studies*, 47(9): 1135–1144.

Freeman, S., Edwards, R. & Schroder, B. (2006) How smaller born-global firms use networks and alliances to overcome constraints to rapid internationalization. *Journal of International Marketing*, 14(3): 33–63.

Freeman, S. & Cavusgil, S. T. (2007) Toward a typology of commitment states among managers of born-global firms: A study of accelerated internationalization. *Journal of International Marketing*, 15(4): 1–40.

Freeman, S., Deligonul, S. & Cavusgil, T. (2013) Strategic re-structuring by born-globals using outward and inward-oriented activity. *International Marketing Review*, 30(2): 156–182.

Freeman, S., Hutchings, K., Lazaris, M. & Zyngier, S. (2010) A model of rapid knowledge development: The smaller born-global firm. *International Business Review*, 19(1): 70–84.

Glaister, A. J., Liu, Y., Sahadev, S. & Gomes, E. (2014) Externalizing, internalizing and fostering commitment: The case of born-global firms in emerging economies. *Management International Review*, 54(4): 473–496.

Goldstein, A. (2009) Multinational companies from emerging economies composition, conceptualization and direction in the global economy. *Indian Journal of Industrial Relations*, 45(1): 137–147.

Gomes, E., Weber, Y., Brown, C. & Tarba, S. Y. (2011) *Mergers, Acquisitions and Strategic Alliances: Understanding the Process*. Hampshire: Palgrave Macmillan.

Greenwood, R., Raynard, M., Kodeih, F., Micelotta, E. R. & Lounsbury, M. (2011) Institutional complexity and organizational responses. *The Academy of Management Annals*, 5(1): 317–371.

Haley, U. C. & Schuler, D. A. (2011) Government policy and firm strategy in the solar photovoltaic industry. *California Management Review*, 54(1): 17–39.

Hall, E. T. (1976). *Beyond Culture*. New York: Anchor Books.

Hånell, S. M. & Ghauri, P. N. (2016) Internationalization of smaller firms: Opportunity development through networks: Internationalization of smaller firms. *Thunderbird International Business Review*, 58(5): 465–477.

Hayton, J. C., George, G. & Zahra, S. A. (2002). National culture and entrepreneurship: A review of behavioral research. *Entrepreneurship Theory and Practice*, 26(4): 33–52.

Hennart, J.-F. (2009) Down with MNE-centric theories! Market entry and expansion as the bundling of MNE and local assets. *Journal of International Business Studies*, 40(9): 1432–1591.

Hofstede, G. (1980) *Cultural Consequences: International Differences in Work-related Values.* Beverly Hills, CA: Sage Publications.

Hofstede, G. (2001). *Culture's Consequences: Comparing Values, Behaviors, Institutions and Organizations across Nations* (2nd edn). Thousand Oaks, CA: Sage Publications.

Hofstede, G., Hofstede, G. J. & Minkov, M. (2010). *Cultures and Organizations: Software of the Mind*. Columbus, OH: McGraw Hill.

Hohenthal, J., Johanson, J. & Johanson, M. (2014) Network knowledge and business-relationship value in the foreign market. *International Business Review*, 23(1): 4–19.

Jansson, H. & Söderman, S. (2012). Initial internationalization of Chinese privately owned enterprises – the take-off process. *Thunderbird International Business Review*, 54(2): 183–194.

Jormanainen, I. & Koveshnikov, A. (2012) International activities of emerging market firms. *Management International Review*, 52(5): 691–725.

Kahiya, E. T., Dean, D. L. & Heyl, J. (2014) Export barriers in a changing institutional environment: A quasi-longitudinal study of New Zealand's manufacturing exporters. *Journal of International Entrepreneurship*, 12(4): 331–364.

Kahiya, E. T. & Dean, D. L. (2016). Export stages and export barriers: Revisiting traditional export development. *Thunderbird International Business Review*, 58(1): 75–89.

Karra, N., Phillips, N. & Tracey, P. (2008) Building the born global firm: Developing entrepreneurial capabilities for international new venture success. *Long Range Planning*, 41(4): 440–458.

Khan, A. W., Freeman, S., Cavusgil, T. S. & Ghauri, P. (2019) *Sense-making Perspectives in Entrepreneurial Opportunity Recognition: Review and Agenda for Future Research* to the AIB US Southeast 2019 Conference in San Antonio, Texas, USA, 17–19 October 2019.

Knight, G. A. & Cavusgil, S. T. (1996) The born global firm: A challenge to traditional internationalization theory, in S. T. Cavusgil & T. K. Madsen (eds), *Advances in International Marketing*, Vol. 8, Greenwich, CT: JAI Press, pp. 11–26.

Knight, G. A. & Cavusgil, S. T. (2004) Innovation, organizational capabilities, and the born-global firm. *Journal of International Business Studies*, 35(2): 124–141.

Kothari, T., Kotabe, M. & Murphy, P. (2013) Rules of the game for emerging market multinational companies from China and India. *Journal of International Management*, 19(3): 276–299.

Kuemmerle, W. (2005) The entrepreneur's path to global expansion. MIT *Sloan Management Review*, 46(2): 42–49.

Lawrence, P. R. & Lorsch, J. W. (1967) *Organization and Environment*. Boston: Graduate School of Business Administration, Harvard University.

Lattemann, C., Alon, I., Spigarelli, F. & Marinova, S. T. (2017) Dynamic embeddedness in Chinese firm internationalization. *Thunderbird International Business Review*, 59(4): 547–559.

Leitch, C., Hill, F. & Neergaard, H. (2010) Entrepreneurial and business growth and the quest for a 'comprehensive theory': Tilting at windmills?. *Entrepreneurship Theory and Practice*, 34(2): 249–260.

Liao, D. & Sohmen, P. (2001). The development of modern entrepreneurship in China. *Stanford Journal of East Asian Affairs*, 1: 27–33.

Lim, J., Sharkey, T. W. & Kim, K. I. (1991). An empirical test of an export adoption model. *Management International Review*, 31(1): 51–62.

Lindstrand, A. & Melen Hanell, S. (2017) International and market-specific social capital effects on international opportunity exploitation in the internationalization process. *Journal of World Business*, 52: 653–663.

Lin, X. & Tao, S. (2012) Transnational entrepreneurs: Characteristics, drivers, and success factors. *Journal of International Entrepreneurship*, 10(1): 50–69.

Liu, X., Xiao, W. & Huang, X. (2008). Bounded entrepreneurship and internationalization of indigenous Chinese private-owned firms. *International Business Review*, 17(4): 488–508.

Liu, Y. (2017). Born global firms' growth and collaborative entry mode: The role of transnational entrepreneurs. *Marketing Review*, 34(1): 46–67.

Lounsbury, M. & Boxenbaum, E. (2013) *Institutional Logics in Action*, Part A. Bingley: Emerald Group Publishing.

Madsen, T. K. & Servais, P. (1997) The internationalization of born globals: An evolutionary process?. *International Business Review*, 6(6): 561–583.

Maekelburger, B., Schwens, C. & Kabst, R. (2012) Asset specificity and foreign market entry mode choice of small and medium-sized enterprises: The moderating influence of knowledge safeguards and institutional safeguards. *Journal of International Business Studies*, 43(5): 458–476.

Martineau, C. & Pastoriza, D. (2016) International involvement of established SMEs: A systematic review of antecedents, outcomes and moderators. *International Business Review*, 25(2): 458–470.

Mathews, J. A. 2006) Dragon multinationals: New players in 21st century globalization. Asia Pacific *Journal of Management*, 23(1): 5–27.

McDougall, P. P. & Oviatt, B. M. (2000) International entrepreneurship: The intersection of two research paths. *Academy of Management Journal*, 43(5): 902–906.

McGrath, R. G., MacMillan, I. C. & Scheinberg, S. (1992). Elitists, risk-takers, and rugged individualists? An exploratory analysis of cultural differences between entrepreneurs and non-entrepreneurs. *Journal of Business Venturing*, 7: 115–135.

McSweeney, B. (2002). Hofstede's model of national cultural differences and their consequences: A triumph of faith – a failure of analysis. *Human Relations*, 55: 89–118.

Mousa, F. T. & Reed, R. (2013) The impact of slack resources on high-tech IPOs. *Entrepreneurship Theory and Practice*, 37(5): 1123–1147.

Narayandas, D. & Rangan, V. K. (2004) Building and sustaining buyer-seller relationships in mature industrial markets. *Journal of Marketing*, 68(3): 63–77.

National Bureau of Statistics of the People's Republic of China (NBSC). (2011). Interim measures for statistical definitions of large, medium and small enterprises. Retrieved from www.stats.gov.cn/statsinfo/auto2073/201310/t20131031_450691.html

National Bureau of Statistics of the People's Republic of China (NBSC). (2014). The third national economic census. Retrieved from www.stats.gov.cn/tjsj/zxfb/201412/t2014 1216_653709.html

Nordman, E. R. & Melén, S. (2008) The impact of different kinds of knowledge for the internationalization process of born globals in the biotech business. *Journal of World Business*, 43(2): 171–185.

Pache, A. C. & Santos, F. (2013) Inside the hybrid organization: Selective coupling as a response to competing institutional logics. *Academy of Management Journal*, 56(4): 972–1001.

Penrose, E. (1959) *The Theory of the Growth of the Firm.* White Plains, NY: Sharpe.

Peteraf, M. A. (1993) The cornerstones of competitive advantage: A resource-based view. *Strategic Management Journal*, 14(3): 179–191.

Pinho, J. C. & Pinheiro, M. L. (2015). Social network analysis and the internationalization of SMEs: Towards a different methodological approach. *European Business Review*, 27(6): 554–572.

Poutziouris, P., Wang, Y. & Chan, S. (2002) Chinese entrepreneurship: The development of small family firms in China. *Journal of Small Business and Enterprise Development*, 9: 383–399.

Prashantham, S. & Dhanaraj, C. (2010) The dynamic influence of social capital on the international growth of new ventures. *Journal of Management Studies*, 47(6): 967–994.

Ramamurti, R. (2009) Why study emerging-market multinationals?, in R. Ramamurti & J. V. Singh (eds), *Emerging Multinationals in Emerging Markets*, Cambridge: Cambridge University Press, pp. 3–22.

Redding, S. G. (1990) *The Spirit of Chinese Capitalism.* Berlin; New York, NY: de Gruyter.

Saxenian, A. (2002) Transnational communities and the evolution of global production networks: The cases of Taiwan, China and India. *Industry and Innovation*, 9(3): 183–202.

Saxenian, A. (2007) *The New Argonauts: Regional Advantage in a Global Economy.* Boston, MA: Harvard University Press.

Sepulveda, F. & Gabrielsson, M. (2013) Network development and firm growth: A resource-based study of B2B Born Globals. *Industrial Marketing Management*, 42(5): 792–804.

Shane, S., Kolvereid, L. & Westhead, P. (1991). An exploratory examination of the reasons leading to new firm formation across country and gender. *Journal of Business Venturing*, 6: 431–446.

Speckbacher, G., Neumann, K. & Hoffmann, W. H. (2015) Resource relatedness and the mode of entry into new businesses: Internal resource accumulation vs. access by collaborative arrangement. *Strategic Management Journal*, 36(11): 1675–1687.

Surdu, I. & Mellahi, K. (2016) Theoretical foundations of equity based foreign market entry decisions: A review of the literature and recommendations for future research. *International Business Review*, 25(5): 1169–1184.

The Economist. (2014) It's like 1997 all over again. *The Economist*. Viewed 10 April, www.economist.com/blogs/freeexchange/2014/01/emerging-markets.

The Economist (2017) Four BRICs don't quite make a wall. *The Economist*. Viewed 7 July, www.economist.com/news/finance-and-economics/21723133-brazil-russia-india-and-china-have-done-even-better-forecastthanks-mainly.

The Economist (2019) Unicorns in winter. *The Economist*. 9 March 2019, pp. 52–53.

Thomas, A. S. & Mueller, S. L. (2000) A case for comparative entrepreneurship: Assessing the relevance of culture. *Journal of International Business Studies*, 31: 287–301.

Trudgen, R. & Freeman, S. (2014) Measuring the performance of born-global firms throughout their development process: The roles of initial market selection and internationalisation speed. *Management International Review*, 54(4): 551–579.

Wadhwa, V., Jain, S., Saxenian, A., Gereffi, G. & Wang, H. (2011) *The Grass is Indeed Greener in India and China for Returnee Entrepreneurs: America's New Immigrant Entrepreneurs* – Part VI, Kansas City, KS: Ewing Marion Kauffman Foundation.

Wang, R. (2012) Chinese culture and its potential influence on entrepreneurship. *International Business Research*, 5(10): 76–90.

Welch, C. & Paavilainen-Mäntymäki, E. (2014). Putting process (back) in: Research on the internationalization process of the firm. *International Journal of Management Reviews*, 16(1): 2–23.

Welter, F. (2011) Contextualizing entrepreneurship-conceptual challenges and ways forward. *Entrepreneurship Theory and Practice*, 35(1): 165–184.

Wernerfelt, B. (1984) A resource-based view of the firm. *Strategic Management Journal*, 5(2): 171–180.

Wright, M. & Stigliani, I. (2013) Entrepreneurship and growth. *International Small Business Journal*, 31(1): 3–22.

Wu, F., Sinkovics, R. R., Cavusgil, S. T. & Roath, A. S. (2007) Overcoming export manufacturers' dilemma in international expansion. *Journal of International Business Studies*, 38(2): 283–302.

Yan, H., Wickramasekera, R. & Tan, A. (2018) Exploration of Chinese SMEs' export development: The role of managerial determinants based on an adapted innovation related internationalization model. *Thunderbird International Business Review*, 1–14.

Zapalska, A. M. & Edwards, W. (2001). Chinese entrepreneurship in a cultural and economic perspective. *Journal of Small Business Management*, 39: 286–292.

Zhang, X., Ma, X. & Wang, Y. (2012). Entrepreneurial orientation, social capital, and the internationalization of SMEs: Evidence from China. *Thunderbird International Business Review*, *54*(2): 195–210.

Zhang, X., Ma, X., Wang, Y., Li, X. & Huo, D. (2016). What drives the internationalization of Chinese SMEs? The joint effects of international entrepreneurship characteristics, network ties, and firm ownership. *International Business Review*, 25(2): 522–534.

Zhu, Y., Freeman, S. & Cavusgil, S. T. (2018) Service quality delivery in a cross-national context. *International Business Review*, 27(5): 1022–1032.

5   Ethnicity and entrepreneurship

Introduction

One of the key elements of international entrepreneurship is ethnic entrepreneurship with a focus on ethnic minority groups, mainly immigrants, operating business in a very different social and cultural environment from their home country. In this chapter, we illustrate the underpinning issues related to ethnic entrepreneurship, including different definitions of ethnic entrepreneurship, related theoretical framework and models, relevant ethnic entrepreneurs' strategies and determinant factors, and the later conceptual advancements regarding ethnic economy and enclave economy as well as transnationalism and entrepreneurship. These concepts provide direction to the arguments and justifications presented in subsequent chapters based on studies on the internationalization of entrepreneurship in Australian society and ethnic entrepreneurship among the Chinese and Jewish people in the process of economic globalization and international migration.

Defining ethnic entrepreneurship and related theoretical frameworks/models

According to Waldinger et al. (1990: 3), ethnic entrepreneurship is "a set of connections and regular patterns of interaction among people sharing common national background or migration experiences". However, the terms 'ethnic entrepreneur' and 'immigrant entrepreneur' cannot be used interchangeably, as explained by Rath (2010: 6): "The entrepreneurs in question are not always immigrants in the true sense because they were not always born in another country". Therefore, for many researchers, ethnic entrepreneurship refers to the ethnic background of these first-generation or second-generation entrepreneurs, and the term 'entrepreneurs' refers to people who are simultaneously owner and manager of an enterprise (Rath, 2010; Rettab, 2001).

With regard to the theoretical framework, literatures in sociology, anthropology and labour economics have each contributed to the development of theoretical frameworks addressing the effect of ethnicity and race on entrepreneurship (Volery, 2007). During the early years, research focused on ethnic business conducted by entrepreneurs serving other members of the ethnic community and satisfying their specific ethnic needs (Greene & Owen, 2004). Most initial theories on ethnic entrepreneurship were developed within the field of sociology, including the disadvantage theory and the cultural theory. The disadvantage theory claimed that most immigrants have significant disadvantages hampering them upon arrival, which at the same time steer their behaviour (Fregetto, 2004). The cultural theory suggested that ethnic and immigrant groups are equipped with culturally determined characteristics such as dedication to hard work, membership of a strong ethnic community, economical living, acceptance of risk, compliance with social value patterns, solidarity and loyalty, and orientation towards self-employment (Masurel et al., 2004).

In addition, the differences in ethnic resources provide an explanation for the different rates of self-employment between equally disadvantaged ethnic groups (Waldinger et al., 1990). For example, cultural aspects can be used to explain the propensity of Chinese people to become self-employed. However, other critical aspects, such as employment alternatives, immigration policies, market conditions and availability of capital can also be seen as important factors determining the rates of self-employment (Volery, 2007).

From an economics perspective, middleman minority theory is the primary explanation for ethnic entrepreneurship. Following the expansion of an ethnic community, the related business can be developed and sustained with a sufficient number of potential consumers purchasing ethnic products. Subsequently, ethnic businesses can start to grow by engaging in trade with entrepreneurs from other ethnic groups. After reaching a critical mass and obtaining acceptance widely, their businesses can expand into high-volume trade engaging the entire local population (Volery, 2007).

Based on the initial development of the ethnic entrepreneurship concept, a number of theoretical models have been developed to explain the phenomenon as a whole, including the interactive model, the mixed embeddedness model, and the model merging the interactive aspects with the entrepreneurial process. The interactive model claimed that the development of an ethnic business could be traced back to multiple interactive factors responsible for the entrepreneurial success of an ethnic group, in particular, a complex interaction between opportunity structures (i.e. market conditions, access to ownership, job market conditions and legal frameworks) and group resources (i.e. cultural traditions and ethnic social networks) (Waldinger et al., 1990). These two dimensions determine the strategies that an ethnic entrepreneur has to implement in order to create a viable business in an alien environment (Pütz, 2003).

The mixed embeddedness model further developed the concept by recognizing the structures of a local economy and the legal-institutional factors that exert a strong influence on the development of ethnic businesses (Razin, 2002). The business environment can be very different from one region to another, hence, spatial variations among the same immigrant groups and variations between different ethnic groups exist in the same economic milieu (Razin & Light, 1998).

Therefore, opportunities should be analysed on a national, regional and local level (Boissevain et al., 1990).

The third model that merged the interactive model with the entrepreneurial process, identified the factors influencing an ethnic entrepreneur. The model emphasized the view that an individual ethnic entrepreneur comes from a different ethnic group and, as a potential entrepreneur, has an ethnic, cultural or religious background which could influence the pursuit of entrepreneurial opportunities. Even among the same ethnic group, individual differences (i.e. psychological characteristics, access to information and knowledge, networks/social relationships, ability/skills, judgement/decision) exist and affect the way individuals in the group recognize and pursue opportunities (Schaper & Volery, 2004). Such an 'ethnic dimension' could influence the 'entrepreneurship dimension' differently, depending on the cultural differences between host and home country, the level of discrimination, the progression of the social integration, the experience in the new environment, and the individual personal background with regard to age, gender and education level (Volery, 2007).

Ethnic entrepreneur strategies

Besides the development of the theoretical framework and models regarding ethnic entrepreneurship, another key area of literature focuses on ethnic strategies. A common tendency of ethnic entrepreneurs is to develop an easily portable and less sophisticated business, allowing them to return to their home countries. Hence, the business is characterized by low levels of technology and innovation, with immigrants having to acquire the skills and capital needed for running such a business. For ethnic entrepreneurs the career and social risks are much lower in comparison with their local counterparts since: (1) ethnic entrepreneurs are new to the environment and expect these challenges; (2) the jobs have relatively low standards and are easy to obtain; and (3) ethnic entrepreneurs work within family or friendship environments and do not risk social exclusion (Schaper & Volery, 2004). Therefore, ethnic communities and networks are crucial for the survival of ethnic entrepreneurs as a central source of 'social capital'.

According to Massey (1988: 384), migration networks are "sets of interpersonal ties that link migrants, former migrants, and non-migrants in origin and destination areas through the bonds of kinship, friendship, and shared community origin". Such networks can substantially improve the efficiency of running new migrant businesses by providing a number of crucial resources. This support can improve the survivability of new migrant businesses when faced with challenges and difficulties (Jones & Ram, 1998) since it helps to reduce economic risks. In addition, other factors, in particular related to individual entrepreneurs' ability to acquire skills through learning-by-doing and to innovate, are also important (Jones & Ram, 1998). Sometimes, hard work and commitment are not sufficient to ensure business success for ethnic entrepreneurs. The inability to delegate responsibilities to non-family employees and establish a succession strategy in order to entrust the business to professional management personnel, could be factors that hinder business growth and expansion in the long run (Basu & Goswami, 1999). This is a valuable lesson for ethnic entrepreneurs to learn. Developing capability through educational attainments and employee training beyond relying on family members could be vital strategy for the long-term growth.

Another challenging issue for business success is related to financing ethnic business. Having sufficient capital to start a small business is one of the biggest challenges in the process of business development. For ethnic entrepreneurs, lack of business 'track record' and good references, plus lack of language capability, can lead to difficulties in obtaining bank loans (Jones & Ram, 1998). Many ethnic entrepreneurs are able to use their own savings or borrow money from relatives or within the ethnic community, but only a small number may be able to acquire a bank loan (Basu & Goswami, 1999). Other methods include the 'rotating credit association' (RCA) within the Chinese ethnic business community as popular financial resources (Bates, 1997). Calomiris and Rajaraman (1997: 208) defined the RCA as "a voluntary grouping of individuals who agree to contribute financially at uniformly-spaced dates towards the creation of a fund, which will then be allotted in accordance with some prearranged principle to each member of the group in turn". In each period, a member can withdraw the cash accumulated in the fund and use it for commercial purposes, but the member is excluded from other funds until the fund is reimbursed at the end of the RCA period (Volery, 2007). Such community-based mutual support funds can play an important role in replacing formal financial institutions to meet the needs of a particular section of the population, namely ethnic groups. This observation leads to the consideration of the ethnic group as one of the important determinants of ethnic entrepreneurship and we will elaborate in greater detail in the following section.

The important determinants of ethnic entrepreneurship

As we discussed earlier, the support of the ethnic community is crucial for the success of ethnic entrepreneurs and their businesses. The concept of 'ethnic donor group' claimed by Rettab (2001) provided more detailed understanding regarding the inter-relationship and interaction between ethnic group/ community and individual ethnic entrepreneurs. According to Rettab (2001: 8), the ethnic donor group is the minority group producing entrepreneurs. The importance of the donor group is that it influences ethnic entrepreneurship's emergence through interaction with the environment and is responsible for an individual engaging in entrepreneurship or not, depending on the group and individual's social and economic endowments (Rettab, 2001: 9). These social and economic endowments can be summarized in the five concepts of capital, including human capital, informational capital, financial capital, social capital (i.e. contacts and networks) and cultural capital (i.e. business attitudes of ethnic entrepreneurship). These interactions between the donor group and the individual based on the availability of the five capitals establish for the ethnic entrepreneur the conditions and constraints under which the labour market and entrepreneurship decisions are taken (Rettab, 2001: 11).

A number of aspects support the overall argument mentioned above. First, the resources produced by donor groups are in unequal amounts, resulting in unequal responsiveness by individuals to entrepreneurship with different outcomes. A comparison between an ethnic group with large-sized households and traditional behavioural patterns, and another ethnic group with predominately single-parent households, demonstrates the difference in human capital and financial resources of the members, which consequently leads to different routes towards entrepreneurship with different outcomes (Rettab, 2001).

Second, individual employment status and labour market circumstances also influence the adoption of particular routes to enter ethnic entrepreneurship. Generally speaking, many new immigrants occupy lower skilled, less professional and lower paid jobs; their unemployment rates are higher and average incomes lower than those of native locals (Rettab, 2001). These trends can be seen as push factors for immigrants to choose to run their own start-up businesses as self-employed individuals rather than being unemployed, under-employed or employed but under paid. These individual immigrants can be categorized as being the 'second-best choice' for entrepreneurship due to mismatches between supply and demand resulting in unemployment, under-employment or dissatisfaction with employment. The 'second-best choice' entrepreneurs are non-voluntary due to their employment status, income level and social exclusion. On the other hand, there is another group of individual immigrants who can be categorized as being 'best choice' entrepreneurs. These individuals are voluntary entrepreneurs and choose self-run businesses with the support and motivation of the donor group to respond to market opportunity, make profit and possess the drive to improve economic conditions (Gold, 1992). These entrepreneurs are more likely to be risk-takers because of the associated opportunity costs (Rettab, 2001: 18). This urge among self-run business entrepreneurs exists because of the many advantages, including an alternative employment opportunity, better income and possibly a better social position and social integration when the business eventually becomes successful.

The above observations lead to the third area for consideration, namely the relationship and trade-off between individual willingness and business opportunity. According to van Praag (1996), opportunity is determined by the availability of start-up capital, entrepreneurial ability and the economic environment, whereby lack of capital is mitigated by entrepreneurial ability. While willingness is determined by the individual evaluation of self-run business versus wage employment, and individual evaluation depends on personal preferences and choices between alternatives among the determinants of financial, psychological, human capital and situational variables. Overall, ethnic entrepreneurs need to build on their current living and working conditions in their donor group as shaped by the market environment, and they need to interact accordingly to manage their endowments. Generally speaking, ethnic entrepreneurs end up in ethnic markets characterized by easy entry, ethnic products, excess supply relatively low return, unstable and uncertain factors, low levels of technology and innovation (Rettab, 2001: 19–20).

The ethnic economy versus the enclave economy

Later conceptual advancements regarding ethnic entrepreneurship focus on re-examining the meaning and analytical distinction of relevant concepts such as the middleman minority, ethnic economy and enclave economy. Ethnic social structures are important for understanding the concepts related to the business operation among ethnic entrepreneurs (Zhou, 2004). As we discussed earlier, the concept of middleman minorities encompasses ethnic entrepreneurs who trade between a society's elite and the masses. They run businesses that are mainly portable and easily liquidated and many then reinvest money elsewhere, often implying a return home (Bonacich, 1973). In the past, they ran businesses in poor minority communities deserted by mainstream retail and service industries; however, in recent years, they have moved to more affluent urban areas and have become involved in the mainstream economy. Generally speaking, these ethnic entrepreneurs have few intrinsic ties to the social structures and social relations of the local communities in which they operate their businesses (Zhou, 2004).

In contrast, enclave entrepreneurs are individuals bounded by co-ethnicity, co-ethnic social structures and location. Historically, they operated their businesses in immigrant neighbourhoods where their co-ethnic group members dominated and were themselves part of the social networks within their self-sustaining ethnic enclave. However, in more recent years, many ethnic enclaves have evolved into multi-ethnic and multi-cultural communities and new ethnic start-up businesses also choose the location in affluent middle-class suburbs. Many of these entrepreneurs can play double roles between middleman minorities and enclave entrepreneurs. Examples provided by Zhou (2004) demonstrate that Chinese immigrants run fast food takeaway shops in a Latino-dominant neighbourhood as middleman minority entrepreneurs, and at the same time, they also run their restaurants in Chinatown as enclave entrepreneurs. These two types of ethnic entrepreneurs are conditioned by different social structures and social relations. Such phenomena lead to the consideration of two different concepts, namely the ethnic economy versus the enclave economy.

Generally speaking, the ethnic economy concept includes any immigrant or ethnic group's self-employed, employers, and co-ethnic employees (Bonacich, 1987). Later, according to Light and others (Light et al., 1994; Light & Karageorgis, 1994; Light & Gold, 2000), the ethnic economy includes two key aspects: (1) the ethnic group has a control over ownership of their businesses and labour (i.e. co-ethnic labour force or unpaid family labour); (2) the ethnic group has a control over the employment network that allows the channelling of co-ethnic members into other organizations, including non-co-ethnic firms or other sectors. Based on these, the ethnic economy concept encompasses businesses owned by middleman minorities, businesses owned by co-ethnics in ethnic enclaves, and all ethnic-owned or ethnic-controlled enterprises in the general economy.

On the other hand, the enclave economy is a special case of the ethnic economy and that is bounded by co-ethnicity and location. Not every group's ethnic economy can be called an enclave economy (Zhou, 2004: 1043). According to Portes and others (e.g. Portes & Bach, 1985; Portes & Manning, 1986), the enclave economy has several unique characteristics: (1) the group involved has a sizeable entrepreneurial class; (2) economic activities are not exclusively commercial, but include productive activities; (3) the business clusters have a high level of diversity with a wide range of economic activities common in the general economy; (4) co-ethnicity epitomizes the relationships between owners and workers as well as patrons and clients; (5) a physical concentration is required within an ethnically identifiable neighbourhood with a minimum level of institutional completeness. The ethnic businesses in the enclave need a co-ethnic clientele, which they initially serve, as well as ethnic resources (e.g. financial information and labour) to support their business (Portes & Manning, 1986).

In addition, the enclave economy also has an integrated cultural component whereby economic activities are governed by bonded solidarity and enforceable trust. These can be seen as the mechanisms of support and control necessary for economic life in the community and for reinforcement of norms and values, and sanctioning of socially disapproved behaviour (Portes & Zhou, 1992), such as cheating. Therefore, a contractual monetary bond maintains the relationships between co-ethnic owners, workers and customers. One good example of the above observations is the Chinatowns in major cities outside China, where many different economic activities occur and new immigrants from China with little knowledge of local languages and few job skills can find work.

Transnationalism and entrepreneurship

In recent years, due to new technological developments, new phenomena have emerged that are unmatched by the historical movements of many immigrant groups. The contemporary movements can be seen as transnational on a larger scale and with more diversity than in the past, and indicating high density and regularity (Zhou, 2004). Increasing numbers of immigrants maintain their roots and involvement in both home country and host country with participation in political, economic and social lives in both locations (Levitt, 2001). This trend leads to the rise of new structures and forces that determine ethnic entrepreneurship and develop a variety of transnational representations of entrepreneurship, including financial services, import/export, cultural enterprises (e.g. music, movies and video products), manufacturing firms operating in one or multiple locations, and overseas returnees operating micro-enterprises and start-ups.

Their transnational lives and networks sustain regular back-and-forth movements, including cyclical migration (Portes & Guarnizo, 1991).

Based on these phenomena, transnationalism is defined as "the processes by which immigrants forge and sustain multi-stranded social relations that link together their societies of origin and settlement" (Basch et al., 1994: 6). Others also argued that it is the intensity of exchanges, not just the occurrences themselves, such as trips or contacts, that become important aspects for investigation. Portes et al. (1999) developed a typology of three sectors of transnationalism (i.e. economic, political and sociocultural) at two levels of institutionalization (high versus low). These researchers defined transnationalism as measurable occupations and activities that require for their implementation regular and sustained social contacts over time across national borders.

In addition, there are other issues associated with the concept of transnationalism, including human capital and other demographic characteristics that determine and affect engagement in transnational activities (Zhou, 2004). For example, highly educated immigrants can leave their well-paid jobs to pursue entrepreneurship because they can utilize their skills, bi-cultural literacy and transnational networks to gain material benefits. On the other hand, low-skilled immigrants can also be engaged in transnational entrepreneurship by converting their meagre wages earned in developed economies and send remittances home to support family and developing new businesses, consequently gaining social status and material benefits in their home countries (Popkin, 1999). In summary, today's immigrants are sensitive to the opportunities of taking and exploiting entrepreneurship opportunities across national boundaries to progress socioeconomically in both host and home countries.

Conclusion

This chapter has highlighted the conceptual evolution of ethnic entrepreneurship. According to different theoretical underpinnings and disciplines, such as sociology, anthropology, labour economics and business entrepreneurship literature, we have observed the changing pattern from focusing on individual immigrant, personal and social disadvantages as driving factors, to a more group-based, community-based, enclave-based and even transnational-based approach to ethnic entrepreneurship. Many of the useful ideas and thoughts expressed here form the foundation for the arguments and justifications presented in the subsequent chapters based on the illustration of internationalization of entrepreneurship in Australian society (Chapter 6), as well as historical evolution and current changes in ethnic entrepreneurship among Chinese and Jewish people (Chapters 7 and 8). We will consolidate the relevant information in order to streamline the understanding regarding internationalization of entrepreneurship and ethnic entrepreneurship in the process of economic globalization and international migration in our concluding Chapter 9.

References

Basch, L., Glick-Schiller, N. & Blanc-Szaton, C. (1994) *Nations Unbound: Trans-national Projects, Post Colonial Predicaments and Deterritorialized Nation States*. Langhorne, PA: Gordon and Breach.

Basu, A. & Goswami, A. (1999) Determinants of South Asian entrepreneurial growth in Britain: A multi-variate analysis. *Small Business Economics*, 13(1): 57–70.

Bates, T. (1997) Financing small business creation: The case of Chinese and Korean immigrant entrepreneurs. *Journal of Business Venturing*, 12: 109–124.

Boissevain, J., Blauschkee, J., Grotenberg, H., Joseph, I., Light, I., Sway, M., Waldinger, R. & Werbner, P. (1990) Ethnic entrepreneurs and ethnic strategies, in R. Waldinger, H. Aldrich and R. Ward (eds), *Ethnic Entrepreneurs: Immigrant Business in Industrial Societies*, London: Sage, pp. 131–157.

Bonacich, E. (1973) A theory of middleman minorities. *American Sociological Review*, 38: 583–594.

Bonacich, E. (1987) Making it in America: A social evaluation of the ethnics of immigrant entrepreneurship. *Sociological Perspectives*, 30: 446–466.

Calomiris, C. W. & Rajaraman, I. (1997) The role of ROSCAs: Lumpy durables or event insurance?. *Journal of Development Economics*, 56(1): 207–216.

Fregetto, E. (2004) Immigration and ethnic entrepreneurship: A U.S. perspective, in H. P. Welsch (ed.), *Entrepreneurship: The Way Ahead*, New York: Routledge, pp. 253–268.

Gold, S. (1992) *Refugee Communities*. Newbury Park: Sage.

Greene, P. & Owen, M. (2004) Race and ethnicity, in W. B. Gartner, K. G. Shaver, N. M. Carter and P. D. Reynolds (eds), *Handbook of Entrepreneurial Dynamics: The Process of Business Creation*, Thousand Oaks, CA: Sage, pp. 26–38.

Jones, T. & Ram, M. (1998) *Ethnic Minorities in Business*. London: Small Business Research Trust.

Levitt, P. (2001) *The Transnational Villagers*, Berkeley, CA: University of California Press.

Light, I. & Gold, S. J. (2000) *Ethnic Economies*. San Diego, CA: Academic Press.

Light, I. & Karageorgis, S. (1994) The ethnic economy, in N. J. Smelser & R. Swedberg (eds), *The Handbook of Economic Sociology*, Princeton, NJ: Princeton University Press, pp. 647–669.

Light, I., Sabagh, G., Bozorgmehr, M. & Der-Martirosian, C. (1994) Beyond the ethnic enclave economy. *Social Problems*, 41: 65–80.

Massey, D. S. (1988) Economic development and international migration in comparative perspective, *Population and Development Review*, 14: 383–413.

Masurel, E., Nijkamp, P. & Vindigni, G. (2004) Breeding places for ethnic entrepreneurs: A comparative marketing approach. *Entrepreneurship & Regional Development*, 16: 77–86.

Popkin, E. (1999) Guatemalan Mayan migration to Los Angeles: Constructing trans-national linkages in the context of the settlement process. *Ethnic and Racial Studies*, 22(2): 267–289.

Portes, A. & Bach, R. L. (1985) *The Latin Journey: Cuban and Mexican Immigrants in the United States*. Berkeley, CA: University of California Press.

Portes, A. & Guarnizo, L. E. (1991) Tropical capitalists: U.S.-bound immigration and small enterprise development in the Dominican Republic, in S. Diaz-Briquets and S. Weintraub (eds), *Migration, Remittances, and Small Business Development: Mexico and Caribbean Basin Countries*, Boulder, CO: Westview Press, pp. 101–131.

Portes, A., Guarnizo, L. E. & Landolt, P. (1999) Introduction: Pitfalls and promise of an emergent research field. *Ethnic and Racial Studies*, 22(2): 217–237.

Portes, A. & Manning, R. D. (1986) The immigrant enclave: Theory and empirical examples, in S. Olzak and J Nagel (eds), *Comparative Ethnic Relations*, Orlando, FL: Academic Press, pp. 47–68.

Portes, A. & Zhou, M. (1992) Gaining the upper hand: Economic mobility among immigrant and domestic minorities. *Ethnic and Racial Studies*, 15(4): 491–522.

Praag, M. C. van (1996) *Determinants of Successful Entrepreneurship*. Amsterdam: Thesis Publisher.

Pütz, R. (2003) Culture and entrepreneurship – remarks on transculturality as practice. *Tijdschrift voor Economische en Sociale Geografie*, 94(5): 554–563.

Rath, J. (2010) Ethnic entrepreneurship: Conceptual paper, European Foundation for the Improvement of Living and Working Conditions, Dublin, Ireland.

Razin, E. (2002) The economic context, embeddedness and immigrant entrepreneurs. *International Journal of Entrepreneurial Behaviour & Research*, 8(1/2): 162–167.

Razin, E. & Light, I. (1998) Ethnic entrepreneurs in America's largest metropolitan areas. *Urban Affairs Review*, 33: 332–360.

Rettab, B. (2001) The emergence of ethnic entrepreneurship: A conceptual framework, EIM Research Report 0103, Zoetermeer, Netherland.

Schaper, M. & Volery, T. (2004) *Entrepreneurship and Small Business: A Pacific Rim Perspective*. Milton: John Wiley & Sons Australia.

Volery, T. (2007) Ethnic entrepreneurship: A theoretical framework, in L. P. Dana (ed.), *Handbook of Research on Ethnic Minority Entrepreneurship: A Co-evolutionary View on Resource Management*, Cheltenham: Edward Elgar, pp. 30–41.

Waldinger, R., Aldrich, H. & Ward, R. (1990) *Ethnic Entrepreneurs: Immigrant Business in Industrial Societies*. London: Sage.

Zhou, M. (2004) Revisiting ethnic entrepreneurship: Convergences, controversies, and conceptual advancements. *International Migration Review*, 38(3): 1040–1074.

6 Australia and its history of immigration and entrepreneurship

Introduction

Perhaps because it is far away from many important centres, or has only 25 million inhabitants, or is seen mainly as a habitat for unusual marsupials, Australia usually attracts relatively little attention about its successful economic management. However, the country's economy is arguably one of the most successful in the 'rich' world. Australia has been growing for 28 years without a recession – a record for any developed country; its cumulative growth over that period is almost triple that of Germany. However, recent bushfires of an unprecedented level in late 2019 and now the Covid-19 pandemic since early 2020 are redressing this situation rapidly. Nonetheless, until these two unprecedented events, the medium income had risen. The median income has risen four times faster than in the United States. While the public debt is at 1 per cent of GDP, it is less than half of that in Britain (*The Economist*, 2018a). Australia is also an ideal location in which to examine immigrant ethnic entrepreneurs due to the country's long history of immigration. A considerable and heterogeneous immigrant population has developed, with people arriving from more than 200 countries during the 200 years of white settlement (Australian social trends, cat no. 4102.0, 2008; Collins, 2003; Evans, 1989). However, there are reforms that Australia should be undertaking and is slowly addressing. For example, indigenous (Aboriginal) Australians suffer from enormous disadvantages, which a succession of governments has found difficult to address. Increasingly, global warming is causing serious damage – droughts and floods have become more frequent and more severe (*The Economist*, 2018a).

Nonetheless, Australia has a unique history with some 29 per cent of its inhabitants born overseas – double the number in the United States (*The Economist*, 2018b). In round terms, about half of all Australians are immigrants or the children of immigrants. Thus, Australia is one of the largest immigrant countries in the Western World, compared to Canada (18 per cent), the United States (11 per cent) and the United Kingdom (10 per cent) (Borooah & Mangan, 2007, Smans, 2006, 2012). Over the past two decades, the major source of immigration has been Asia, rapidly changing the country's traditional ethnic mix. This large immigrant population stands in contrast to that in the United

States, United Kingdom and Italy, where far smaller inflows have generated resentment among a large proportion of the electorate, and in Japan, where allowing immigrants to settle in any numbers is politically resisted. In Australia, both main parties – the governing Liberal–National coalition (right-of-centre) and the main opposition Labor party (left-leaning) – argue that admitting significant numbers of skilled migrants is essential to the health of the economy not only through their labour contribution but also through new business development and entrepreneurship (*The Economist*, 2018a and 2018b).

Immigrants to Australia began arriving in the late eighteenth to early nineteenth century, the majority from the British Isles. It was not until the gold rush of the mid-nineteenth century that immigrants began arriving from all over the world, primarily Europe (particularly Italy) as well as Asia (mostly from China) (Collins, 2003; Cresciani, 2003). As immigrants grew, reservations concerning wage competition and hostility towards immigrants led to the Australian government enacting the Immigration Restriction Act No. 17 in 1901, refusing entry to the illiterate or unskilled employment. Therefore, the majority of immigrants continued to have Anglo-Saxon roots right up to the mid-1970s (Cresciani, 2003; Evans, 1989; Smans, 2012).

Following World War II, the Australian government decided to increase the population to improve the nation's defence capacity and to rapidly expand the industrial and agricultural sectors of the economy (Mascitelli & Battiston, 2008). At the same time, millions of people displaced by war-ravaged Europe were seeking refuge outside Europe (Cresciani, 2003; Smans, 2012). Between 1947 and 1971, the Australian government commenced a campaign to induce immigrants, primarily European and preferably British, to come to Australia. Immigrants were offered assisted passage, resulting in 2.4 million Britons and 800,000 non-English speaking people immigrating to Australia during this period (Cresciani, 2003; Smans, 2012).

During the 1970s and 1980s, changes in policy shifted focus and the number of skilled Asian immigrants and refugees in Australia grew steadily (Evans, 1989; Smans, 2012). From the 1990s, the configuration of arrivals continued to change, reflecting global humanitarian needs and the changing Government Migration Program. This development included the introduction of a skilled stream to assist economic development by attracting highly skilled immigrants bringing with them skills, business expertise and capital (Australian social trends, cat no. 4102.0, Australian Bureau of Statistics, 2007; Smans, 2012). The number of arrivals from Europe began to decrease while those from New Zealand, China, India and sub-Saharan Africa increased (Australian social trends, cat no. 4102.0, Australian Bureau of Statistics, 2007; Borooah & Mangan, 2007; Smans, 2012).

Immigration and entrepreneurship in Australia have a long history. Post-World War II Australia received around 6.5 million migrants (Australian social trends, cat no. 4102.0, Australian Bureau of Statistics, 2007; Smans, 2012). Collins (2003: 138) observed that "many of Australia's post-war immigrants ... moved into entrepreneurship" and based on the 1996 census data, some groups demonstrated higher levels of entrepreneurship than those demonstrated by the broader Anglo-Saxon community. For example, in 1996, while the Italian dias-pora represented merely 2.0 per cent of the population of Australia, 22.2 per cent of employers and 18.0 per cent of self-employers as owners of fruit and veget-able shops in New South Wales were Italian-born immigrants (Collins, 2003; Smans, 2012).

More recently, in response to the ongoing debate about the economic impact of Australian immigration, Low (2008) examined the economic contribution of Asian born female immigrant entrepreneurs in Australia. This empirical study showed the significant economic contribution of these entrepreneurs to the cre-ation of new businesses and jobs in addition to other non-quantifiable economic benefits to Australia (Low, 2008). Another example in which Australia appears to 'stand out' from other countries, is the fact that at a time when governments around the world are 'souring' on immigration, seeking to send 'some home', Australia has admitted 190,000 newcomers every year since the 1990s – nearly three times as many (relative to the population) as the United States (*The Eco-nomist*, 2018a, 2018b).

In part, this perceived tolerance of outsiders may reflect another remarkable feature of Australian society: the solvency of its welfare state. Complaints about foreigners using the system are rare. Public debt amounts to just 41 per cent of GDP. This is one of the lowest levels in the 'rich' world, reflected in Australia's enviable record in terms of growth and history of perceptive policymaking. Nearly 30 years ago, the government refurbished the pension system. Since then workers have been obliged to save for their retirement through private invest-ment funds. The modest public pension covers only those without adequate savings (*The Economist*, 2018a, 2018b). Therefore, since half of all living Australians were born abroad or are children of parents born abroad, and given the rich immigration history and economic contribution of immigrants, Australia continues to be a poly-ethnic society that provides the ideal setting to explore immigrant ethnic entrepreneurship.

Different groups in Australian immigration and their impact on entrepreneurship

Italians in Australia

Since the 1800s Italians have been encouraged by the Italian government to pursue employment and economic opportunities abroad (Baldassar & Pesman, 2005). Many settled in Australia, becoming "strongly entrenched in the Australian business community, particularly as small businesses" (Battiston & Mascitelli, 2007, p. 28). The Italian community has prospered in Australia for over 200 years with more than 420,000 arrivals (Cresciani, 2003; Smans, 2006). In spite of bureaucratic restrictions initially imposed on Southern Italians, from the end of World War II until 1973, 305,000 immigrated to Australia, forming the largest non-English speaking national group (Cresciani, 2003). The peak of Italian-born arrivals was recorded in 1971 with 288,300 people, and subsequently steadily decreased as the Italian-born population aged and deaths exceeded new arrivals (Australian social trends, cat no. 4102.0, 2008; Smans, 2006).

With the Italian government's 'push', the poor living standards, under-employment, an agricultural crisis and two world wars, Italians emigrating *en masse* to other countries in Europe, the Americas and Oceania (Smans, 2012). Baldassar and Pesman (2005) highlighted that while around "fifty-seven million Italians live in the [Italian] peninsula; another five million live abroad, as do as many as seventy million children and grandchildren of Italian emigrants" (p. 20). While Australia received approximately 280,570 Italian immigrants (Battiston & Mascitelli, 2007) from 1947 to 1976, the business activities of these immigrants received little attention (see Lampugnani, 1993; Lampugnani & Holton, 1989). Instead, the focus remained on issues of identity and culture (Baldassar & Pesman, 2005; Cresciani, 2003; Smans, 2006). Sequeira and Rasheed (2006: 371) highlight that

> a promising area for future research is the international dimension of immigrant economies ... [and] the international linkages that exist among geographically dispersed enclaves of a given immigrant community [that] may bestow upon that community a competitive advantage in an era of increasing globalization.

Although the reasons for immigrating to Australia may have changed over the years – from spiritual fulfilment as missionaries, the gold fields in the 1850s/1890s, to improving social and economic status in the post war years – Italians have always played an important role in the Australian economy (Cresciani, 2003; Smans, 2006, 2012) having "created continent-wide networks [diaspora] along which circulated information on work opportunities and the state of the labour market" (Baldassar & Pesman, 2005: 25). This has led to Italian immigrants achieving various levels of economic success, as both a source of labour and as self-employers through immigrant entrepreneurship (Smans, 2012).

Italians as a labour source

The pre-World War II wave of Italian immigration consisted largely of illiterate or semi-literate peasants seeking economic security and prepared to accept poor working conditions and renumeration in order to own their own land (Cresciani, 2003; Smans, 2012). Many worked in the Victorian goldfields in the 1890s as miners, woodcutters, labourers, cooks and waiters, or in infrastructure (Cresciani, 2003; Smans, 2012). In 1891, Italians were explicitly identified as a labour source, leading to, for example, 335 Italians from the Piedmont region of North-ern Italy being offered assisted passage to work on sugar plantations in North Queensland as cheap labour because slave work had recently been banned (Andreoni, 2003). During the period between the late nineteenth century and World War II, many of the immigrants were fishermen or peasants who had skills in farming, market gardening, poultry and pig farming, and traditional crafts (e.g. terrazzo, shoe making and carpentry). However, arriving with no capital meant they had to find work "as labourers for a period of time in order to build up sufficient capital and hence be able to achieve the economic independence they were looking for in the first instance" (Lampugnani, 1993: 159).

Post-World War II, Italian immigrants continued to arrive as unskilled or semi-skilled labourers into manufacturing, building and construction, or agricultural activities, such as fruit picking or cane cutting (Collins et al., 1995; Smans, 2012). Italian immigrants also worked in large industrial development projects such as the Trans-Australian railway, the Snowy Mountains Hydro Electric Scheme, and in the car manufacturing industry (Cresciani, 2003; Smans, 2012). Over time, the situation changed. Burnley (2005) noted that between 1971 and 2001, the percentage of first-generation Italian male manual workers dropped from 67 per cent to 49 per cent. By 2001, less than a quarter of first-generation males were employed in semi and unskilled manual labour, compared to 15 per cent of second and third generation Italian males (Smans, 2012). Although Italian immigrants in Australia were initially a source of labour, as they amassed capital, many subsequently became self-employed entrepreneurs.

Italians as self-employers

The 1800s saw the initial Italian immigrants forming communities and developing small commercial enterprises to cater for their needs. For example, the first macaroni factory at Daylesford, Victoria, catered for the Italian community on the goldfields (Cresciani, 2003; Smans, 2012). By 1947, 50 per cent of Italian-born males and 44 per cent of females were classified as self-employed. While this figure reduced by 1981 to 24 per cent of males and 17 per cent of females, it was still higher than participation rates of the Australian-born population (Collins et al., 1995). Small businesses emerged in building, construction and retail industries, particularly clothing and furniture stores, grocers, fish and chip shops, bread and cake shops, tobacconists, barbers, confectioners and milk bars (Smans, 2012). The strongest presence was fruit and vegetable shop owners, with Italians owning one in three businesses, despite being merely 2 per cent of the Australian population (Collins et al., 1995). The nature of these small businesses reflected traditional links to farming, old trades and skills (barbers, cobblers and terrazzo workers) and fashion (e.g. clothing stores) (Lampugnani, 1993; Cecilia, 1987).

Studies explain that the Italian immigrants' preference for self-employment stemmed from the Venetian tradition of small-scale industrialization and commerce, combined with

> limited English language skills, the refusal of Australian authorities to recognize pre-migration qualifications and experience, racial antagonism and the sponsorship system, all of which meant that Italian migrants were unlikely to rise through the ranks of Australian labour hierarchies.

Self-employment, therefore, often appeared to provide the best hope for a secure future.

(Baldassar & Pesman, 2005: 92)

Many post-World War II Italian immigrants were peasants, leaving Italy to escape debt, poverty and lack of land ownership. Australia offered opportunities to avoid being a source of labour and enabled them to become small-scale famers (Collins et al., 1995). In Griffith, New South Wales, for example, early Italian immigrants were farmers and applied their skills and knowledge to reju- venate farms abandoned by former Anglo-Celtic Australians because of the high salt content or wetlands (Jordan, Krivokapic-Skoko & Collins, 2009). "Their desire for land and their rural backgrounds, the traditional economic practices that treated the family as a labour unit dependent on cooperation and group solidarity, their willingness to take on gruelling work, and the long-established habits of frugality and saving all contributed to the likelihood that the Veneti could achieve success in environments that other farmers shunned" (Baldassar & Pesman, 2005: 66–67).

In conclusion, Italian immigrants in Australia have a long history of self- employment and substantial contributions to the economy. Italian small-scale farmers became central to Griffith introducing new industries, such as wine, responsible for the region's future economic success (Jordan, Krivokapic- Skoko & Collins, 2009). Interestingly, research on Greek and Italian immig- rants in Australia reveals intergenerational differences. Burnley (2005) reported changes in occupational status between first and second generation immigrants. Typically, the first generation established a business with the second generation employed as managers or executives. Alternatively, they started their own firms. Entrepreneurship was, therefore, evident in the first, second and third generations, particularly in the construction and building industries, with specialization in tiling, artisan work and furniture making (Burnley, 2005; Smans, 2012).

The shift to Asian immigration in Australian: the Vietnamese

The story of Kien Ly sounds improbable. Born in Saigon in 1955, he was the son of an officer in the South Vietnamese army. Having qualified as an engineer, before the war, he felt there were few prospects left at home after the fall to the Communist North. In 1981 he built a boat and fled with 54 fellow compatriots, was rescued from the South China Sea and was later interned in a camp in Indonesia. However, destiny intervened. The right-wing Australia gov- ernment at the time admitted 70,000 refugees from Indochina between 1975 and 1982. This was a significant departure from the recently dismantled White Australia policy, which ultimately led to the arrival of Kien Ly in Sydney. Ten years later Ly joined the local council as a member of the Labor Party. By the 1980s, stories like Kien Ly's became common. Australia's population at the time was merely 17 million. The government began to admit 100,000 people a year, resulting in a population in 2019 of 25 million, with a proposed annual quota of 190,000 immigrants a year. Largely due to this influx, Australia has been growing by 1.5 per cent a year, a third faster than Canada and twice as fast as the United States (*The Economist*, 2018b).

One factor currently helping to drive entrepreneurial activity in Australia is the young age of immigrants, which gives Australia a median age comparatively well below that of most European countries. Estimates by the International Monetary Fund (IMF) suggest that by reducing the rate at which the population ages, the new arrivals will boost GDP growth by as much as 0.5–1 percentage points a year until 2050. This trend is likely to last while immigration continues at the current rate in Australia and is an important feature of the economy given the average annual growth rate has been below 3 per cent for some time (*The Economist*, 2018a, 2018b).

Immigrants now comprise a third of the population of all Australia's state capitals except for Hobart, the capital of the largest island off the southern eastern tip of Australia. Interestingly, Kien Ly has observed that in the ten years he has lived in Fairfield, an inner-city in Sydney, which includes Cabramatta, the area has become largely a Vietnamese and Arab community. Kien Ly says with a laugh, "In Cabramatta, if you see a European, they're probably a tourist!" (*The Economist*, 2018b: 9). Overall, the public acceptance of high levels of immigration in Australia relies on the perception of a strong border policing policy in Australia, with a very low tolerance for illegal immigrant vessels landing on the country's coasts with 'would be' asylum seekers. Both major political parties broadly support the policy suggesting it is likely to continue, according to a recent Melbourne-based research organization, the Lowy Institute. However, the October figures for the number of immigrants arriving in 2018 were slightly down on recent years at around 162,000, perhaps indicating the trend may slow (*The Economist*, 2018b).

Modern Australian immigration

Nonetheless, a new picture of modern immigration in Australia has slowly emerged, one that now focuses on attracting immigrants offering skills when they are just entering their peak. One recent example includes a young couple from Brazil, now based in Queensland. Both are engineers specializing in asset integrity in the gas, oil and power sectors. The wife, Ana Luiza, works in a Brisbane-based company in high-end biology cell treatment while her husband, Rafael, is the Asia-Pacific sales manager for an engineering company. Both offer high skill-based capabilities and are at the idea age; as Rafael commented: "If I was over 30 years old (when I applied), I couldn't have the visa" (The Weekend Australia, 2018: 17). Recent statistics show that the picture has slowly changed with regard to skilled immigrants. While these immigrants comprised a fraction of the total immigration in the early 1980s, with family reunion being the main category, this trend had reversed by the mid-1990s. More specifically, over the past decade, skilled immigration has dominated, rather than the family stream as a rationale for immigration by an average ratio of 2 : 1. For example, during the 2016–2017 period, the skilled stream accounted for about 124,000 places compared with merely 56,000 in the family stream. Research suggests many of these immigrants will go on to run their own businesses. Immigration policy is no longer concentrated on conveying parents, grandparents and siblings to Australia; the focus is now directed towards partners, spouses and finance visas, which account for a substantial 85 per cent of total migration in the family category (*The Weekend Australian*, 2018).

The source countries have also changed dramatically since the 1970s, with the top three immigration countries in 2016–2017 comprising India (21 per cent), China (15 per cent) and Britain (now only 9 per cent). Even as little as a decade ago, Britain was second behind southern Asia and by contrast, Chinese Asia was a very close third. Another reason that Australia has focused on attracting skilled immigrants rather than the humanitarian (refugee) category, is that the latter have fewer skills and poor English proficiency and thus find it harder to secure employment. A recent 2017 survey of refugees by the Australian Department of Social Services found that only 16 per cent had a university degree, trade or technical qualification. A mere 27 per cent had secured employment within a year of arriving (*The Weekend Australian*, 2018). However, based on other evidence, such as studies of earlier waves of Italian unskilled immigrants, while many experienced difficulties in finding skilled jobs, they were very successful at setting up small businesses. Waves of Italian immigrants originating from the industrial districts of Northern Italy, especially the Veneto region, arrived in Griffith in regional New South Wales and in the inner-city suburb of Carlton in Melbourne, Victoria, making a name for themselves as hard-working immigrant entrepreneurs. Entrepreneurial proclivity was evident in first, second and third generation Italian immigrants, particularly in the construction and building industries (Burnley, 2005). Vietnamese immigrant entrepreneurs have followed a similar pathway, illustrated, for example, by many small businesses flourishing in the restaurant trade, supermarkets, furniture, arts and crafts and fresh produce markets in Richmond in Melbourne's inner-city. Both immigrant groups imported produce, machinery and materials from home markets into Australia to support business development and growth.

While the humanitarian refugee program has continued in Australia, it has only included approximately 15,000 refugees per year in the past decade, well below 10 per cent of total immigration. By contrast, skilled immigrants have rapidly and successfully transitioned into the work force, with others setting up businesses in a short period of time. Since 2009, the Australian Department of Home Affairs has undertaken a continuous survey of migrants, revealing that six months after arrival, nine out of ten skilled immigrants were employed. Over three-quarters of these immigrants were working full-time and more than six out of ten were employed in skilled jobs (*The Weekend Australian*, 2018).

Australian migration trends: implications 'at home' and in the region

There is little doubt that Australia's people, cities and composition of immigration categories will continue to experience considerable change over the next two decades. Australia's external environment will be influenced by demographic shifts that will see greater pressure on urbanization and continued high rates of people movements. By 2030 the world's population is estimated to be approximately 8.6 billion, up from 7.6 billion in 2017 according to a recent Federal Government 2017 Foreign Policy White Paper (DFAT, 2018). It is predicted that, similar to highly developed countries, the populations of Africa and South Asia will rise quickly. China's population is, however, ageing rapidly. The challenge for governments in the region will lie in whether this rising population will assist or constrain economic growth. How well governments are prepared for these challenges will vary depending very much on how they support education and training, health, employment and infrastructure (DFAT, 2018). This population growth is also predicted to increase (irregular) refugee migration in the region. This development is likely to raise other transnational security challenges.

The above suggests that the increased flow of displaced persons is likely to drive strong trends towards urbanization, including in the Indo-Pacific regions, which is likely to bring many export opportunities for Australian minerals and energy, and other goods and services, especially education. According to the United Nations estimates, globally there are likely to be 41 mega-cities (i.e. cities with more than ten million people) by 2030 (DFAT, 2018). Forecasts for increases in urban population from 2010 to 2030 indicate eight countries in the region will be most impacted. In descending order, China is estimated to have an additional 330 million people, followed by India with an additional 210 million, Indonesia 65 million, the Philippines and Vietnam both at around 40 million, Thailand at 38 million, the Republic of Korea at 8 million and Japan at around 3–5 million additional people (DFAT, 2018).

This suggests that increased flows of displaced persons and irregular migration will continue to present a range of challenges for Australia. The world is now witnessing an ever-increasing flow of people displaced by conflicts and environmental disasters that result in their movement within and across country borders. It is estimated that around 65 million displaced people now exist worldwide, a number close to that following World War II (DFAT, 2018). This situation is causing challenges that many countries find overwhelming and feel ill-equipped to handle at a cultural, social, economic, political and legal level. The sheer scale demands new approaches for dealing with such widespread challenges to support immigrants in humanitarian as well as skilled categories, as has always been adopted by Australia. However, while the social and cultural arguments are essential to the overall discussion, the economic benefits will be important to Australia's future economic growth, productivity and prosperity (DFAT, 2018). There seems little doubt that irregular refugee (humanitarian) migration will continue, with implications for the management of border security. Such movements are frequently supported by digital communication, inexpensive transport and people smuggling operations (DFAT, 2018). The future is both fragile and one of opportunity, with the history of immigrant entrepreneurship a very strong and ongoing reminder of the reason for Australia's economy and society having benefitted and continuing to benefit from immigration policies.

Technological advances will continue to drive change. E-commerce provides new ways for immigrant entrepreneurs to enter markets and access consumers. The new digital economy and the governance of this economy are of continuing interest to Australian businesses, as is the relocation of value chain activities for competitive advantage. Additional challenges around lower-cost robotics and new technologies, including additive manufacturing, are expanding opportunities for firms that are based in higher-wage economies such as Australia (DFAT, 2018). Given the likely rise in skilled immigrants entering Australia, the new businesses evolving around global manufacturing and global value chains will have significant implications for inbound and outbound trade and investment. Due to its pivotal role in manufacturing, China will continue to exert considerable influence regionally and globally. As the economy advances further, it is likely that production of many goods and services will be centralized (DFAT, 2018). However, the likelihood also exists of a shift to other countries for cost and strategic reasons that may open further opportunities for Australian immigrant entrepreneurs, providing important local and international networks for business opportunity recognition and subsequent business development and growth.

Australia: exports and future opportunities for immigrant entrepreneurs

Australia is an export nation. In 2016, AU$337 billion in goods and services were exported, comprising one fifth of all economic activity. Broadly speaking, Australia can be described as a mineral and energy superpower. Approximately AU$160 billion in minerals and energy were exported to major markets in 2016. For iron ore and coal, lead export markets include India, Japan, China and Republic of Korea (DFAT, 2018). Australia is arguably one of the world's biggest exporters of coal and iron ore as well as LNG. It is also home to the largest deposits of metals and minerals comprising gold, iron ore, lead, nickel, zinc and uranium. The past 60 years have witnessed the significant role of Australia in supporting Asia's economic growth and industrialization. During this period, exports of iron ore to the Republic of Korea, followed by Japan and China, represented Australia's largest trading partners in 2017 (DFAT, 2018). The growth in immigrant entrepreneurial businesses in the advanced manufacturing sectors in Australia is an illustration of what business development and growth are offering with immigrant entrepreneurs able to use their home market and ethnic networks as part of a global diaspora to expand business opportunities internationally.

Australia is also one of the ten most successful agricultural exporters globally. In 2016, Australia exported more than AU\$47 billion in agricultural and fish products, representing more than two-thirds of its agricultural production. In addition, Australia is the largest exporter of beef and wool with a reputation of producing safe high-quality food and is arguably the industry leader globally (DFAT, 2018). Again, the growth in this area has been supported by the increasing number of immigrant entrepreneurs using their ethnic home-based networks and ethnic ties to their globally located diaspora as well as network ties. Services now comprise an increasing share of exports, comprising more than AU\$75 billion or approximately one fifth of the country's exports in 2016. Australia is the third-largest provider of education to international students, attracting more than 550,000 students from over 180 countries in 2016. Over 8.5 million tourists visited Australia in 2016–2017. In the previous financial year, international tourists contributed over AU\$34 billion to the economy and supported the employment of over 580,000 people. The growth of many tourist-related service businesses has thus been promoted not only directly in tourism, but also in hospitality and the arts. In 2016, China was the largest source of inbound tourists (1.25 million, up by 10 per cent from the previous year), followed by the United States (0.75 million), the United Kingdom (0.73 million), Japan (0.42 million) and the Republic of Korea (0.29 million).

Manufacturing comprises up to AU\$44 billion or 13 per cent of Australian exports. The rapid growth in high-tech and knowledge-intensive Australian manufacturing is driven by the commodity sectors which recognize Australia as a well-known exporter. New business development and growth has been rapid in the past two decades, connecting Australian-based businesses with global value chains and developing other high-end value-adding products and services, including research and development, design and engineering. These sectors have increasingly moved into the advanced manufacturing sectors with global connections often created through the ethnic ties of immigrant entrepreneurs. More than four out of five Australian manufacturing businesses are SMEs (DFAT, 2018), many of which were developed by first, second and third generation immigrant entrepreneurs. Australian manufacturing businesses now rank fifth among advanced economies for business innovation, development and growth.

Government sectoral initiatives have been directed towards a range of key sectors to support the Australian economy's transition into the 'smart', high-value and export-focused industries. Australian industry-led growth centres have been increasingly developed to drive collaboration, commercialization, international engagement, skills and regulation reform. The Entrepreneur's Program is designed to provide practical advice and support to businesses. A further priority has been directed by the establishment of Government growth centres for the following sectors: advanced manufacturing, food and agribusiness, medical technologies and pharmaceuticals, mining equipment, technology and services, oil, gas and energy resources, and cyber security. As part of this strategic effort to develop a smarter and more advanced business base, the various state governments of Australia, are quickly developing international linkages through key cities and regional centres. This effort has been well supported by the large immigrant communities in Australia that have grown significantly in the last decade, as have the number of Australians now working overseas. Companies trading and investing globally have grown rapidly in the same period. Education and tourism strongly connect the market to other markets globally. Thus, globalization means that greater use of soft power – through Australia's efforts to influence the behaviour or thinking of others through the power of attraction and ideas – is becoming more important to Australia. Increasing the use of soft power is helping to shape its external environment and therefore enable the country to pursue more effectively its interests internationally (DFAT, 2018).

The rise of indigenous Australian entrepreneurs

While research on immigrant entrepreneurship in Australia is significant, research on indigenous small business entrepreneurship in Australia is scant. Research suggests that 'push' factors tend to be the main motivator for setting up businesses and this is turn is very strongly linked to improving the sense of severe disadvantage due to poor economic circumstances and racial stereo-typing which is both negative and discriminatory. There is thus a sense of trying to escape poverty, prejudice and address the needs of the community. However, there are many barriers to developing such businesses. The main barriers highlighted throughout Australian indigenous entrepreneurship research include a lack of adequate and formal education, prior work experience, language proficiency, cultural conflicts and the inability to locate adequate finance (Wood & Davidson, 2011; Maritz & Foley, 2018; Foley, 2008). Female indigenous entrepreneurs face both gender and racial discrimination making the challenges for them as a group more acute (Wood & Davidson, 2011). Thus, special challenges exist for Australian indigenous entrepreneurs which can be explored through indigenous entrepreneurship, networks and ecosystem integration with distinct differences between indigenous and non-indigenous entrepreneurship in Australia.

Special challenges

Australian indigenous businesses and people face special challenges in participating in Australian society as first nation people, warranting a separate investigation from other disadvantaged minorities (Closing the Gap, 2015; Denny-Smith & Loosemore, 2017). Indigenous entrepreneurship (Colbourne, 2018) has unique dimensions: community, spirituality and sustainability, linked to social entrepreneurship (Roundy, 2017). The greatest inhibitors to business growth for indigenous Australians include networking and financial literacy, limited working capital, inadequate planning, poor networking and family support (Carter, Kuhl,

Marlow, et al., 2017), and deficiency in access to equity funding and joint venture partners (Foley, 2017; Marlow & Martinez, 2017).

The link to indigenous entrepreneurial education ecosystems correlates increased indigenous employment with higher levels of education and networking (Foley, 2017). Additional beneficial outcomes of indigenous entrepreneurial education ecosystems include cultural captivity of entrepreneurship, inclusive development (Stam & Spigel, 2017), indigenous knowledge and indigenous wisdom (Foley, 2017; Marlow & Martinez, 2017). Yet, the greatest inhibitor to business growth is racism, illustrating the extent of commercial restrictions that racial inequality places on indigenous Australians. Moreover, indigenous women face gender discrimination (Foley, 2017) and more complex approaches to family, encompassing broader, long-term responsibilities. The impact of gender and racial discrimination (inequality) represents a greater barrier to entrepreneurial activity for women than for men.

Future research would be welcome in areas of cross-cultural management, entrepreneurship and international business that address two broad questions. First, how can Australia, as a case example, reduce inequality faced by Australian indigenous entrepreneurs, especially indigenous women entrepreneurs, who are the most vulnerable and marginalized? Second, what are appropriate indigenous entrepreneurial education ecosystems that support greater participation in employment, and social and economic values for indigenous entrepreneurs, especially for indigenous women entrepreneurs, in Australian society?

The body of research on entrepreneurship, networks and ecosystem integration is significant; not so for indigenous entrepreneurship (Roundy, 2017; Maritz & Foley, 2018). Social and economic disadvantages faced by first nation indigenous Australians are well-documented (Foley, 2017), implying entrepreneurial and ecosystem integration will be different. Key dimensions distinguish entrepreneurial networking between both cultures: family members rarely understand Aboriginal networking with non-Aboriginal people, often sabotaging networking effectiveness with non-indigenous business partners. While non-indigenous families encourage wide networking, the indigenous network predominantly within the dominant settler society. Indigenous women entrepreneurs face additional challenges: balancing family and business life, difficulties gaining access to capital, lack of information and business/management assistance, and financial discrimination (Maritz & Foley, 2018). Family bonds include not only children, but siblings and extended family. It is therefore not surprising that provision for family is a major motivator for indigenous women entrepreneurs' entry into business, with 72 per cent having dependent children (Foley, 2017). The glass ceiling leading to underdevelopment of management and financial skills is frequently experienced by women in business (Marlow & Martinez, 2017) making the scope and outcomes of studies in this field potentially relevant to all women entrepreneurs (Maritz & Foley, 2018). However, investigation of this experience where it is most acute (i.e. for indigenous women entrepreneurs), is a special case. Future research that explores the temporal dynamics of gender and entrepreneurial ecosystems would be timely.

Several research questions could be explored more specifically. First, why do some emerging indigenous entrepreneurial ecosystems fail to develop? Second, why are the processes that result in the revitalization of indigenous entrepreneurial ecosystems in decline? Third, how is gender experienced in such situations? Outcomes in this field of research would be relevant to all first nation indigenous entrepreneurs, especially for indigenous women entrepreneurs.

A starting place requires definitional research that is still being refined. For example, a recent definition of an Australian indigenous entrepreneur has been proposed by Maritz and Foley (2018: 3) using an indigenous perspective through extensive case studies pertinent to business settings in a city, or within a regional or rural-remote-based context. Indigenous entrepreneurs and Australian indigenous entrepreneurs were used in the above study interchangeably, reinforcing contextual interpretations that Australian indigenous entrepreneurs are representative of global indigenous entrepreneurs:

> The Indigenous Australian entrepreneur alters traditional patterns of behaviour, by utilizing their resources in the pursuit of self-determination and economic sustainability via their entry into self-employment, forcing social change in the pursuit of opportunity beyond the cultural norms of their initial economic resources.
>
> (p. 3)

Future research that documents Australian indigenous entrepreneurs through case studies would be welcome as these would provide practical implications and policy recommendations for promoting indigenous business creation and growth.

It is interesting to note that indigenous chambers of commerce are on the rise. Indigenous networking is growing through these chambers, promoting guidelines for integration of indigenous and non-indigenous entrepreneurs. While non-indigenous entrepreneurs see networking as informal relationships and an extension of their family, indigenous entrepreneurs see relationships as essential tools for success (Maritz & Foley, 2018). However, power imbalances operate within this context (Maritz & Foley, 2018) because indigenous entrepreneurs largely rely on non-indigenous network partners. Research that leads to outcomes focusing on the different processes of international entrepreneurship ecosystems and network building for indigenous entrepreneurs, especially indigenous women entrepreneurs, through indigenous and non-indigenous chambers of commerce would be especially timely. Entrepreneurial ecosystems as a recent framework proposed by Maritz and Foley (2018), present a context where entrepreneurial activity is likely to expand. Research into entrepreneurial ecosystems has the advantage of suggesting pathways for combining social, political, economic and cultural elements within regions supporting development and growth of innovative start-ups, encouraging nascent entrepreneurs and others to take the risks inherent to starting, funding, and assisting high-risk ventures (Stam & Spigel, 2017). Research that investigates how to promote Australian indigenous entrepreneurs, using methodologies such as case studies examining indigenous chambers of commerce and how these might drive integration of indigenous and non-indigenous business networks, is likely to be welcomed by policymakers and entrepreneurs, thereby contributing to creating and revitalizing indigenous entrepreneurial ecosystems.

Foley (2017) emphasizes the limitations of the social, human and financial capital of Australian indigenous entrepreneurs, highlighting that their experiences are markedly different to those of non-indigenous entrepreneurs. Australian indigenous entrepreneurs experience significantly lower life expectancies, due to poorer overall health, often characterized by medical conditions of a chronic nature, consistent with global indigenous communities (Denny-Smith & Loosemoore, 2017; Colbourne, 2018). While scholars of indigenous entrepreneurship research highlight an incongruence of economic and social justification (Bodle et al., 2018; Maritz & Foley, 2018; Foley, 2017), few identify specific mechanisms and initiatives to enhance entrepreneurship education. A recent commentary in the Australian popular press by Pascoe, a well-known indigenous author who published a book on the history of the white invasion of Australia, *Dark Emu*, first published in 2014 and now in its 28th printing, is about to be included nationally in schools as part of the curriculum on Australian history (Guilliatt, 2019). This non-academic research and commentary in the popular press of historical accounts remarks on the earlier entrepreneurial activity of Australian indigenous entrepreneurs who "cultivated crops, built large villages and devised sophisticated dams and aquaculture systems" that signal a "sweeping revisionist view, one that still gets some eminent professor very hot under the collar. But it has captured the public imagination!" (Guilliatt, 2019, p. 1).

In summary, current research into Australian indigenous entrepreneurs (Bodle et al., 2018; Maritz & Foley, 2018; Foley, 2017) suggests that these individuals continue to commence business with poorer entrepreneurial ecosystems than non-indigenous entrepreneurs, with notably less business expertise (social capital), lower education qualifications (human capital), lower capital resources (financial capital), restricted access to finance, nominal to no access to working capital resources, and little to no real property for bank security, little financial wealth, and nominally established commercial networks. These factors combine to severely retard indigenous entrepreneurship, in particular in the case of indigenous female entrepreneurs.

By contrast, research suggests that non-indigenous Australian entrepreneurs enjoy better social positioning in all facets of networking, enjoying much more positive business positioning. Non-indigenous people also do not suffer the debilitating impact of racism, which is by far the greatest hindrance to commercial activity and personal well-being experienced by most indigenous entrepreneurs. Foley (2017) provides implications regarding pedagogy and learning for Australian indigenous entrepreneurs and for academically advancing this research stream in international entrepreneurship. Colbourne (2018) identifies significant opportunities for Australian indigenous entrepreneurs to build a vibrant indigenous economy that supports sustainable economic development and well-being. Research that seeks to build on this stream by linking factors that drive development and growth in indigenous entrepreneurial ecosystems through a specific framework that integrates indigenous entrepreneurship ecosystems and targets Australian indigenous entrepreneurs, particularly indigenous female entrepreneurs, is likely to offer significant advances in the field of indigenous entrepreneurship specifically, and indigenous international entrepreneurship in general.

It is important to build awareness in research that entrepreneurial activity does not happen in a vacuum; it occurs within families and households (Carter et al., 2017) and where team-led ventures are commonplace (Marlow & Martinez, 2017). Even sole proprietors cannot create and operate ventures alone (Maritz & Foley, 2018). Research addressing context-bound activities ensuring the 'voices' of female and male Australian indigenous entrepreneurs, is a next step forward to better social inclusion and cultural tolerance with supporting policy direction underpinned by research into appropriate program development in terms of entrepreneurial networking and financial training. In order to address 'contextualization' by, for and about Aboriginal people, adoption of the recent indigenous entrepreneurship ecosystem education framework (Maritz & Foley, 2018) helps to ensure appropriate interviewee selection, process and analysis that "consists of justification, legitimization, validation, dynamic dimension integration, geographic, qualified scholars, flexibility, adaptability, and contemporary approaches" (Maritz & Foley, 2018: 7) as well as adding appropriate methodological schemes to this research stream.

Recent estimates of Australian indigenous unemployment indicate a figure of 46 per cent (KPMG, 2016). Stimulating growth and accomplishment of indigenous businesses, not only creates employment and economic growth but also brings other social benefits (Foley, 2017) as planned outcomes. The Women in Global Business Survey (Australian International Business Survey, 2016) reports Australian Women Entrepreneurs are finding it harder than men to access networks and capital to create successful businesses. Lack of access to networks diminishes access to financial as well as information resources. Policy initiatives that promote workshops and activities involving chambers of commerce and other indigenous institutions, will empower indigenous men and women, especially the latter, encouraging enhanced entrepreneurial leadership roles.

The concept of entrepreneurial ecosystems has emerged in recent years as a framework to understand the nature of places in which entrepreneurial activity flourishes. The idea of entrepreneurial ecosystems is a recent framework; we still do not know how various elements in entrepreneurial ecosystems enhance entrepreneurship (Roundy, 2017; Stam & Spigel, 2017; Audretsch, Mason, Miles & O'Connor, 2018). Moreover, within that structure, discourse around indigenous entrepreneurship, and women and gender is silent. There is also an underlying problem in viewing women entrepreneurs (either as a separate category or individuals) as typical gendered research subjects, as this view may contribute to an imagined construct of the female entrepreneur (Marlow & Martinez, 2017). Attempts to examine motivations, activities and outcomes of female entrepreneurs, separate from the relationships and institutions within which they participate and enact gender (Marlow & Martinez, 2017), limit the scope of such investigations. Why is context so important to indigenous entrepreneurs, women and gender discourse?

Future studies that wish to address the above problem could begin by exploring the following question: How can the above-mentioned interactions be mapped and analysed within the context of women and gender? Certain approaches in the discipline adopt a 'pipelines' perspective (Audretsch et al., 2018), investigating the extent, role and significance of the external networks of entrepreneurial ecosystems. Specifically, we highlight the complete absence of research examining indigenous women and gender in entrepreneurial ecosystem research. Entrepreneurial ecosystem studies integrating women and gender and the network tipping points, critical densities and vitality that assist to explain complex system behaviour would be valuable (Marlow & Martinez, 2017). Currently, the link to indigenous research is missing from entrepreneurship in general and, in particular, from international entrepreneurship (Maritz & Foley, 2018; Foley, 2017).

Conclusion

Australia is a remarkable location for examining not only business creation and growth, given its long history of trade, but also the equally long history of immigration, providing an exceptional and unique context to observe the immigrant ethnic entrepreneur and the activities around government immigration policy, industry development and cultural, social and economic inclusion. Nearly a third of all Australian inhabitants were born overseas (*The Economist*, 2018b). However, the pattern of immigration to Australia has changed significantly, from its original British 'invasion' in the late 1770s and subsequent settlement in the 1840s, to the European immigrant waves resulting from the first and second World Wars, mostly consisting of Italian and Greek immigrants as well as many others fleeing persecution in Europe at the time. These waves then gave way to Asian immigrants in the early 1970s, first from Vietnam and then in the late 1990s, from other Asian cultures, with Middle Eastern and African immigrants now more prevalent. The change from unskilled immigrants from Europe, Asia, Middle East and Africa in the early 2000s, to highly skilled, young immigrants in the last decade, has presented the Australian government and society with unique and numerous challenges. Entrepreneurship has always been a very large part of the immigrant experience in Australia, initially with unskilled labourers after the two World Wars seeking a new way of life to escape serfdom and realize land ownership and economic independence through the creation of their own businesses. The end of the official White Australia policy in the early 1970s with the humanitarian immigration of many Vietnamese and then the move to greater immigration through the skilled visa category in the early 2000s, have seen the rapid expansion of professional services, tourism, hospitality, education and the arts. The last census in 2018 demonstrated the changing nature of Australian culture, with Chinese and Indians representing the largest cultural race in Australia. Immigrant ethnic entrepreneurship linking country of origin and ethnic diaspora continues to play a significant role in the shape and location of Australian business development, growth and activity. Increasingly, indigenous Australian entrepreneurs and female entrepreneurs, including indigenous, non-indigenous and ethnic entrepreneurs, are finding a 'voice'. Their contribution to entrepreneurial activity takes on an added dimension of self-determination in contemporary Australian society.

References

Andreoni, H. (2003) Olive or white? The colour of Italians in Australia. *Journal of Australian Studies*, 27(77): 81–92.

Audretsch, D., Mason, C., Miles, M. P. & O'Connor, A. (2018) The dynamics of entrepreneurial ecosystems. *Entrepreneurship & Regional Development*, 30(3–4): 471–474.

Australian International Business Survey (AIBS) (2016) Australian International Business Survey 2016, www.austrade.gov.au/Australian/How-Austrade-can-help/Trade-services/women-in-export

Australian social trends, cat no. 4102.0 2008, ABS, Canberra.

Australian social trends, cat no. 4102.0 Australian Bureau of Statistics 2007, ABS, Canberra.

Baldassar, L. & Pesman, R. (2005) *From Paesani to Global Italians: Veneto Migrants in Australia* (1st edn). Crawley: University of Western Australia Press.

Battiston, S. & Mascitelli, B. (2007) Migration, ethnic concentration and international trade growth: The case of Italians in Australia. (Report). *People and Place*, 15(4): 2–11.

Bodle, K., Brimble, M., Weaven, S. K. A., Frazer, L. & Blue, L. (2018) Critical success factors in managing sustainable indigenous businesses in Australia. *Pacific Accounting Review*, 30: 35–51.

Borooah, V. K. & Mangan, J. (2007) Living here, born there: The economic life of Australia's immigrants., *European Journal of Political Economy*, 23(2): 486–511.

Burnley, I. H. (2005) Generations, mobility and community: Geographies of three generations of Greek and Italian Ancestry in Sydney. *Geographical Research*, 43(4): 379–392.

Carter, S., Kuhl, A. & Marlow, S., et al. (2017) Households as a site of entrepreneurial activity. *Foundations and Trends in Entrepreneurship*, 13: 81–190.

Cecilia, T. (1987) *We Didn't Arrive Yesterday*. Victoria: The Sunnyland Press.

Closing the Gap (2015) Prime Minister's Report. Australian Government, Canberra.

Colbourne, R. (2018) Indigenous entrepreneurship and hybrid ventures. *Advances in Entrepreneurship, Firm Emergence and Growth*, 19: 93–149.

Collins, J. (2003) Cultural diversity and entrepreneurship: Policy responses to immigrant entrepreneurs in Australia. *Entrepreneurship & Regional Development*, 15: 137–149.

Collins, J., Gibson, K., Alcorso, C., Castles, S. & Tait, D. (1995) *A Shop Full of Dreams: Ethnic Small Business in Australia*, Pluto Press Australia, Leichhardt, NSW.

Cresciani, G 2003, *The Italians in Australia*. Cambridge: Cambridge University Press,.

Denny-Smith, G. & Loosemoore, D. (2017) Integrating indigenous enterprises into the Australian construction industry. *Engineering, Construction and Architectural Management*, 23(4): 428–447.

DFAT (Department of Foreign Affairs) (2018) 2017 Foreign Policy White Paper, "Opportunity Security Strength", Australian Government, Published in November 2018, pp. 1–122. ISBN: 978-1-74322-411-3.

Evans, M. D. R. (1989) Immigrant entrepreneurship: Effects of ethnic market size and isolated labor pool. *American Sociological Review*, 54(6): 950–962.

Foley, D. (2008) Does culture and social capital impact on the networking attributes of indigenous entrepreneurs? *Journal of Enterprising Communities: People and Places in the Global Economy*, 2(3): 204–224.

Foley, D. (2017). The dark side of responsible business management, in A. K. Verbos, E. Henry & A. M. Peredo (eds), *Indigenous Aspirations and Rights: The Case for Responsible Business and Management*, Auckland: Greenleaf Publishing, pp. 22–33.

Guilliatt, R. (2019) Turning history on its head. *The Weekend Australian Magazine*, May 25, p. 1.

Jordan, K., Krivokapic-Skoko, B. & Collins, J. (2009) The ethnic landscape of rural Australia: Non-Anglo-Celtic immigrant communities and the built environment. *Journal of Rural Studies*, 25(4): 376–385.

KPMG. (2016) *Collaborative Ideas for Igniting the Indigenous Economy*. Sydney: KPMG, October.

Lampugnani, R. (1993) The impact of South Australian Italians on the economy: Italian businesses, in D. O'Connor & A. Comin (eds), *The Impact of Italians in South Australia*, Adelaide: Flinders University of South Australia, pp. 15–32.

Lampugnani, R. & Holton, R. (1989) *Sociological Profile of the Italian Business Profile*, Ethnic Business in South Australia, Centre of Multicultural Studies, Adelaide: Flinders University of South Australia.

Low, A (2008) Economic outcomes of female immigrant entrepreneurship. *International Journal of Entrepreneurship and Small Business*, 5(3–4): 224–240.

Maritz, A. & Foley, D. (2018) Expanding Australian indigenous entrepreneurship education ecosystems. *Administrative Sciences*, 8(20): 1–20.

Marlow, S. & Martinez, A. (2017) Annual review article: Is it time to rethink the gender agenda in entrepreneurship research? *International Small Business Journal: Researching Entrepreneurship*: 1–20. DOI: 10.1177/0266242617738321

Mascitelli, B & Battiston, S 2008, *The Italian expatriate vote in Australia: democratic right, democratic wrong or political opportunism?* (1st edn). Ballan, Australia: Connor Court Publishing.

Roundy, P. P. (2017) Social entrepreneurship and entrepreneurial ecosystems: Complementary or disjoint phenomena? *International Journal of Social Economics*, 44: 1252–67.

Sequeira, J. & Rasheed, A. (2006) Start-up and growth of immigrant small businesses: The impact of social and human capital. *Journal of Developmental Entrepreneurship*, 11(4): 357–375.

Smans, M. (2006) It's all buono mate! Perceptions of third-generation Italian-Australians by a peer-related cohort of non-Italian background informants in South Australia: Mapping trends in the interaction, cultural maintenance and stereotyping of third-generation Italian-Australians in South Australia. Department of Language (Italian Section), Bachelor of Arts (Honours) thesis, The Flinders University of South Australia.

Smans, M. (2012) The internationalisation of immigrant ethnic entrepreneurs, PhD thesis, Business School, Faculty of the Professions, The University of Adelaide, Adelaide, Australia.

Stam, E. & Spigel, B. (2017) Entrepreneurial ecosystems, in R. Blackburn, D. De Clercq, J. Heinonen & Z. Wang (eds), *Handbook for Entrepreneurship and Small Business*, London: Sage.

The Economist (2018a) Aussie rules: The stellar performance of the Australian economy holds encouraging lessons for the rest of the world, October 27, p. 11.

The Economist (2018b) Immigration: Not huddled, but masses in Special Report Australia, *The wonder down under: Can Australia's boom last?* October 27, pp: 8–10.

The Weekend Australian (2018) Growing pains hit home in an age-old dilemma. *The Inquirer*, April 14–15, p. 17.

Wood, G, & Davidson, M. (2011) A review of male and female Australian indigenous entrepreneurs: Disadvantaged past – promising future? *Gender in Management: An International Journal*, 26(4): 311–326.

7 Internationalization of Chinese entrepreneurship

Introduction

The internationalization of Chinese entrepreneurship can be seen as a very complex and dynamic phenomenon with a relatively long history. In the seventeenth century, ethnic Chinese merchants established themselves in the colonial port cities of Batavia (Jakarta), Penang, Singapore and Malacca to act as the bridge-heads for Chinese migrants looking for work and opportunities outside China (Pan, 1998: 54–57). In the nineteenth and early twentieth centuries, these merchants began to establish a business system covering vast areas of coastal China, Hong Kong and major ports in the Southeast Asian region (Yen, 2013) as well as other Asian (e.g. Japan and Korea) and Western (e.g. Australia, Canada, Europe and the US) countries. With the influence of Confucian values and clannish organizations, the merchants were able to develop effective business networks in the region. Given the poor economic background of earlier generations of immigrants, survival-driven behaviours such as hard work, flexibility and adaptability, self-sacrifice and risk-taking, the merchants were able to adapt to the new political and economic environments and successfully develop their business systems. One of the key factors was their ability to continue the process of reform and modernization of ethnic Chinese business practices by bringing up new generations with bilingual capabilities and cross-cultural understanding. Later generations of ethnic Chinese who were born, worked and lived overseas had received both Chinese and Western educations, and had been constantly trying to mould their value systems into a hybrid and possibly superior structure (Yen, 2013). The first part of this chapter will focus on an elaboration of the earlier years of ethnic Chinese entrepreneurs as the first generation, as well as their children and grandchildren as the second and third generations, conducting their business activities overseas, predominately in the Southeast Asian region. By doing so, the unique value system, personal and organizational characteristics, social and business networks of these entrepreneurs, and their unique patterns of entrepreneurship can be identified and illustrated.

The recent wave of Chinese entrepreneurs emigrating from mainland China overseas has been influenced by the Chinese government's open door policy and economic reform. Since 1980, new policy initiatives have enabled Chinese citizens to run privately-owned businesses (Zhu et al., 2010) and this has led to the emergence of a new class of entrepreneurs running their own businesses in China and overseas. Many newly developed business owners seek expansion into overseas markets by diversifying their business operations and maximizing market share internationally. At the same time, they also look for better living conditions and education opportunities for their children. Immigrating to other developed economies, such as Australia, Canada, EU, Japan, New Zealand, Singapore and the US, not only enhances business expansion into developed markets, but also offers better education to the younger generation. The new wave of Chinese immigration has not only occurred in developed economies, but also in developing economies, such as in Africa, Southeast Asia, Middle East and South America (Zhou, 2017). There are different reasons for people choosing to emigrate to these developing countries, but fundamentally the motives are rooted in economic and social ties with these countries. For instance, many choose African countries due to previous work experience in those countries under government funded aid projects. After the completion of these projects, some stayed on to develop their own businesses by using the established social and business networks (Shen, 2017). Others choose Southeast Asian countries for business migration mainly due to the existing social networks with family and friends operating businesses in those countries. By engaging with these networks, entrepreneurs expect to expand their domestic business in China into international markets (Dai, 2017; Chin, 2017).

These new business entrepreneurs have a better educational background and enjoy better economic conditions compared with early generations of ethnic Chinese immigrants moving to Southeast Asian regions and other Western countries in earlier years as indicated above. These entrepreneurs may represent different patterns and systems of ethnic Chinese business with some unique characteristics in comparison with earlier generations of business immigrants. The focus of the second part of this chapter will focus on these particular entrepreneurs with the intention of contrasting and comparing the different generations of ethnic Chinese entrepreneurs operating businesses outside China.

The third focus of this chapter is the recent wave of ethnic Chinese entrepreneur business activities returning from overseas to China. Given the rapid economic development over four decades, China has become the second largest economy globally with an increasingly larger middle class and market size. By seizing business opportunities in such a large market, many successful ethnic Chinese operating overseas through business activities or professional development such as university education, obtain advanced managerial skills, knowhow and financial capabilities, using these advantages back in China. From small start-ups with innovative ideas and advanced technology, to medium and large trading companies, R&D centres and manufacturing facilities, a variety of business operations have been established by Chinese 'overseas returnees' referred to as *haigui*. These entrepreneurs may have similar but different characteristics compared with the other two groups mentioned above. Therefore, the third part of this chapter will focus on an analysis of this unique group of entrepreneurs with regard to their business development, characterized by the so-called 'returning home' phenomenon.

Earlier generations of ethnic Chinese entrepreneurs

Earlier generations of ethnic Chinese entrepreneurs operating businesses outside China were predominately *nanyang huaqiao*, that is, overseas Chinese settled in Southeast Asia, following the significant number of ethnic Chinese immigrants (mainly from the southern part of China) who moved to Southeast Asian from the early seventeenth century to late nineteenth century (Dahles, 2017; Yen, 2013). From a historical perspective, the overall norms and institutions associated with Chinese communities in general, and business communities in particular, are presumed to condition the development of individual family-based enterprises as well as the broader structures of Chinese business networks (Folk & Jomo, 2003). Apart from the fact that ethnic Chinese communities adopted a great many Confucian values and practices, ethnic Chinese are distinctly different from the indigenous communities in Southeast Asia and from the European communities in the West and in Australia (Yen, 2013). An immigrant mentality and harsh overseas environments drove many to become involved in business, and it was business that offered them quick progress in upward social mobility (Yen, 1986). At the same time, the European colonial administrations treated *nanyang huaqiao* as second class citizens, using bureaucratic measures to block opportunities to climb the social ladder. These two factors combined to account for the predominant position of ethnic Chinese in business when they emigrated overseas countries during the earlier years. In fact, both cultural (Redding, 1990) and institutional (Whitley, 1992) factors worked in parallel, influencing the survival of early generations of ethnic Chinese immigrants operating businesses in their new land.

Two systems existed side-by-side in Chinese immigration to Southeast Asia and other parts of the world: (1) kinship-based immigration, and (2) the credit-ticket system (Yen, 2013). The former was based on traditional kinship ties, while the latter operated on a system of credit. In order to maintain family businesses in the new environment, successful Chinese entrepreneurs needed to find honest and trustworthy staff. The simplest way was to recruit their relatives or kinsmen from their home villages in China. Generally speaking, the owners paid for their relatives' or kinsmen's passages and provided them with food and lodgings in the new countries in return for hard work in the owners' business sites as apprentices and assistants. After several years accumulating business experience and money, the former new arrivals could run their own businesses. Further expansion of their businesses led to the recruitment of more relatives or kinsmen from China. Hence, the trend of immigration based on kinship was developed and became one of the most important patterns characterizing the earlier years of ethnic Chinese immigration (Yen, 2013).

The credit-ticket system involved much wider social and economic networks. Given the poor economic conditions, many Chinese immigrants could not afford to pay their passage overseas. Their passage money was advanced by labour brokers, captains of junks or labour agencies. After arriving at overseas ports, the credit-ticket immigrants were made available to employers who needed labourers. The employers paid the passage money owed by the immigrants in exchange for a verbal or written contract for the repayment of the debts in the form of labour. After working for a fixed period of time, the credit-ticket immigrants were freed from their obligations and were able to move around seeking new employment opportunities. This practice was another common method for bringing a major portion of the ethnic Chinese immigrants to overseas countries, predominately to the Southeast Asian region, during the nineteenth century (Yen, 2013).

In the nineteenth century, the new Chinese immigrants formed groups based on dialect association, clan organization and secret societies in order to develop mutual support social groups (Skinner, 1957; Yen, 1986). The overseas Chinese business communities also formed business guilds in the major ports and cities based on strong regional and kinship affiliations. This trend was mainly a response to religious and economic needs in the new countries, and extended to a variety of businesses such as import-export companies, grocery stores, clothing, tea, restaurants, among others (Hua, 1977). Hence, economic interests and mutual aid were the principal functions of the ethnic Chinese business guilds. The desire to minimize competition and maximize profit brought together a group of far-sighted business leaders who founded the guilds, and the desire was incorporated into the guilds' rules and regulations through negotiation among members (Fewsmith, 1983). Business guild members shared common needs such as mutual aid for business survival. The guilds were also used as a platform to settle internal disputes among members as well as a network for introducing new business opportunities and contacts.

Given the weak formal institutions and the vulnerability of Chinese communities operating in an environment with politically sanctioned suspicion and hostility, informal institutions among Chinese entrepreneurs and local people based on trust and reciprocity played an important role in reducing transaction costs and social risk over time. Due to the uncertain business environment in the early years, Chinese entrepreneurs could only hope to make money quickly with short-term goals and expectations of returning to China with money, rather than with long-term commitments and more productive investment in the local economy. Particularly during the transition period from colonial order to post-colonial regimes, Chinese businesses were disrupted with increasing unpredictability, resulting in a rising anxiety and mistrust between the businesses and the local political elites (Bardsley, 2003). In order to survive, Chinese business communities helped organize the distribution of credit and facilitated a social network that linked and supported individual entrepreneurs within the context of a weak formal market mechanism and political institutions.

With political consolidation under strong interventionist states in many Southeast Asian countries, certain Chinese businesses, particularly large enterprises, found it advantageous to strategically cultivate rent-generating political connections as a basis for business expansion and diversification (Bardsley, 2003). In addition, in terms of management style, many Chinese entrepreneurs had tended to incorporate Western-style corporate forms and norms as well as impersonal management practices which were rooted in Chinese family business traditions, such as the paternalist management style. With the support of government policies which were more favourably disposed towards business development, Chinese entrepreneurs were spurred to reinvent existing networks as flexible production systems within competitive industries. By doing so, the Chinese business communities in general and individual Chinese entrepreneurs in particular, could accommodate the still-prevalent personalistic social relations in Southeast Asia with the strictures and opportunities presented by the new economic globalism (Folk & Jomo, 2003).

The type of business predominating among ethnic Chinese entrepreneurs was the small scale family owned company with a number of characteristics: (1) subcontracted arrangements with large firms which allowed small business entrepreneurs to link their businesses to national development and larger scale business activities; (2) social networks and *guanxi* which allowed small business entrepreneurs to interact with other small and larger businesses as well as political elites, certain interactions being market/opportunity driven and relatively impersonal; (3) traditional family business management practices, such as paternalism and patriarchal power, together with a low level of capitalization which may have jeopardized long-term development of small ethnic Chinese family businesses; and (4) mobile small business entrepreneurs who could easily leave a particular country if the politics of ethnicity and labour markets were not favourable (Nonini, 2003).

On the other hand, the business expansion of larger ethnic Chinese family business conglomerates was based on the cultivation of links and partnerships with key political elites (Rivera, 2003). Challenges emerged from time to time, such as inter-generational succession, increasing dependence on the skills of professional managers, the relative diffusion of political power, and the necessity of adapting to a more competitive regional and global business environment (Rivera, 2003). Given the dramatic changes after the 1997/1998 Asian financial crisis, the political economy gradually shifted towards a more 'liberal' and 'democratic' oriented direction in many Southeast Asian countries. Their sociopolitical system also gradually transformed from the 'bureaucratic polity' towards a more pluralistic one with a broadly based 'liberalization coalition' and many large Chinese family business owners emerging as part of such a coalition (Niyomsilpa, 2003).

As for individual ethnic Chinese entrepreneurs, Yen (2013: 189) defines these as a people who bring capital, labour and management together, and create an enterprise with a capitalist attitude – the love of money and pursuit of profit, courage to take initiatives and risks, and the determination to implement new ideas, as well as a strong will to succeed. An ethnic Chinese entrepreneur also possesses foresight, business acumen and imagination that can contribute to the success of an enterprise with the quality of innovation and leadership; thus this entrepreneur is not just a creator, but also a perpetuator of an enterprise.

Ethnic Chinese entrepreneurship could be defined as a new type of modern Chinese entrepreneurship which has a strong Chinese cultural input as well as interaction and integration with Western business practices (Yen, 2013). The blending of Chinese and Western values and business practices progressed to a higher level in the second and third generations of ethnic Chinese entrepreneurs given their experience of studying in the West that provided a better chance to maintain and expand their business operations. Returning from the West with knowledge and experience also enhanced their business practices by combining Chinese and Western ways of conducting modern business successfully. An important outcome seen in Southeast Asia, with the exception of Singapore, is that although ethnic Chinese are numerical and political minorities, they hold a dominant position in the economic sphere (Yeung, 2004: 13). The economic success of ethnic Chinese entrepreneurs can be seen in the on-going effort of both older and younger generations who may have similar but different ways of undertaking their entrepreneurial activities.

Compared with older generation ethnic Chinese entrepreneurs operating in Southeast Asia as illustrated earlier, the younger generations of ethnic Chinese entrepreneurs, namely, second and third generations, are considered to have similar as well as different characteristics of entrepreneurial style and ways of conducting business operations. The common characteristics, such as a hard-working spirit, networking arrangements and respect for authority, have been deemed to have played an important role in this regard (Redding, 1990; Weidenbaum & Hughes, 1996). However, the 'older' styles of ethnic Chinese business conducted no longer hold. Education brings new ideas and "younger generations do things according to business studies, contracts and the law" (Koning & Verver, 2013: 337). A number of cases reveal that notions of seniority, family loyalty, saving, hierarchy and informality are questioned (ibid). In general, the younger generations make it clear that they do not need or want the safety of the family anymore and prefer more independent inter-actions with the local market and society. However, interestingly enough in most cases the family (parents and children) provides start-up capital or resources while the importance of the family or ethnic network is expressed in terms of knowledge and advice (wealth of business expertise) and (trust-worthy) information on business opportunities within the Chinese business community circle (ibid).

Another remarkable difference in conducting business among the younger generations of ethnic Chinese entrepreneurs is breaking intra-ethnic business networks but embracing the inter-ethnic business networks (Gomez, 2007). In other words, younger people would like to do business and develop new ven-tures with other nationalities, rather than only within the ethnic Chinese groups as was normally done by the first generation. Working with business partners who have a similar class background is more important than having a similar ethnic background. Inter-ethnic partnerships are usually people with 'class resources' (Light & Gold, 2000); that is, people who are well-educated and have financial means. As Gomez (2007: 172) argued, the importance of ethnic identity claimed by transnational theory is only valid at the point of migration. Immigrants feel that ethnic identity is helpful for fitting into the new environment and searching for new business opportunities. However, when these immigrants settle and become used to the new environment, ethnicity is no longer an important business tool. Guercini et al. (2017: 269–270) claimed that new immigrant entrepreneurs faced with the uncertainties associated with internationalization, can rely on their social networks, which are predominately linked with family and friends, to acquire information and reliable partners. However, business ties may replace social ties in consolidating insidership in new business settings and in the discovery, evaluation and exploitation of new opportunities. Business networks have no boundaries and the basis is economic, rather than sociological. Therefore, when immigrant entrepreneurs overcome the early stage of 'foreignness', they can build wider business networks mainly outside their own ethnic circle for business expansion. The same situation can be seen among the second and third generations of ethnic Chinese entrepreneurs, who are more outward looking and embrace business opportunities beyond the ethnic Chinese boundary. In fact, many of them have mainly developed inter-ethnic business networks and partnerships, and have emerged into the mainstream business networks in their business operating environment (Gomez, 2007).

Another interesting phenomenon is that younger generations of ethnic Chinese entrepreneurs were born overseas, not on mainland China. Therefore, their connection with China is less significant compared with the first generation of Chinese immigrants (Dahles, 2017). Indeed, the younger entrepreneurs have hardly had any connections to mainland China based on relatives or legacies that they can exploit. Although they recognize that China's economic growth offers market opportunities for the local economy, these younger entrepreneurs do not reveal any personal relatedness with these developments (Tejapira, 2009: 276). Appreciation of China's growing influence and the subsequent revaluation of Chinese language and culture have been noted (Vatikiotis, 1998: 226–227). For the younger generation, stressing local national identity has seemed more compelling than dwelling on relations with China or ethnic Chinese identity. Although Chinese cultural events are celebrated and seen as important, it is expected that this trend will disappear with the coming generations. There is a strong tendency among the younger generations to emphasize that ethnic Chinese are highly integrated into the local societies (Koning & Verver, 2013).

These trends lead us to consider the important impact of current economic globalization on the younger generation of entrepreneurs not only in terms of the second and third generations of ethnic Chinese born overseas, but also the new generation of Chinese business immigrants who left China in recent years and are now working and living outside China in order to expand their business activities.

New wave of business immigration of ethnic Chinese entrepreneurs operating overseas

As discussed above, the new wave of business immigration by ethnic Chinese entrepreneurs represents a new process of internationalization of entrepreneurship with similar as well as different characteristics and patterns of conducting entrepreneurial activities compared with those of older generations. Most of these entrepreneurs belong to emerging new rich and upper middle classes benefiting from the economic reform and 'open door' policy in China since the 1978. As Zhou (2017: xi) defined, post-1978 Chinese immigrants, commonly referred to as new Chinese immigrants or *xi yimin*, are now spreading to every corner of the globe and developing diasporic communities wherever they set foot. The total number of immigrants from mainland China has exceeded 8 million since 1978 (Wang & Zhuang, 2011) with little sign of slowing down.

According to a report by the Chinese Academy of Sciences entitled "Global Politics and Security", China is fast becoming the largest supplier of immigrants to many other countries, with a third big wave of immigration since the implementation of the Chinese Open Door Policy in 1978. Both macrostructural factors and individual reasons have generated the new wave of Chinese immigrants seeking more 'liveable' societies. Macro factors include: (1) the open door policy and economic reforms which encouraged foreign investment in China, overseas Chinese diaspora being a part of this trend, helping to restore transnational family ties and rebuild migration networks (Portes & Zhou, 2012); (2) removal by the Chinese government of barriers to emigration, easing requirements to obtain passports and allowing citizens with overseas sponsors to emigrate; (3) academic exchanges and overseas study undertaken by scholars and students, many of them remaining overseas after the completion of study; and (4) increasingly visible state and private capital investments overseas and business investment migrant status granted to investors (Zhou, 2017). With regard to individual reasons, many new rich and upper middle class citizens want to live in a country that enables them to have a better life-style. These immigrants are known as 'life-style migrants' (Spoonley et al., 2009) and they immigrate in order to secure wealth with the protection of more mature legal systems, benefit from a better education system, and enjoy social benefits, cleaner air, and greater food safety, as well as enjoy convenience when travelling to other countries (Liu, 2017). In particular, in contrast to the situation of the late 1970s, most new Chinese immigrants have become financially successful and socially established in recent years (Modern Express, 2010).

The aforesaid changed situation is confirmed by a report indicating that 60 percent of Chinese 'high net worth individuals' (HNWIs) – entrepreneurs who have investable assets greater than US$1.5 million – have considered or have undertaken investment immigration (Bain.com, 2011). Australia is one of the most popular destinations for Chinese migrants, with Australian Government figures showing that about 40 to 60 percent of immigrants to Australia each year originate from China, and more than 70 percent are business immigrants (Deng, 2012).

The motives for immigrating overseas, in particular to Western English-speaking countries, such as Australia, Canada, New Zealand and the US, include taking the opportunity to access a better English education system and life-style for children and the entire family. Various factors have been taken into consideration when a business immigrant finally makes a decision to start a business in a new environment. While some consider the amount invested, others count on the benefits and advantages of utilizing their business skills, experiences and resources obtained in China to help them run businesses in a foreign country (Deng, 2012). However, some people have been unable to make such beneficial connections when starting businesses in a new foreign market. In many cases, due to the different business environment and language barrier in the foreign country, the business experience and skills obtained in China could not be immediately transferred into the new reality.

Language is a major challenge for business immigrants. Although English language proficiency is not required for business immigrants in many countries, most people have found English language abilities to be very important in running their business smoothly. Those with limited English skills are also limited in the scope of businesses they feel able to choose. Takeaway restaurants and convenience stores that require limited English skills have thus become popular among these immigrants.

Despite these challenges, most business immigrants who have gone through both stages (i.e. building business in home country and then leaving for overseas to build a new one) of the process have found the experience to be a difficult journey, but a worthwhile one with no regrets about the immigration decision. People have highlighted a number of benefits, such as gaining different experiences, having another chance in life in a place of fair play, improving management skills and English capacity, and enjoying an improved life-style (Deng, 2012).

Most Chinese business immigrants rely on the local Chinese community to hunt for business opportunities. The business resources are introduced by migration agents, business brokers, friends, or friends of friends. Hundreds of small businesses are advertised as being for sale weekly in Chinese local community newspapers. Nevertheless, most of these businesses on the market are limited to milk bars, convenience stores, takeaway foods and other small retail outlets previously owned by older generation Asian and European immigrants. A small portion of businesses are also recycled among previous business immigrants (Deng, 2012).

On the one hand, new immigrants can be overwhelmed by biased business information and sometimes endure unpleasant experiences. On the other hand, there is a lack of investment access for Chinese business immigrants with regard to genuine local businesses in advanced technology, innovative manufacturing or other industries that may have more potential to bring a long-term business investment return. Hence, there is an urgent need to build such business investment and cooperative bridges between local business communities and Chinese business immigrants. It is important for Chinese business people to gain business knowledge by working with local business people in order to better apply their skills and experiences in a foreign environment. It is also essential for local businesses to access the China market through Chinese business immigrants (Deng, 2012).

In the case of new business immigrants to European countries, other phenomena also need to be addressed here. For example, immigrants from Wenzhou region in Zhejiang province of east China have developed their garment and textile industries in Prato, Italy, for many years (Guercini et al., 2017). In the beginning, the immigrant entrepreneurs, faced with the uncertainties associated with internationalization, could only rely on their own social networks to acquire information and find reliable partners with whom to conduct their business (Lin et al., 2016; Xie & Amine, 2009). However, when they gradually developed other business ties based on the initial social ties, the business ties based on intra-ethnic networks replaced the initial social ties in consolidating new business opportunities (Guercini et al., 2017). New business immigrants also confront on-going challenges, in particular related to understanding and following local institutional rules and cultural norms; language barriers are an important factor for deep engagement with local communities. The challenges faced by business immigrants are common to many other European countries, such as Czech Republic (Horalek et al., 2017) and Spain (Li, 2017).

New business immigrants to other developing countries, such as African and Southeast Asian countries, may have different reasons and motivations, and may experience different barriers and challenges compared with new immigrants to the developed economies discussed earlier. For example, many Chinese who initially went to Africa were part of large public construction projects under the Chinese government aid initiatives. After the projects were completed, some Chinese stayed on and used their relationships with locals to open wholesale or retail shops, or to establish factories in countries such as Zimbabwe (Shen, 2017). These Chinese could be seen as the first generation of new Chinese immigrants. Once their businesses developed, these immigrants invited their families, relatives and friends to join them and run new businesses together. The new Chinese community developed, albeit in a slow and gradual manner. Shen (2017: 82) indicates three types of immigrant in these contexts: (1) owners of small and medium-sized enterprises who invest in manufacturing; (2) private business people engaged in catering, recreation, tourism, and wholesale and retail trading; and (3) Chinese employees hired by the former Chinese SOEs, who stayed on after completing their initial contracts. Given their business background and income level, the new business immigrants choose these relatively expensive locations as their residential and business location for developing new business ties and markets for their products. By supporting newly established Chinese business associations, information of business opportunities is shared among the members, and new business ties among themselves as well as with other mainstream business networks can also be established (Shen, 2017). However, some common problems also exist such as the language barrier, self-isolation and not actively engaging in local politics, thus presenting challenges for business development and wellbeing as residents living in Africa.

There are many well-established Chinese business communities in Southeast Asia. In recent years, there have been new waves of new business immigrants coming from mainland China to Southeast Asia for new business opportunities. Many of these immigrants had developed trade ties and others were engaged in relocating labour-intensive manufacturing factories from China to some Southeast Asian countries where labour costs were lower than in China. Private mining companies were also becoming interested in exploring new gold mines in the region. As Chin (2017: 187) pointed out, the new Chinese business community is vastly different from the old one in Cambodia with a mixed new business immigration from mainland China, Hong Kong, Macau and Taiwan. After political turmoil and civil wars in Cambodia, the new government of Cambodia began relaxing restrictions on the Chinese community in 1989 and allowed more freedom for developing Chinese-language based education. Once peace was restored, new Chinese immigrants started to arrive. Some of these new Chinese immigrants arrived by virtue of their ties of kinship and dialect, and others came with special skills working for Chinese government aid projects or carrying out their own professional businesses, such as dentistry, medicine, cooking and Chinese language teaching (Chin, 2017: 191). Therefore, the new Chinese immigrant community in Cambodia is highly diversified socially, professionally as well as in terms of provenance. Some new immigrants came from remote inland places such as Xinjiang and Qinghai.

A key characteristic of successful Chinese business communities operating in Southeast Asia in general, and Cambodia in particular, can be summarized as ongoing transformation from inward looking to outward looking by engaging in the mainstream political, business and social networks. In other words, the new Chinese business immigrants transformed their diversified community into one protected and assisted by different networks intertwining with each other. By collaborating with the ruling elite, these new Chinese business immigrants successfully established themselves locally and become deeply embedded in the local society (Chin, 2017). The new Chinese business immigrants also maintained close social and business ties with their former business partners, and relatives and friends in mainland China. Transnational social and business engagement between host and home countries was more frequent and active in comparison with the older generation.

The overall phenomenon of new Chinese business immigrants shows that these individuals possess some unique characteristics in comparison with the old generation, such as better education and better developed social and business ties not only within the Chinese communities, but with other ethnic business communities, in particular mainstream communities and elites. In addition, ties with the home-country are much closer in comparison with the older generation of Chinese immigrants and their children and grandchildren who were born overseas. The active engagement in transnational business engagement will be further elaborated in the next section by using the examples of established overseas Chinese entrepreneurs returning home.

New wave of overseas Chinese students returning home as entrepreneurs

The third key area of this chapter focuses on the new phenomenon of overseas Chinese students returning home as entrepreneurs, referred to as the 'reverse brain drain' (Zhou, 2018). This is a more recent wave due to further opening of the Chinese economy to the world with more business opportunities in China, in particular in the areas of start-ups and venture capital. According to the Ministry of Education, more than 608,400 students from China went abroad while more than 480,900 returned in 2017. This brings the total number of returnees to over 3.13 million since 1978. To date, nearly 80 per cent of students have chosen to return to China after completing overseas studies, up from 30 per cent in 2007 and about 5 per cent in 1987 (*The Straits Times*, 2018).

With continuing economic growth, China has better opportunities for developing new businesses as well as obtaining better careers in comparison with major Western economies where economic slowdown has made fewer opportunities available for finding good jobs and careers among young graduates (Koiviola, 2017). In addition, in order to attract the overseas returnees, the Chinese government has provided for incentive policies, such as generous allowances to move back to China, as well as housing, health care and other benefits. A growing number of returning young professional Chinese, so-called *haigui* (Chinese for overseas returnees and translated into English as 'sea-turtles') (*The Economist*, 2018), have answered the call for 'innovation-driven development' to establish new businesses in many sectors, including technology, internet, telecommunications and media, and help revitalize many traditional industries. Enterprises started by returnees are now part of the mainstream high tech economy in China with 47 per cent of businesses started by returnees in the scientific field and 44 per cent holding patents (UN Chronicle, 2013).

Another key area to which returnees have made significant contribution is the introduction of venture capital mechanisms in China. In fact, venture capital firms are totally new to the Chinese economy, but are critical for new start-up firms which lead the development of China's new economy. The returnees have played a key role in this area with almost all international venture capital companies in China being managed by returnees (Wang et al., 2011). Their injections of capital have supported new domestic business in China, as well as older firms founded by returnees who planned to list their company quickly. Most importantly, many new venture capital firms prefer to support China's private sector, given this sector has been under-funded and has experienced difficulties in obtaining loans from state-owned banks. Through the effort of these new venture capital firms, private firms, many of them SMEs, have found it possible to go global (Wang et al., 2011).

These returnees have also been the main drivers of overseas listings of China's high tech companies in the US financial markets. For example, in 2009 alone, a record 33 Chinese companies were listed on the NASDAQ, with a total of 124 Chinese companies listed on the stock market. Most of these listed Chinese companies were either funded or run by Chinese returnees (UN Chronicle, 2013). Another key area to which returnees have made significant contributions is in the management of MNCs in China. Given most of the world's top 500 MNCs are now operating in China, the demand for talented people with management skills and transnational networks to bridge the East-West divide has been growing. China faces a serious shortage of middle and high-level managers. The new waves of Chinese returnees who have overseas work experience and have worked for MNCs and leading companies abroad, now fill many of the top management positions in MNCs, often as in-country directors, CEOs, Vice Presidents and in other senior posts. These experienced returnees are able to put new strategies into practices with local knowledge and networks, and facilitate MNCs' localization strategy, improve the country's overall industrial structure, and help local partner companies move up the value chain in world trade (UN Chronicle, 2013).

The last but not least important area of contribution by returnees is leading the drive towards globalizing China in accordance to the government's new initiative of 'going global' (*The Economist*, 2018). In fact, returnee entrepreneurs often have maintained connections, personally and professionally, in the foreign countries in which they received education, training and/or working experience. These connections have helped the returnees to secure access to funding, updated technology and the marketplace (Wang et al., 2011). Both Chinese SOEs and private firms bear the heavy burden of 'liability of foreignness' in the global marketplace; in particular SOEs face challenges as legitimate players in a foreign environment. However, legitimacy should be less of a problem for returnees; the global stock markets are more likely to accept returnee enterprises than SOEs. Therefore, as key players in realizing the national 'going global' strategy, returnees have been playing a crucial leadership role in the new wave of internationalization of Chinese firms. In playing such a unique role, many returnees have not stayed permanently in China, but travel between China and other countries, earning the label of 'seagulls'. This tendency marks a new trend of transnationalism, namely returning from overseas to China and at the same time, continuing to flit back and forth between East and West (*The Economist*, 2018).

Conclusion

In this chapter, we have presented three areas related to ethnic Chinese entrepreneurs engaging in the process of internationalization. Firstly, we have discussed the early generation of Chinese immigrants who left home for overseas as the first generation of ethnic Chinese immigrant entrepreneurs, and their children and grandchildren as the second and third generations of entrepreneurs who were born overseas with different characteristics, ethnic identity and ties with mainland China. Secondly, we have illustrated the new wave of Chinese immigrants operating businesses overseas after China adopted economic reforms and the open door policy. The new business immigrants present a different picture from the older generation of ethnic Chinese entrepreneurs as well as their children and grandchildren operating businesses outside China. Thirdly, we have focused on the new phenomenon of young Chinese students obtaining an overseas education and returning China for better business and career opportunities. This group of new generation entrepreneurs also present a very different trend of engaging in entrepreneurship through a 'multiple-way' transnationalization.

Based on the study of the outcomes of the similar and different characteristics, and the process of internationalization of ethnic Chinese entrepreneurship, we summarize a number of key implications related to the development of literature in the IB field as well as relevant policy and practices.

First, based on the development trajectory of different generations of ethnic Chinese entrepreneurs, we observe different patterns and trends of transnationalism. Our findings show that the new generation of ethnic Chinese entrepreneurs do not follow the older generation by focusing either on the host country or the home-country as their business focus, but undertake 'multiple-way' transnationalism. Among the younger generation, there are also differences between China-born business migrants, overseas-born second and third generations of ethnic Chinese entrepreneurs, and the new generation of Chinese returnees who were born in China, educated overseas and then returned to China. Generally speaking, the differences in ethnic identity, sense of belonging and ethnic ties among different generations as well as within the younger generation of ethnic Chinese entrepreneurs have added to the complexity in the argument regarding transnationalism which emphasizes one specific way of presenting identity, ethnic ties and a sense of belonging (Gomez & Benton, 2003).

Second, with regard to the effectiveness of social networks and business networks, our findings identify a common trend; namely, in the early stage of business development in a foreign environment, new migrants tend to rely on social networks to conduct their businesses with a relatively safe and stable environment, and after their businesses become established with the possibility of expansion, then a gradualist transition is seen towards developing new business ties with other non-Chinese based networks, in particular the main stream business networks, since the new migrants have accumulated a certain degree of local knowledge and contacts during their early years of business operation. Therefore, we would claim that both social ties and business ties are equally important but function with different effect at different stages of business development. This also leads to the consideration of expanding business connections beyond intra-ethnic groups through the engagement of inter-ethnic business networks as an important step towards long-term growth among ethnic business entrepreneurs.

The issue regarding business ties is also related to the business location. For many new ethnic Chinese migrants, Chinatown is the natural starting place for running a new business. However, we have observed a new phenomenon indicating that new generation entrepreneurs go beyond this boundary by developing new businesses in the main stream marketplace with cutting edge technology or high quality services. Generational differences in terms of location chosen and sense of belonging lead to differences in other areas, such as business model, market identification and strategy and cross-cultural communication. In addition, differences in ethnic identity and ties with China also lead to a different kind of business development, with some entrepreneurs being more host country-oriented and others more home country-oriented, while others may focus on both ways or even multiple orientations.

The above interesting phenomena reflect on the changing world and influence individuals in their response to their surrounding environments. The next chapter will focus on another important ethnic group, namely ethnic Jewish entrepreneurs, in the process of internationalization. We may find similar as well as different patterns, trends and processes of entrepreneurship between these two important ethnic groups.

References

Bain.com (2011) 2011 China Private Wealth Report, China Merchant Bank and Bain & Company, www.bain.com/Images/2011_China_wealth_management_report.pdf [accessed 5 January 2019].

Bardsley, A. G. (2003) The politics of 'seeing Chinese' and the evolution of a Chinese idiom of business, in K. S. Jomo and B. C Folk (eds), *Ethnic Business: Chinese Capitalism in Southeast Asia*, London and New York: Routledge, pp. 26–51.

Chin, J. K. (2017) Ethnicized networks and local embeddedness: The new Chinese migrant community in Cambodia, in M. Zhou (ed.), *Contemporary Chinese Diasporas*, Singapore: Palgrave, pp. 187–206.

Dahles, H. (2017) Chinese capitalisms in Southeast Asia: Diverging institutional legacies of Southeast Asian Chinese business communities, in J. Nolan, C. Rowley and M. Warner (eds), *Business Networks in East Asian Capitalism: Enduring Trends, Emerging Patterns*, Amsterdam: Elsevier, pp. 191–210.

Dai, F. (2017) Chinese immigration to the Philippines, in M. Zhou (ed.), *Contemporary Chinese Diasporas*, Singapore: Palgrave, pp. 167–186.

Deng, L. (2012) The aspirations of Chinese business migrants in Australia: Barriers, opportunities and implications for government policy development. *Migration Australia*, 2: 52–57.

Fewsmith, J. (1983) From guild to interest group: The transformation of public and private in late Qing China. *Comparative Studies in Society & History*, 25: 617–740.

Folk, B. C. & Jomo, K. S. (2003) Introduction, in K. S. Jomo and B. C Folk (eds), *Ethnic Business: Chinese Capitalism in Southeast Asia*, London and New York: Routledge, pp. 1–9.

Gomez, E. T. (2007) Family firms, transnationalism and generational change: Chinese enterprise in Britain and Malaysia. *East Asia*, 24: 153–172.

Gomez, E. T. & Benton, G. (2003) Transnationalism and the essentializing of capitalism: Chinese enterprise, the state, and identity in Britain, Australia, and Southeast Asia. *East Asia*, Winter: 3–28.

Guercini, S., Milanesi, M. & Ottati, G. D. (2017) Paths of evolution for the Chinese migrant entrepreneurship: A multiple case analysis in Italy. *Journal of International Entrepreneurship*, 15: 266–294.

Horalek, A., Cheng, T. J. & Hu, L. (2017) Identity formation and social integration: Creating and imagining the Chinese community in Prague, the Czech Republic, in M. Zhou (ed.), *Contemporary Chinese Diasporas*, Singapore: Palgrave, pp. 263–284.

Hua, W. (1977) *Xinjiapo Huazu Huiguan Zhi (Chinese Associations in Singapore)*, Volume 3, Singapore: South Seas Society.

Koiviola, Z. (2017) Why Chinese overseas students are now returning home in record numbers, bringing China closer, 28 April 2017, https://gbtimes.com/why-chinese-overseas-students-are-now-returning-home-record-numbers [accessed 24 March 2019].

Koning, J. & Verver, M. (2013) Historicizing the 'ethnic' in ethnic entrepreneurship: The case of the ethnic Chinese in Bangkok. *Entrepreneurship & Regional Development*, 25(5–6): 325–348.

Li, M. H. (2017) New Chinese immigrants in Spain: The migration process, demographic characteristics and adaptation strategies, in M. Zhou (ed.), *Contemporary Chinese Diasporas*, Singapore: Palgrave, pp. 285–308.

Light, I. and Gold, S. J. (2000) *Ethnic Economies*. San Diego: Academic Press.

Lin, S., Mercier-Suissa, C. & Salloum, C. (2016) The Chinese born globals of the Zhejiang province: A study on the key factors for their rapid internationalization. *Journal of International Entrepreneurship*, 14(1): 75–95.

Liu, L. S. (2017) New Chinese immigration to New Zealand: Policies, immigration patterns, mobility and perception, in M. Zhou (ed.), *Contemporary Chinese Diasporas*, Singapore: Palgrave, pp. 233–259.

Modern Express (2010) The new immigration wave out of China: A sign of China's failure?, *Modern Express* (China) 9 June 2010, www.echinacities.com/china-media/the-new-immigration-wave-out-of-china-a-sign-of-china-s.html [accessed 15 January 2019].

Niyomsilpa, S. (2003) Telecommunications, rents and the growth of a liberalization coalition in Thailand, in K. S. Jomo and B. C Folk (eds), *Ethnic Business: Chinese Capitalism in Southeast Asia*, London and New York: Routledge, pp. 182–210.

Nonini, D. (2003) All are flexible, but some are more flexible than others: Small-scale Chinese business in Malaysia, in K. S. Jomo and B. C Folk (eds), *Ethnic Business: Chinese Capitalism in Southeast Asia*, London and New York: Routledge, pp. 73–91.

Pan. L. (1998) Western expansion into China and Southeast Asia, in L. Pan (ed.), *The Encyclopedia of the Chinese Overseas*, Cambridge (Mass): Harvard University Press, pp. 54–57.

Portes, A. & Zhou, M. (2012) Transnationalism and development: Mexican and Chinese immigrant organizations in the United States. *Population and Development Review*, 38: 191–220.

Redding, G. (1990) *The Spirit of Chinese Capitalism*. Berlin, New York, NY: Walter de Gruyter.

Rivera, T. C. (2003) The leading Chinese-Filipino business families in post-Marcos Philippines, in K. S. Jomo and B. C Folk (eds), *Ethnic Business: Chinese Capitalism in Southeast Asia*, London and New York: Routledge, pp. 92–104.

Shen, X. L. (2017) Integration of newcomers into local communities: An analysis of new Chinese immigrants in Zimbabwe, in M. Zhou (ed.), *Contemporary Chinese Diasporas*, Singapore: Palgrave, pp. 79–102.

Skinner, G. W. (1957) *Chinese Society in Thailand: An Analytical History*, Ithaca, New York: Cornell University Press.

Spoonley, P., Meares, C., Ho, E. & Bedford, R. (2009) Attracting, supporting and retaining skilled migrants: Experiences of recently arrived British and South African Migrants, *Rising Dragons, Soaring Bananas International Conference*, the University of Auckland, Auckland.

Tejapira, K. (2009) The misbehaving jerks: The evolving regime of Thainess and Sino-Thai Challenges. *Asian Ethnicity*, 10(3): 263–83.

The Economist. (2018) Turtles and seagulls: What happens when Chinese students abroad return home. *The Economist*, 17 May 2018, www.economist.com/special-report/2018/05/17/what-happens-when-chinese-students-abroad-return-home [accessed 23 March 2019].

The Straits Times. (2018) Better job prospects in China bring more overseas students home. *The Straits Times*, 20 August 2018, www.straitstimes.com/asia/east-asia/better-job-prospects-in-china-bring-more-overseas-students-home [accessed 23 March 2019].

UN Chronicle. (2013) China's return migration and its impact on home development, UN Chronicle, September 2013, https://unchronicle.un.org/article/chinas-return-migration-and-its-impact-home-development [accessed 23 March 2019].

Vatikiotis, M. (1998) Thailand, in L. Pan (ed.), *The Encyclopedia of the Chinese Overseas*. Richmond, Surrey, England: Curzon, pp. 218–27.

Wang, H. Y., Zweig, D. & Lin, X. H. (2011) Returnee entrepreneurs: Impact on China's globalization process. *Journal of Contemporary China*, 20(70): 413–431.

Wang, W. & Zhuang, G. (eds) (2011) *An Overview of Chinese Overseas*, Beijing: World Affairs Publisher.

Weidenbaum, M. & Hughes, S. (1996) *The Bamboo Network: How Expatriate Chinese Entrepreneurs Are Creating a New Economic Superpower in Asia*, New York: The Free Press.

Whitley, R. D. (1992) *Business Systems in East Asia: Firms, Markets, and Societies*, London: Sage.

Xie, Y. H. & Amine, L. S. (2009) Social networks and internationalization of Chinese entrepreneurs. *Global Business Organisation Excellence*, 29(1): 61–78.

Yen, C. H. (1986) *A Social History of the Chinese in Singapore and Malaya, 1800–1911*, Singapore: Oxford University Press.

Yen, C. H. (2013) *Ethnic Chinese Business in Asia: History, Culture and Business Enterprise*. New Jersey: World Scientific.

Yeung, H. W. C. (2004) *Chinese Capitalism in a Global Era: Towards a Hybrid Capitalism*. London, New York: Routledge.

Zhou, M. (2017) Preface, in M. Zhou (ed.), *Contemporary Chinese Diasporas*. Singapore: Palgrave, pp. xi–xxvi.

Zhou, Y. Y. (2018) Reverse brain drain: Chinese students increasingly return home after studying abroad, *Quartz*, 29 July 2018, https://qz.com/1342525/chinese-students-increasingly-return-home-after-studying-abroad/ [accessed 24 March 2019].

Zhu, Y., Webber, M. & Benson, J. (2010) *The Everyday Impact of Economic Reform in China: Management Change, Enterprise Performance and Daily Life.* London and New York: Routledge.

8 Ethnic entrepreneurs in the West vis-à-vis those in the East

Jewish entrepreneurs' experience

Introduction

This chapter discusses the contribution of ethnic minority entrepreneurs to economic growth, in particular the contribution made by Jews. There is no a priori reason why entrepreneurship should be evenly distributed in terms of ethnic groupings. However, we find empirical evidence to indicate that there is an asymmetric distribution over historical time. Historians have selected specific ethnic groups over the historical past that appeared to have contributed more than proportionately to entrepreneurship. We find it interesting that some ethnic group contributions may be praised or condemned according to the prejudices of the observer. In this chapter, we will deal mainly with ethnic groups in the West as opposed to those in the East who will be covered in another chapter. The contribution of these respective ethnic groups varies across time and space.

A major illustration of Western entrepreneurial activity over the course of modern economic history has been the role of Jewish entrepreneurs in Western Europe, Britain, the United States and elsewhere. However, the number of Jews globally is relatively small compared with the overseas Chinese who outnumber their Jewish counterparts many times over. Today, with changing patterns of urbanization and social mobility, the role of such entrepreneurs is changing as many of their offspring aspire to the professional classes such as doctors and lawyers, with other ethnic groups becoming more and more important, for example, South Asian and other new immigrants in Britain and the United States. This chapter will draw conclusions with respect to both theoretical and empirical implications of such entrepreneurial evolution.

Defining the Jewish entrepreneur

We will first clarify the term 'Jewish entrepreneur'. A great deal depends on how we define 'Jewish' and 'entrepreneur'. We must also distinguish between those who are regarded as 'stereotypes' and others. There were two main groups of Jews, the Ashkenazis from Northern Europe and the Sephardis who came mainly from Southern Europe and the Middle East. The former accounted for around seven in ten of the total population and as many were decimated by the

Holocaust. Of those who are described as Jews, a number may not be practising or may be non-believers. Our studies found that a minority of those historical figures had been baptized. Moreover, the businesses they established may not have employed co-religionists. We found that many businesses that were described as 'Jewish' and 'entrepreneurial' displayed no particular religious characteristics. In many cases, the so-called entrepreneurs were actually managers or other kinds of professionals. Few, over the centuries, were inventors. It has been pointed out elsewhere that in the final analysis, Jewish entrepreneurs were no more likely to have successful businesses and remain in business, than non-Jews.

Many argue that it was Jews who had a comparative advantage in occupations that needed literacy or numeracy skills, in turn leading to their specialization as merchants, traders and moneylenders. In particular, one writer, Pascali (2016), studied the presence of Jewish communities in medieval Italy and indicated that financial institutions and knowledge had been present in the country over centuries. As the growth premium associated with the presence of Jews only emerged after 1600, it is argued that the high level of human capital among Jews did not promote economic growth in the Middle Ages per se, when Jewish economic activity was relatively limited and long-distance trade was weak and restricted to a few commodities. Positive interaction between Jewish human capital and city growth only surfaced when institutions with more open access helped Jews participate more freely in the main European economies (North, Wallis & Weingast, 2009).

Other researchers, such as Johnson and Koyama (2016) studied whether cities in Europe between 1400 and 1850 with Jewish communities expanded faster than cities which did not have Jewish communities. To measure this, they matched up data on city populations. The results suggested that cities with Jewish communities grew about 30 per cent faster than comparable cities that did not have Jews. These studies provided evidence that the advantage of cities with Jews came about in part from the onset of Jewish emancipation and their ability to exploit market access after 1600.

Although Europe's Jewish communities were a small percentage of the continent's population, they were said to be disproportionately represented in trade and commerce. It was surmised that this disproportion arose from their cultural, linguistic and religious links across the region. In Amsterdam, for instance, Portuguese Jews were heavily involved in Atlantic trade, particularly in sugar, tobacco and diamonds. In Poland, Jews were said to be prominent in river trade with Russia, the Ottoman Empire and the Baltic. In Germany, Jews were known for being prominent in cattle trading (see Bell, 2008: 127–129). Sephardic Jews, in particular, fostered international trade and helped to promote cross-cultural merchant networks.

Jews also played a prominent role in the textile and tobacco trades in Eastern Europe. Furthermore, Jews were involved in the later building of railroads across Europe but not in the early seminal period of such development in Britain, as we shall see later. Well-known Jewish bankers were among the major movers in this regard. Jewish financiers, such as the Rothschilds, were active in promoting railroad construction throughout the nineteenth century in Europe, starting in the north of France. Jewish capital and entrepreneurs were also active in the industrialization of the Russian Empire, which included parts of Poland, particularly in the textile and sugar industries towards the end of the nineteenth century. However, the Jewish proletariat were mainly concentrated in small-businesses.

Max Weber, the Protestant ethic and the role of the Jews

The contribution of the Jewish entrepreneurial model must be seen against the backdrop of economic history over the last millennium. A major figure in this debate was the German sociologist Max Weber (1864–1920) who linked the so-called 'Protestant Ethic' to the rise of Capitalism, a view which, we may suggest, diverted attention from a discussion of the contribution of the Catholic south of Europe, as well as the role of non-Protestants in the north of Europe. In his book, *The Protestant Ethic and the Spirit of Capitalism* (Weber, 2002 [1904]), Weber referred to 'pariah capitalism', amongst other issues, in referring to the Jewish contribution. He set out the idea that the Jews are, in essence, a 'pariah people', capable of offering no more than a 'pariah capitalism'. Weber developed this case in response to Werner Sombart's book, *The Jews and Modern Capitalism* (1913), in which the author presented an alternative to Weber's argument, which had been based on the Protestant view of the origin of modern capitalism (see Barbalet, 2006).

The Austrian economist, Joseph Schumpeter (1883–1950) argued that capitalism began in the south of Europe, in fact in Italy in the fourteenth century, not in the Protestant north of Europe (Schumpeter, 1954). According to the French historian Fernand Braudel,

> all historians have opposed this tenuous theory [the Protestant Ethic], although they have not managed to be rid of it once and for all. Yet it is clearly false. The northern countries took over the place that earlier had been so long and brilliantly been occupied by the old capitalist centres of the Mediterranean. They invented nothing, either in technology or business management.
>
> (1977: 65–66)

Jewish entrepreneurs in the Industrial Revolution

It is rather surprising that Jewish entrepreneurs played a rather limited role in the Industrial Revolution in Britain in the eighteenth century. Among the major players, such as the characters featured in the study *The Lunar Men* (Uglow, 2002), none appear to have been Jewish. Whether we look at the Agricultural Revolution or the Industrial Revolution during this period, we find little trace of

Jewish entrepreneurs, except as peripheral players. However, in time, Jewish financiers began playing a supportive role.

Mokyr (2011) notes:

> The pace of innovation, however, accelerated during the Industrial Revolution to the point where a term such as 'revolution' seems apt. By 1850, technological innovation had become a central source of economic change. Yet despite their huge head start economically, Jews played an almost imperceptible role in the history of science and technology before and during the early Industrial Revolution.

If we look at the Industrial Revolution, we find that Jews are not prominent amongst the major innovators for the most part. Adam Smith (1723–1790) for instance, did not mention Jews, Judaism or Jewish business at all in writings such as *The Wealth of Nations* (1776) in which we recently carried out an online word-search. David Ricardo (1772–1823), himself a Jew, was the first to use the term 'Capitalism' but says little about his co-religionists in that period in his *Principles* (1817).

One explanation for the above is the very small number of [Sephardi] Jews in Britain in the late eighteenth century and early nineteenth century. Having been expelled from Britain several centuries earlier, the number of Jews in the country at the time of the Industrial Revolution was low, amounting to about 600 at the start of the eighteenth century. By the 1880s, the figure had risen to 60,000. At the beginning of the nineteenth century, there were only around 2,000 Jews in London and even fewer, around 700, in Birmingham. However, these numbers were to grow dramatically in the course of the nineteenth century, with the Eastern European [Ashkenazi] immigration (see Vaughan, 1994). By 1881, there were no more than 36,000 Jews in Britain but many left their homes in Eastern Europe between 1881 and 1914, hoping for a better and safer life, resulting in around 100,000 settling in London's East End, near the docks where they had arrived. The majority worked in skilled trades like tailoring and shoe making. By 1900, Jews formed around 95 per cent of the population in the Wentworth Street district of Spitalfields, in the East End of London.

Living in densely packed urban slums concentrated in London and New York, Jews predominantly took up two or three occupations – the so-called 'immigrant trades'. Above all, however, in both London's East End and New York's Lower East Side, immigrant activity was overwhelmingly dominated by the clothing industry. The industrialization of garment production in the late nineteenth century did not go beyond sewing machine mechanization. Using simple machines, clothing firms were mostly small and easily set up. The path to entrepreneurship in the garment industry was therefore said to be broader than in almost any other sector and Jewish firms often competed by cutting labour costs.

The tipping point with respect to the role of Jewish entrepreneurs in modern economic history came with the mass immigration at the end of the nineteenth century from East to West. It was at this time that a significant dynamic arose from the 'critical mass' of potential entrepreneurs. When such a significant core encounters a favourable economic environment, it is able to make its mark. In urban conurbations such as London and New York, entrepreneurial energies can be unleashed. Immigration to America was not unique to the Jewish people, but they definitely made a huge impact in the New World. The Jews constituted an extremely large portion of the overall immigration to America, particularly in the late 1800s and early 1900s (see Mokyr, 2011).

As Godley (2004: 1) points out:

> Between 1880 and 1914, more than 2.5 million Jews left Eastern Europe. Almost 2 million settled in the United States and about 150,000 came to Britain. They were the poorest of all arrivals, yet today the average Jewish household in the US and in the UK enjoys a top decile income, partly because half of the employed Jews there today are professionals earning professional salaries. But the professionalization of American and British Jewry is only relatively recent – a third-generation phenomenon. What was truly remarkable about first and second-generation Jewish immigrants in the West was just how many were entrepreneurs.

By the late nineteenth century, a number of Jews in London had found a place to live in the city, but most Jewish immigrants worked in the poorer East End districts in unskilled trades, such as tailoring, known as 'sweated labour'. These trades also included food-preparation, furniture-making and petty-retailing. Petticoat Lane emerged at this time as a major marketplace. Jews then spread from the East End of London to the West End and the suburbs. With regard to wealthier Jews, by 1880 about 10 per cent worked in finance, almost 0 per cent worked in manufacturing and 20 per cent were merchants, with the rest, about 70 per cent, constituting the working class, although the accuracy of these census statistics is uncertain. Many Jews were able to become entrepreneurs due to small grants from Jewish charities.

If it can be said that there was a disproportionate number of Jews who were small and large entrepreneurs, by the same token there were many who were not and who became members of the 'proletariat'. By 1914, a substantial Jewish working class had formed with socialist sympathies. Entrepreneurship in the United Kingdom, as well as in the United States, demonstrated a distinct spatial pattern, which in turn changed with urbanization and social mobility, particularly after World War II, as many of the entrepreneurs' offspring went to college and became professionals, and new ethnic groups become entrepreneurs.

Four mini case studies

We will now deal with four mini case studies involving Jewish entrepreneurship:

the first is the 'Banking Revolution', unleashed by the Rothschild Dynasty in the nineteenth century, which is still ongoing.

The second is the 'Retail Revolution', which was created by British and United States Jewish entrepreneurs in the early and mid-twentieth century.

The third is the 'Entertainment Revolution', which was stimulated by Jewish entrepreneurship in the United States, in particular, in Hollywood.

The fourth is the 'Silicon Valley Revolution' of recent times.

All four revolutions constituted an important *demarche* in modern economic history, each involving three distinct sets of Jewish entrepreneurs.

The first revolution was led by individuals who were to become Jewish 'aristocrats' in their respective societies and went into banking, such as the Rothschilds. The second revolution was spurred by people of more modest backgrounds, who were poor immigrants to the United Kingdom and United States in the late nineteenth century and early twentieth century, and who developed new forms of retailing, such as Marks and Spencer. The third revolution emerged from the entrepreneurial actions of the aforesaid group who established Hollywood and studios such as Metro-Goldwyn-Mayer. The fourth revolution was begun by the offspring of the latter group who became highly educated, particularly in information technology, and set up businesses in Silicon Valley, as in the case of Google and the like.

The mini case studies provide examples of new and innovative economic activities undertaken by Jewish entrepreneurs, and also reveal the industrial sectors in which such ethnic entrepreneurs were not in fact involved.

1 Banking

In the history of European economic development, including banking, we find that a number of countries, religions and ethnicities played an important role. Innovations in banking took place in Renaissance Italy in Florence, with the Catholic Medici family creating a major banking empire in the fifteenth century and extending its activities across Europe. With the expulsion of the Jews from Spain in 1492, many Jews settled in Italy and became important players in the local commercial life and indeed in banking. However, Jews did not achieve key historical permanence until much later in the eighteenth century when the Jewish Rothschild family built an international network of banks run by family members in five major European centres, namely, in London, Paris, Frankfurt, Vienna and Naples. Mayer Amschel Rothschild (1744–1812) became one of Europe's most significant bankers in the Landgraviate of Hesse-Kassel in the Holy Roman Empire. One son, the fourth, Nathan Mayer, went to England in 1799, first setting up a banking branch in Manchester in 1805 – and later moving to London in 1811.

The Rothschild Archive notes:

> Nathan Mayer Rothschild's increasingly successful business provided a model for his brothers back in Frankfurt. In 1812, James Mayer Rothschild

(1792–1868) established a banking house in Paris. Salomon Mayer Rothschild (1774–1855) settled in Vienna in 1820. Carl Mayer Rothschild (1788–1855) set up business in Naples in 1821, leaving Amschel Mayer (1773–1855), to head the Frankfurt bank.

(Rothschild Archive, 2018)

It is probably true to say that the Rothschilds invented 'modern' international banking and reproduced in a new form in modern times what the Medici had done centuries earlier. The former developed an organizational model that was unprecedented in modern banking, unaided by economists or business school academics.

Since the Rothschild financial empire had such a wide geographical spread, we will concentrate in this mini case study on the British branch. This branch of the family was established too late to have influenced the Industrial Revolution in the eighteenth century in Britain but was significantly involved in the early cotton trade in Manchester. The family soon had had an enormous influence on subsequent developments.

Ferguson (1999) points out:

> The French Revolution was not the only revolution to transform Mayer Amscher's life and business. The British Industrial Revolution, in its first phase by the 1780s if not before, exerted an equally important influence. For although Mayer Amschel had already begun building up his banking business by the late 1790s, this did not imply a winding up of his previous coin-dealing business, which continued in a small way even after his death; and nor did it preclude expansion into other potentially profitable fields of business activity. Of these, none was more profitable in the late eighteenth century than that generated by the English revolution in textile manufacturing. In particular, the dramatic growth of (partly) mechanized cotton spinning, weaving and dyeing in Lancashire signalled an unprecedented and genuinely revolutionary change in the pace of economic life.
>
> (1999: 3)

During most of the nineteenth century, the Rothschild family's role was considerable both at home and abroad. The Rothschild Archive (2018) also notes that:

> With Nathan's death in July 1836, the City of London lost a financier whose name had become legendary in his own lifetime. However, N M Rothschild & Sons would continue to prosper and grow at the centre of the London financial world, and his sons continued the business under the name N M Rothschild & Sons.

The Rothschild business specialized in foreign loan issues, bullion trading and the finance of public utility companies, notably foreign railways, while maintaining in the first half of the nineteenth century a certain volume of merchant trade in commodities such as quicksilver, tobacco, sugar and cotton. The firm operated through a worldwide network of agents, among them August Belmont (New York, est. 1837), Weisweiller & Bauer (Madrid, est. 1835), Lionel Davidson (Valparaiso, est. 1843), and S. Bleichröder (Berlin, documented from 1850).

The firm acquired the lease of the Royal Mint Refinery in 1852, refining bullion until the sale of the business in 1967. In the late nineteenth century N. M. Rothschild & Sons specialized in the financing of mining companies, notably De Beers, through the Exploration Company of which the bank was a founder, and also acted as bankers to the governments of Brazil, Chile and Egypt.

The first non-family partner was admitted in 1960 and the firm was incorporated as a limited liability company, N. M. Rothschild & Sons Limited, in 1970 (see www.rothschildarchive.org/business/n_m_rothschild_and_sons_london/). The bank still plays an active role in the City of London and now functions as the British division of Rothschild & Co, a global enterprise, with 57 offices around the world.

Ferguson concludes:

> For most of the nineteenth century, N. M. Rothschild was part of the biggest bank in the world, which dominated the international bond-market. For a contemporary equivalent, one has to imagine a merger between Merrill Lynch, Morgan Stanley, J. P. Morgan and probably Goldman Sachs too – as well, perhaps, as the International Monetary Fund, given the nineteenth-century Rothschild's role in stabilizing the finances of numerous governments.
>
> (1999: 479)

2 Retail

The East European Jewish immigrants built on the entrepreneurial base of an earlier generation of German Jewish immigrants in both retailing and services. Both Montague Burton (men's clothing) and Simon Marks (Marks and Spencer's stores and women's clothing) saw very rapid growth from a low base during the 1920s and 1930s (see Briggs, 1984). The businesses generated several successful imitators, largely from the Jewish immigrant community, which together revolutionized the distribution of clothing and, through the impact on supply chains, clothing manufacturing.

Strictly speaking, Marks and Spencer is only 'half-Jewish' in its origin, as the second partner was a Christian. Michael Marks (1859–1907) and Thomas Spencer (1852–1905) met in Leeds in the North of England and were inseparable thereafter.

Marks was born in 1859 into a Polish-Jewish family living as refugees in a Jewish ghetto at Slonim in the Russian-Polish province of Grodno. Thomas Spencer was born in Skipton, Yorkshire, in 1851.

In 1894, Michael Marks joined Thomas Spencer as a business partner, with the latter paying £300 for a half-share in the business. A decade earlier, Marks, had opened his first stall on a trestle in Leeds market, offering a gamut of cheap goods, every item priced at a penny. Thomas Spencer had been a cashier for a Leeds textile trader named Isaac Jowitt Dewhirst (1863–1937) and was an efficient book-keeper. Dewhirst supported Marks by teaching him a little English and assisted him with small loans; Spencer's wife went on to help Marks improve his new language skills (see Briggs, 1984).

Marks and Spencer were part of the retail revolution in British commerce and were very entrepreneurial from the start with their market stall 'Penny Bazaar' in 1884 in Leeds, with the slogan "Don't ask the price, it's a penny'. Once underway, the two never looked back, moving to Manchester's Cheetham Hill and many market locations. Marks and Spencer are known colloquially as 'Marks and Sparks' or 'M&S'. In 1998, the company became the first British retailer to record a pre-tax profit of over £1 billion, although the company's fortunes subsequently slumped into a sudden slide.

Today, the enterprise is one of the top companies in Britain, with over 80,000 employees, although it has lost ground in recent times to cut-price competitors. Marks and Spencer became prominent in the sale of clothing, home products and luxury food products, with an operating income of £690.6 million by 2017.

Although productivity in British retailing overall had remained significantly below American (but not German) levels, these entrants were fast to gain a substantial slice of the market. Such entrepreneurial growth may be seen as exceptional in British retailing at that time. Limited consumer mobility and only a very limited level of urban change was to offer such incumbents much greater market power to deter new entrants from acquiring top High Street sites.

"A Short History of Marks & Spencer" in the M & S Company Archive, sets out the company time-line as follows:

- Marks & Spencer was formed in 1884 when Michael Marks, a Polish refugee opened a market stall in Leeds, with the slogan 'Don't ask the price, it's a penny'.
- In 1894 Marks went into partnership with Thomas Spencer, a former cashier from the wholesale company, Dewhirst.
- In 1904 Marks & Spencer opened their first shop in a covered arcade in Leeds.
- In the 1920s we adopted the revolutionary policy of buying directly from suppliers.
- In 1926 Marks and Spencer Limited became a public company.
- In 1930 the flagship Marble Arch store was opened.
- In 1931 a food department was introduced, selling produce and canned goods.
- In 1933 a staff welfare service was set up to provide pensions, subsidised staff canteens, health & dental services, hairdressing and even camping holidays!

- In 1934 we were the first British retailer to set up its own research laboratory to pioneer new fabrics.
- In 1948 M&S launched its own Food Technology department to work closely with suppliers, producers and farmers.
- In 1954 the research lab undertook the first ever systematic survey of women's leg sizes, to create a new and improved sizing system for stockings.
- The same year saw M&S's 'Operation Simplification', which reduced internal paperwork by 25million items per year.
- In 1974 Indian and Chinese foods were introduced.
- In 1975 the first stores opened in continental Europe in France and Belgium.
- In 1985 our Chargecard was launched.
- In 1986 we opened our first edge of town store at the Metrocentre, Gateshead.
- In 1999 online shopping was introduced via our website.
- In 2001 the first Simply Food stores opened in Surbiton and Twickenham and the Per Una range, designed by George Davis, was launched.
- In 2002 the Blue Harbour men's range was launched, and the Limited Collection launched the following year.
- In May 2004 Stuart Rose was appointed Chief Executive of Marks & Spencer. He became Executive Chairman in 2008.
- In November 2009 it was announced that Marc Bolland, then chief executive of Wm Morrison, would be the new Chief Executive of Marks & Spencer.

(see https://marksintime.marksandspencer.com/download?id=996)

While the board and management of the company may have comprised many members of the Jewish faith, the majority of the employees were more likely to be drawn from other religions, with the exception of company sites in towns or cities with a high Jewish population. It must be borne in mind that the clothing manufacturing industry was heavily Jewish in many parts of the United Kingdom and offered a familiar network of suppliers. M&S also supported many Jewish charities and Zionist causes. Today, the enterprise is facing a tense future. On 22 May 2018, it confirmed that over 100 stores will be closed by 2022 in a 'radical' strategy to save the company from the High Street contraction now facing British retailers.

3 Hollywood

The third case study in the chapter focuses on Jewish entrepreneurship and Hollywood, with entrepreneurs transferring skills from the retail trades to the new mass entertainment market. Jewish entrepreneurs became involved in the mass-production of garments in the clothing industry and entertainment in the movie industry.

Louis B. Mayer (1884–1987), a Jewish immigrant, was a major founder of the Hollywood movie industry. He started life running a small theatre in Boston. When he moved to Los Angeles, he met Irving Thalberg, who became his principal producer and was a very gifted figure. Mayer ran the studio in terms of setting budgets and approving new productions, while Thalberg, still in his twenties, supervised all MGM productions. The two proved to be a brilliant team, with Thalberg aspiring to make high quality movies. Mayer's breakthrough came in April 1924 when Marcus Loew, who owned Loew's movie chain, merged Metro Pictures, Samuel Goldwyn's Goldwyn Pictures Corporation and Mayer Pictures into one studio, Metro-Goldwyn. Loew had acquired Metro and Goldwyn a few months before, but could not find anyone to manage his new holdings on the West Coast. Mayer would hold this job for the next 27 years.

Before the year had passed, Mayer added his name to the corporation with Loew's blessing, and renamed it Metro-Goldwyn-Mayer or MGM. In 1932, with his chief collaborator recovering from a heart attack, Mayer replaced him with producer David O. Selznick. Thalberg died in 1936, aged 37. At its peak in the 1940s, MGM as a corporation employed 6,000 staff and covered 185 acres in Culver City, California, which was just outside Los Angeles. Mayer was reputedly a first class CEO; some said he could have run General Motors (see French, 1969).

Many of the studios were run by individuals from a Jewish immigrant background, such as Marcus Loew, Adolph Zukor, Sam Goldwyn, Carl Laemmle, the Selznicks, Jesse Lasky, William Fox, the Warner Brothers, B. P. Schulberg and Harry Cohn, as well as Louis B. Mayer. By the 1930s, six of the eight major studios were controlled and run by Jewish entrepreneurs. In addition, persons of Jewish birth were eminent among the second and third level of business-oriented producers, managers, assistants, agents and lawyers. A number of top managers and film directors were also of Jewish origins; however, few films had an ethnic flavour; the movies they made highlighted white, male, middle-class Christian values. Jewish content in these movies was scarce and was not directed at a Jewish market, either in the United States or internationally, which remains the case up to the present (see www.myjewishlearning.com/article/jews-in-hollywood-1930–1950/).

Hollywood peaked in the late twentieth century and it was soon to be overtaken by new media, such as TV and more recently the Internet, where Jewish entrepreneurial talent soon became evident, both in the United States and abroad.

4 Silicon Valley

Looking at what we can broadly call Silicon Valley (a term that dates back to 1971) and the so-called 'Fourth Industrial Revolution', it is clear that, in many cases, the founders of the leading companies may indeed have been Jewish entrepreneurs. Silicon Valley is located south of San Francisco, California, and is home to over 2,000 tech companies. It originally sprung up in the Palo Alto/ Menlo Park/Stanford University area. FAANG is an acronym for the five most popular and best performing tech stocks in the market, namely Facebook, Apple, Amazon, Netflix and Alphabet's Google. The nomenclature was born out of the original acronym, FANG, which did not include Apple when CNBC's Jim Cramer coined the term.

Facebook, under the leadership of Mark Zuckerman (1984–), may be classed as having Jewish origins, as well as Google, under the leadership of Sergei Brin (1973–) and Larry Page (1973–). However, Apple, under Steve Jobs (1955–2011), clearly does not fit the description (although co-founders Andy Herzfield and Steve Wozniak may be included among Jewish entrepreneurs) and neither does Amazon, founded by Jeff Bezos (1987–). Marc Randolph at Netflix has Jewish roots, as the great-nephew of Sigmund Freud, but co-founder Reed Hastings does not. Bill Gates (1968–) at Microsoft, is another exception. Tim Berners-Lee (1955–), inventor of the World Wide Web, is also not Jewish. Most people would not identify the founding fathers of the Valley or their firms as stereotypically 'Jewish', although neo-Nazi 'hate' websites often do so. Several of these firms do have close links with Israel, which makes them vulnerable to such postings, especially Google. Immigrants are also said to be twice as likely to start new firms in the United States as American-born citizens. Brin, co-founder of Google, is a good example, as he is Russian-born and came to the United States at the age of six. Over half the scientific and engineering workers in the Valley are described as being of immigrant origin. More recently, Israeli immigrants have become more numerous (Gold, 2018).

As of 20 March 2018, the market capitalization of these companies added up to $472.38B + $760.36B + $888.66B + $136.92B + $757.54B = $3.015 trillion. *The Economist* recently suggested that FAANG's fortunes may have peaked, Apple just missing a $1 trillion dollar capitalization (*The Economist*, 2018). It is hard to predict the future trajectories of such 'Unicorns'. Many jobs hang in the balance, indeed, over one million and half in the Valley itself, but also many subcontracted jobs at home and abroad.

Ethnic immigrants in the West versus those in the East

The number of Jews residing in Israel and in the diaspora is relatively small compared with the overseas Chinese who total approximately 50 million, and if you include those in Taiwan (23.5 million or so) and Hong Kong (7.5 million or so), number many times as many overseas Jews. The worldwide Jewish population is approximately 15 million, if the highest American estimates are assumed, and may be close to 20 million if we include those with half-Jewish origins. Jewish population growth worldwide is low, although the ultrareligious The Haredi community is growing. Currently, close to nine million Jews live in the diaspora and over six million in Israel. Just about half of the world's Jews reside in the Americas, with about 46 per cent in North America.

Approximately 37 per cent of worldwide Jewry lives in Israel. The country's Jewish population recently rose, while the diaspora population dropped, including in the Asian territories of the Russian Republic and Turkey, accounting for about 12 per cent of the total population. Fewer than 2 per cent of the world's Jews live in Africa and Oceania.

A larger proportion of Jews are in professional and higher managerial jobs than any other religious group in England and Wales, according to newly released data from the 2011 census. The Jewish community also has the lowest percentage of long-term unemployed. According to the census statistics, 9.9 per cent of the population in England and Wales occupy professional and higher managerial and administrative roles, while the long-term unemployed rate is only 1.5 per cent. However, the percentage of Jews in better-paid jobs is said to be more than twice the national average at 19.1 per cent and the long-term unemployed constitute only an insignificant percentage.

- Overall, the median household net worth in the United States is said to be around $99,500 but among American Jews it is $443,000.
- Even though Jews constitute 1.7 per cent of all Americans, they allegedly account for 20 of the 50 richest people and a third of the top 400.
- Despite being just 0.2 per cent of the global population, Jews have won a fifth of all Nobel prizes.

Social networks – particularly kinship and ethnic networks – appear to have played an important role in entrepreneurship throughout much of history. A large share of new international market developments over the last two centuries has been generated by networks of entrepreneurs in diasporas, including Jews, Greeks, Indians, Arabs, Chinese and others (Hamilton, 2011). Hamilton (2011) describes the importance of extensive family networks for Chinese entrepreneurs in pooling capital for new ventures. In the United States, immigrant Jews in the early twentieth century formed informal and formal credit organizations to finance small business and trade when access to bank credit was not a possibility. For a comparison of Jewish and Chinese entrepreneurs, see www.afbes.ust. hk/public/userfiles/files/HKUST-Family-Business-Proceedings-Succession-and-Innovation-in-Family-Businesses-final-lr.pdf.

In a recent account, Windolf (2015) claims that:

> In the early twentieth century, a dense corporate network was created among the large German corporations ('Germany Inc.'). About 16% of the members of this corporate network were of Jewish background. At the centre of the network (big linkers) about 25% were Jewish. The percentage of Jews in the general population was less than 1% in 1914. What comparative advantages did the Jewish minority enjoy that enabled them to succeed in the competition for leading positions in the German economy? Three hypotheses are tested: (1) The Jewish economic elite had a better education compared to the non-Jewish members of the network

(human capital); (2) Jewish members had a central position in the corporate network, because many of them were engaged in finance and banking;
and (3) Jewish members created a network of their own that was separate
from the overarching corporate network (social capital). The density of
this Jewish network was higher than that of the non-Jewish economic elite
(embeddedness). Our data do not support any of these hypotheses. The
observed correlation between Jewish background and economic success
cannot be explained by a higher level of education, a higher level of social
capital, or a higher proportion of Jewish managers engaged in (private)
banking.

Nevertheless, Roberts (2016), a professor at MIT, maintained that the study,
with its bias toward success, would have been more balanced had it included
stories of entrepreneurial failure. He notes that:

> Only a small percent of new companies survive for many years, Jewish or
> not", and continues: "Data from my own research shows that Jews have
> been disproportionately likely to start new companies, relative to their Prot-
> estant and Catholic co-workers in the United States. But the same data do
> not indicate a disproportionate percentage of successes from those startups.

According to Roberts:

> Only a small percent of new companies survive for many years, and even
> fewer become great successes. So the wrong lesson might be learned that
> success follows attempt. That is only true in a small fraction of cases,
> Jewish or not.
>
> (Prince, 2016)

Discussion

The impact of national culture on entrepreneurship has recently been tested
historically in a comparative study of Eastern European Jews who emigrated
to London and New York in the late nineteenth century. Godley (2004) argues
that the Jewish immigrants to New York were much more likely to move into
entrepreneurial occupations than those in London, despite coming from
similar backgrounds. He suggests that in both countries the Jews assimilated
many host-country values. This novel methodology of using Jewish immigrants as the 'control group' seems to provide robust evidence of differences
between American and British cultures in terms of how each of these valued
entrepreneurship.

   This comparison of east European Jews in both the United States and in
Britain suggests that as Jewish immigrants assimilated host-country cultural
values, their preference for entrepreneurship was to change. Those in Britain
began to move increasingly into craft employment, rather than pursuing petty

business careers for any given wage and profit level. With very limited options for self-advancement, British working class culture presented strong and conservative craft values, erecting hurdles to pursuing entrepreneurship. With fewer competitive challenges from either immigrants or from aspirant men from below, incumbents remained unthreatened and in place. However, the real entrepreneurial outsiders were immigrants; some were already established in business before they arrived, especially those from the Dominions, but the majority had been brought over by their parents earlier in the waves of east European Jewish immigration. These mostly second-generation Polish and Lithuanian Jews collectively greatly changed much of the British economy from the 1930s through to the 1970s

Conclusion

It is clear that the role of Jews in the evolution of capitalism is a complex one. While this specific ethnic group has been more than proportionately represented in entrepreneurial activity, its role has often been possibly overestimated. There has been an excessive emphasis on Jewish entrepreneurial stereotypes. We have seen how sparse the part these Jews played in the Industrial Revolution in Britain in the eighteenth century was and how they played only a limited role in Colonial America. It is not until the mass waves of immigration from Eastern Europe to Western Europe, Britain and the United States, that we find a substantive impact on economic life (see Jones & Wadhwani, 2006). The phenomenon described above extended from the late nineteenth century to the present and culminates in today's Silicon Valley. However, the range of immigrant groups from many ethnic backgrounds is wider, for instance, the Chinese as well as the South Asian diaspora, which are now making their mark as entrepreneurs, not only in Britain but also in the United States.

References

Barbalet, J. (2006) Max Weber and Judaism: An insight into the methodology of the Protestant ethic and the spirit of capitalism, http://maxweberstudies.org/kcfinder/upload/files/MWSJournal/5–2-6–1pdfs/013%20Jack%20Barbalet.pdf [accessed 5 April 2018].

Bell, D. P. (2008) *Jews in the Early Modern World*. Lanham: Rowman & Littlefield Publishers INC.

Braudel, F. (1977) *Afterthoughts on Material Civilization and Capitalism*. Baltimore and London: The Johns Hopkins University Press.

Briggs, A. (1984) *Marks & Spencer: A Centenary History*. London: Octopus Books.

Ferguson, N. (1999) *The House of Rothschild, The World's Banker, 1849–1999*. New York: Viking.

French, P. (1969) *Movie Moguls. An Informal History of the Hollywood Tycoons*. London: Weidenfeld & Nicolson).

Godley, A. (2004) *Immigrant Entrepreneurs and the Emergence of London's East End as a Clothing and the Modern Metropolis*. Oxford and New York, NY: Berg.

Gold, S. J. (2018) Israeli infotech migrants in Silicon Valley. *The Russell Sage Foundation Journal of the Social Sciences*, 4(1): 130–148.

Hamilton, G. G. (2011) *Asian Business Networks*. New York, NY: de Gruyter.

Johnson, N. D. & Koyama, M. (2016) Jewish Communities and City Growth in Pre-industrial Europe. GMU Working Paper in Economics No. 16–22, pp. 1–39.

Jones, G. G. & Wadhwani, R. D. (2006) Entrepreneurship and business history: Renewing the research agenda, *Working paper series*, Cambridge, MA: Harvard Business School.

Mokyr, J. (2011) The economics of being Jewish. *Critical Review*, 23(1–2): 95–206.

Pascali, L (2016) Banks and development: Jewish communities in the Italian Renaissance and current economic performance, posted online 4 March 2016, www.mitpressjournals. org/doi/abs/10.1162/REST_a_00481 [accessed 20 August 2018].

North, D. C., Wallis,, J. J. & Weingast, B. R. (2009) *Violence and Social Orders: A Conceptual Framework for Interpreting Recorded Human History*. Cambridge and New York, NY: Cambridge University Press.

Prince, C. J. (2016) Jewish entrepreneurs explain how to succeed in business – by trying. 13 September 2016. www.timesofisrael.com/jewish-entrepreneurs-explain-how-to-succeed-in-business-by-trying/

Roberts, D. (2016) Jewish entrepreneurs, www.timesofisrael.com/jewish-entrepreneurs-explain-how-to-succeed-in-business-by-trying/ [accessed 20 May 2018].

Rothschild Archive (2018) www.rothschildarchive.org/contact/faqs/origins_of_the_ rothschild_family_business [accessed 25 May 2018].

Schumpeter, J. (1954) *History of Economic Analysis*. London: Allen and Unwin.

Sombart, W. (1913) *The Jews and Modern Capitalism*. London: Fisher Unwin (translated by M. Epstein).

The Economist (2018) The tech giants are still in rude health. *The Economist*, www. economist.com/business/2018/08/04/the-tech-giants-are-still-in-rude-health

Uglow, J. (2002) *The Lunar Men*. London: Faber and Faber.

Vaughan, L. (1994) The Jews in London 1695 & 1895 – UCL Discovery discovery.ucl. ac.uk/659/1/Vaughan_1994.pdf [accessed 10 May 2018].

Weber, M. (2002) [1904] *The Protestant Ethic and the Spirit of Capitalism*. Los Angeles: Roxbury Publ. (translated by S. Kalberg).

Windolf, P. (2015) *The German-Jewish Economic Elite (1900–1933)*, Uni Trier www. uni-trier.de/fileadmin/fb4/prof/SOZ/APO/WindolfMS577June10.pdf [accessed 10 June 2018].

9 Conclusion

Comparative analysis of internationalization of entrepreneurship

Introduction

The book so far has illustrated complex issues of internationalization of entrepreneurship by reviewing underpinning theories and illustrating multiple cases with contextual background and different types of entrepreneurial internationalization patterns, processes and activities, in particular using different examples, such as entrepreneurial internationalization in Australia, different generations of Chinese entrepreneurial internationalization, and the historical evolution of Jewish entrepreneurial internationalization. The purpose of the book has been to provide a holistic analysis of a wide range of influential factors in philosophical, historical, cultural, social, political and economic domains, that form and shape different models of internationalization of entrepreneurship in different parts of the world. The book also represents an endeavour to enrich understandings of international business and internationalization of entrepreneurship theories and practices in the East and West.

At the beginning of the book, we developed a number of key research questions that provided direction to the subsequent chapters. In this concluding chapter, we start our discussion by summarizing the overall responses to these questions based on the analysis and discussion of the relevant underpinning literatures and case studies. By doing so, we present a general comparative analysis of key characteristics of internationalization of entrepreneurship, which in turn enables the identification of different patterns or models within the context. Based on these patterns, we further develop a general comparative platform with a number of important characteristics that distinguish internationalization of entrepreneurship among different ethnic groups as well as different generations of entrepreneurs operating in different parts of the world. Finally, the conclusion highlights major challenges for further development of research and practices in the internationalization of entrepreneurship globally.

Responding to the key questions

In Chapter 1, we developed key questions related to the causes, patterns/models and processes of the internationalization of entrepreneurship. Hence, this concluding chapter's first primary task is to address these issues.

With regard to the underpinning conceptual thinking influential in the literature on entrepreneurship and international business, we observed deep rooted impact from several phenomena, including entrepreneurial activities based on taking advantage of opportunities and exploiting these opportunities across national borders. In particular, cultural mechanisms (i.e. values and beliefs, and formal and informal cultural norms), individual characteristics (i.e. previous experience, education and personality traits), and entrepreneurs' activity and behaviour embedded in the social, economic and institutional contexts, impact the process of international entrepreneurship. A number of key characteristics of internationally oriented entrepreneurship were identified, such as: (1) activities based on former experience and the important role of social and business networks; (2) activities based on innovative and proactive behaviours with the capability of taking risks and coping with uncertainties; (3) internal factors (e.g. resources) and external factors (e.g. formal and informal institutional environments) influencing decisions, actions and processes; and (4) a new breed of entrepreneurs with international experience and mind-set. In summary, the ultimate goals of international entrepreneurship are to achieve the common, shared view of opportunity and create social values based on different stakeholders' efforts.

Therefore, from the beginning of this book, we have highlighted a comparison between past and present international entrepreneurship as well as cross-country examples with cultural, regional and generational differences. By doing so, we have been able to provide a comparative, holistic approach towards internationalization of entrepreneurship with an analysis of time, space, generation and culture.

In terms of the underpinning literature and schools of thought, Chapter 2 presented different definitions of 'entrepreneurship' and 'entrepreneurs'. One of the key elements of consensus-building is that entrepreneurship is more than a process of wealth creation; it also involves doing something new and different for the purpose of creating wealth for the individual and adding value to society. In the international business literature, entrepreneurship can be seen as 'business exchange' rather than 'production'. Given the current technological progression in general, and the impact of digital technology on new entrepreneurship in particular, many new digital start-ups have been developed globally with individual entrepreneurs as a core 'micro-foundation' (Coviello, Kano & Liesch, 2017: 1151). Therefore, definitions regarding entrepreneurship have shifted from time to time and between different disciplines, but the key elements of these definitions describe entrepreneurship as: (1) the process of making change; (2) requiring great effort in order to achieve sustainability; (3) needing the pursuit of opportunity beyond the resources under the current control; (4) the discovery and/or creation of relevant opportunities by entrepreneurs; and (5) encompassing important contextual variables. Hence, in order to have a clearer understanding of the entrepreneurial journey required to distinguish the field horizontally from research on creativity and strategy, and vertically from research on more practical business functions or more abstract systems-level concepts, we define entrepreneurship as "a process and opportunity recognition as part of an entrepreneurial process that takes place over time and in a range of locations, including home and host markets, as well as virtual markets". To provide further understanding of the extensive range of views and lenses that might influence perceptions of the role, drivers and characteristics of entrepreneurs and internationalization, we have provided a model of ten different schools of thought that offer a more theoretically reflective framework from which to consider future research on entrepreneurship in an international context than is currently available.

With regard to the links between international business and international entrepreneurship, we have defined the area of internationalization of entrepreneurship as a bridge between the notion of entrepreneurship and the concept of international business. This definition emphasizes the challenge of operating business in a foreign land and confronting a different set of institutional contexts. A number of key issues have been identified in this regard in Chapter 3, such as transnational entrepreneurship and institutional perspective on entrepreneurship in international business (Yeung, 2002). So far, three aspects have dominated the research areas, including: (1) entrepreneurial internationalization; (2) international comparisons of entrepreneurship; and (3) international comparisons of entrepreneurial internationalization (Jones, Coviello & Tang, 2011). A number of key elements have also involved significant debate, such as the similarity and difference between the born-globals and INVs (i.e. global start-ups), international vs. global orientation of entrepreneurship, the importance of critical incidents, episodes and events that trigger international entrepreneurial activities, entrepreneurs' market creation and co-creation capability, eco-systems for entrepreneurial internationalization and related business networks.

Following our discussion of the above general themes regarding the concepts and theoretical frameworks of entrepreneurship in relation to international business and international entrepreneurship, we shifted the focus to the current international business and entrepreneurial challenges, namely the important role of emerging market MNCs, many of whom are SMEs and increasingly playing a crucial role in global trade and investment. By explaining the innovation-oriented nature of export-oriented Chinese SMEs as an example, Chapter 4 illustrated recent developments and explored some of the reasons for the increase of Chinese SMEs' internationalization, and the reasons for innovation having risen so quickly in this economy. The relevant key concepts and issues were also discussed, including home and host country environments and values, attitudes and needs that are driving the new wave of international entrepreneurship among emerging market SMEs (Wang, 2012; Liu, 2017; Yan et al., 2018). The evidence shows that the social and institutional linkages help to explain why entrepreneurs cannot accomplish goals alone but depend on others, and how and why people behave in accordance with their values, culture and entrepreneurial behaviour. This evidence also helps to explain how the home and host country environments drive entrepreneurial recognition and opportunity exploitation and how smaller MNCs in emerging markets ensure international competitiveness in foreign markets in their pre and post-internationalization development (early growth through to maturity and change).

We then shifted the focus to case studies of different ethnic entrepreneur groups in Chapter 5, concentrating on the illustration of the relevant key concepts and issues regarding ethnicity and entrepreneurship. One key element of international entrepreneurship is related to ethnic entrepreneurship. A number of important aspects have been discussed, including defining 'ethnic' and 'immigrant' entrepreneurship, relevant theoretical frameworks and models, strategies and determinant factors, and conceptual advancements, such as ethnic economy, enclave economy and transnationalism. Key underpinning theoretical issues have been elaborated along the lines of sociology, anthropology and labour economics that collectively contribute to the notion of ethnic entrepreneurship. A number of key influential factors and models have been identified, such as cultural, economic and overall contextual factors, as well as models described as interactive, mixed embeddedness and interactive with entrepreneurial process (Waldinger et al., 1990; Razin, 2002).

With regard to ethnic entrepreneur strategies, a number of aspects have been discussed. The strategies range from those used in easy and less sophisticated businesses to those implemented in more challenging businesses at a later stage. The latter strategies initially support the businesses through social ties (within the community) and then through business ties (beyond their own community), learning-by-doing and then innovative ways acting, capability building through education and training, sharing responsibility with non-family members, financing business via rotating credit associations and other community-based mutual support funds. It is also important to be aware of the transformation from an ethnic economy (within an ethnic community) to an enclave economy (engaged with wider communities) through the development of 'co-ethnic groups'. Finally, transnationalism represents a variety of entrepreneurial activities in financial services, trade, cultural firms, manufacturing, micro-firms and start-ups in both home and host countries, as well as back-and-forth movement of entrepreneurs, such as cyclical migration (Zhou, 2004; Levitt, 2001; Portes & Guarnizo, 1991).

These underpinning observations led us to consider a number of examples of immigration and entrepreneurship. In Chapter 6, we provided a history of immigration and entrepreneurship in Australia, noting that 29 per cent of the total population was born overseas. Immigration has influenced the entire social transformation and different generations of migrants have made their mark on the historical evolution, particularly through their entrepreneurial activities. We took Italian and Vietnamese immigrants as examples to illustrate the post-World War II migration wave and post-Vietnam War migration wave respectively, and observed a very dynamic trend of immigrations being involved in overall economic development as unskilled and semi-skilled workers, farmers as well as self-employed small business owners. The final focus of this chapter is on the current trend of immigration in relation to entrepreneurial activities in Australia. We have seen a more globally oriented source of new immigrants coming to

Australia, including people from Latin America and Africa who are different from previous immigrant groups who came mainly from Europe and Asia, though the latter are still dominant in the overall immigrant numbers (e.g. Chinese and Indian immigrants). Many of these new immigrants have better education, skills and English proficiency. A certain proportion of them have been able to secure a job within one year after immigration (27 per cent), but many have undertaken entrepreneurial initiatives by developing export and import businesses between Australia and their home countries, in particular using online platforms for new business engagements.

Following an illustration of case studies of immigrant entrepreneurs in Australia, we focused on different generations of ethnic Chinese entrepreneurs' internationalization in Chapter 7, which is divided into three parts. The first part elaborated the earlier years (seventeenth to twentieth centuries) of ethnic Chinese entrepreneurs as the first generation, as well as their children and grand-children as the second and third generations, conducting their business activities overseas, predominately in the Southeast Asian region. The second part of Chapter 7 illustrated the more recent wave of Chinese entrepreneurs immigrating overseas from mainland China since the 1980s when new policy initiatives enabled Chinese citizens to run privately owned businesses (Zhu et al., 2010), leading to the emergence of a new class of entrepreneurs running their own businesses in China and overseas. The third part of this chapter discussed the new trend of transnationalism among overseas ethnic Chinese entrepreneurs who developed new business overseas and who 'returned home' by undertaking trade and investment in China using the links of their overseas host countries.

A number of implications of the above observations have been discussed. First, the evidence shows that the new generation of ethnic Chinese entrepreneurs do not follow the older generation in focusing on either the host country or home country as their business focus, but rather carrying out 'multiple-ways' of transnationalism. Generally speaking, the differences in ethnic identity, sense of belonging and ethnic ties among different generations as well as within younger generations of ethnic Chinese entrepreneurs have added complexity to the issue of transnationalism, which places emphasis on one way of presenting identity, ethnic ties and sense of belonging (Gomez & Benton, 2003). With regard to the effectiveness of social networks and business networks, the evidence identifies a common trend, namely in the early stage of business development in a foreign environment, new migrants tend to rely on social networks to conduct their business in a relatively safe and stable environment, and once their businesses become established with a possibility for expansion, a gradual transition is evident towards developing new business ties with other non-Chinese based networks, in particular main stream business networks. This leads to the consideration of expanding business connections beyond intro-ethnic groups through the engagement of inter-ethnic business networks as an important step for developing long-term growth among ethnic business entrepreneurs. We also observed a new phenomenon indicating that new generation entrepreneurs go beyond the boundary of 'Chinatown' by developing new business in main stream locations with cutting edge technology and high quality services. In addition, differences in ethnic identity and ties with China also lead to different kinds of business development, some being more host country oriented and others more home country oriented, while others may have focus on both ways or even multiple ways.

These interesting phenomena reflect on the changing world as well as changing individuals in responding to their surrounding environments, leading to the next chapter in this book, namely Chapter 8, which focused on another important ethnic group represented by ethnic Jewish entrepreneurs in the process of internationalization. Jewish communities in general, and ethnic Jewish entrepreneurs in particular, can be seen as a specific ethnic group that over the historical past has contributed more than proportionately to entrepreneurship. Evidence shows that Jews have had a comparative advantage (for example, priority on education) in occupations that require literacy or numeracy skills and that led to their specialization as merchants, traders and money lenders. During the earlier years in Italy with the growth of cities, new institutional environments allowed the development of financial institutions and enabling Jewish business development in the financial field due to Jews' readiness to provide the required knowledge and skills (Pascali, 2016). From the 1600s, many Jews were highly involved in trade and commerce in Amsterdam, Poland and Germany given the advantages of Jews in the areas of cross-cultural and linguistic communications as well as religious links with other parts of Europe, including Mid-East Europe (i.e. Russia, the Ottoman Empire and the Baltic countries). Two groups of Jews were engaged in particularly different businesses; namely, in South Europe the Sephardic Jews were actively engaged in cross-cultural trading, while in North and East Europe, the Ashkenazi Jews were involved in textile and tobacco trades, and later building railways across Europe, which heavily depended on the financial institutions being developed by many generations of Jewish bankers and financiers. However, Jews did not play a major role in the Industrial Revolution in the UK due to the low number of Jews living there. However, during the period between the late 1800s and early 1900s, a large portion of Jewish migrants went to the United States (Mokyr, 2011).

In comparison with the older generation of ethnic Jewish entrepreneurs, the new generation (i.e. the third) were better educated and earned higher incomes as successful entrepreneurs and highly skilled professionals. There are a number of similarities between ethnic Chinese and Jewish entrepreneurs in terms of entrepreneurial characteristics and generational differences. These observations have led us to the final section in this book which discussed a number of key fundamental issues with comparative perspectives as well as possible future research directions.

Discussion

We have responded to the key research questions with examples presented in the previous chapters and a number of case illustrations. In addressing these issues, we observed some similar as well as different patterns in two key areas, namely: (1) key research aspects regarding internationalization of entrepreneurship (i.e. the three key areas identified in Chapters 2 and 3); and (2) key similarities and differences between different generations of entrepreneurs and between different ethnic groups (i.e. historical evolution of entrepreneurial activities from the early generations operating businesses in different parts of the world in different ethnic groups in comparison with later generations of entrepreneurs in different ethnic groups). We summarize the first area in Table 9.1 and the second area in Table 9.2 in order to elaborate these in greater detail.

Table 9.1 illustrates the key research aspects and related themes and examples which have been presented in the previous chapters. With regard to the issue of entrepreneurial internationalization, we have identified a number of different types and models of entrepreneurial internationalization. For example, we have discussed immigrant entrepreneurs in Australia, highlighting cases of Italian and Vietnamese entrepreneurial activities. Other detailed examples have included Chinese and Jewish entrepreneurial activities in different countries/ regions.

The second theme in this research area is emerging market MNE and SME internationalization; we used the example of Chinese MNE and SME inter- nationalization. Pull and push factors have been discussed in detail in the rel- evant chapters, together with a number of implications that are significant for other emerging MNEs and SMEs engaging in internationalization, including selecting business model, entry mode, effectively obtaining support from a wide

Table 9.1 Illustrations of key research aspects with themes and examples

Key research aspects	Themes and examples presented in this book
Entrepreneurial internationalization	– Different types and models of entrepreneurial internationalization: e.g. immigrant entrepreneurs in Australia, Chinese and Jewish entrepreneurial activities in different countries/regions.
	– Emerging market MNE and SME internationalization: e.g. Chinese MNE and SME internationalization.
	– Causes and factors influencing the process of internationalization: e.g. survival-driven approach vs. developmental-driven approach in different contexts.
International comparison of entrepreneurship	– Comparing entrepreneurial activities in Australia, China, SE Asia and other Western countries among different groups of entrepreneurs, e.g. different ethnicity, age, location and time.
International comparison of entrepreneurial internationalization	– Comparing entrepreneurial internationalization activities in different countries and regions, e.g. SMEs in Australia, and Chinese and Jewish entrepreneurial internationalization with time differences (past vs. present) and generational differences.

range of stakeholders and controlling/managing resources, identifying and creating opportunities, and developing risk assessment and mitigation capabilities.

The third theme relates to the causes and factors influencing the process of entrepreneurial internationalization. Examples used included different approaches toward entrepreneurial internationalization, such as the survival-driven approach for certain types of entrepreneurs with particular contexts (e.g. earlier generation entrepreneurs, economic difficulty and lack of employment opportunity), in comparison with the developmental-driven approach for others in different contexts (e.g. better educated entrepreneurs with capability, financial resources and international connections).

In the preceding chapters, we also tackled the aspect of international comparison of entrepreneurship by comparing entrepreneurial activities in Australia, China, Southeast Asia and other Western countries among different groups of entrepreneurs, focusing on different ethnicity, age, location and time. The analysis is also linked with the aspect of the international comparison of entrepreneurial internationalization by comparing entrepreneurial internationalization activities in different countries and regions, such as SMEs in Australia, and Chinese and Jewish entrepreneurial internationalization with time differences (past vs. present) and generational differences. A number of meaningful outcomes have been presented and we summarize those outcomes in the following sections as well as in Table 9.2.

Table 9.2 illustrates the generational differences in the process of entrepreneurial internationalization with different ethnic and contextual backgrounds, history and locations. A number of key observations can be summarized here:

1   Most early generations of entrepreneurs (e.g. the first generation) chose entrepreneurial activity as a survival strategy given the lack of education, resources and employment opportunities. These entrepreneurs relied on community support in the beginning stages of their businesses, such as kinship and ethnic networks as well as community-based credit associations, for doing business. Therefore, intra-ethnic business operations dominated their entrepreneurial activities.

2   Younger generations of entrepreneurs (e.g. the second and third generations) tended to be better educated with family-accumulated resources as well as individual professional knowledge and skills. Undertaking entrepreneur activities could be seen as a matter of choice, rather than a necessity, in comparison with their older counterparts. Although kinship and ethnic networks (including credit associations) played an important role in business success, the younger generations could develop business ties and rely on business networks beyond their own ethnic communities (i.e. they were capable of developing co-ethnic group identities and of building multi-ethnic networks). Hence, kinship and ethnic networks become less significant in achieving business success compared to the situation of older entrepreneurs.

3   The current generation of entrepreneurs who start new businesses in the current wave of globalization, indicates a number of unique characteristics;

for example, many were educated overseas with good knowledge, global mind-set and cross-cultural capability. Many new born-global start-ups have been developed by the current generation as well as new patterns of trans-nationalism have been engaged by building business ties and developing entrepreneurial activities between home country and other host countries. Ethnic identity and ethnic ties have become less significant but new ideas and cutting edge technology have become crucial for business success.

Therefore, according to the development trajectory of different generations of ethnic entrepreneurs, we observe different patterns and trends of trans-nationalism. Our findings show that the new generation of ethnic entrepren-eurs do not follow the older generation in focusing either on the host country or the home country as their business focus, but undertake 'multiple-way' transnationalism. Generally speaking, the differences in ethnic identity, sense of belonging and ethnic ties among different generations as well as within the younger generation of entrepreneurs have added complexity to the argument regarding transnationalism, which emphasizes one specific way of presenting identity, ethnic ties and a sense of belonging (Gomez & Benton, 2003).

The above interesting phenomena reflect the changing world and influence indi-viduals in their response to their surrounding environments through the develop-ment of entrepreneurial activities locally, internationally and transnationally. The next concluding section will focus on future research areas with regard to the internationalization of entrepreneurship.

Table 9.2 Illustrations of generational differences in the process of entrepreneurial inter-nationalization

Generations	Business contexts and entrepreneur's characteristics presented in this book
Early generation (e.g. first generation)	– The first generation immigrant entrepreneurs in Australia, e.g. Italian and Vietnamese ethnic entrepreneurs: e.g. entrepreneurial activities for survival; low level of skills but hard-working; initial community-based support with later expansion to inter-ethnic business ties. – The first generation of Chinese immigrant entrepreneurs in SE Asia: e.g. facing tough business environments in a foreign land; low level of skills but hard-working; entrepreneurial activities for survival; ethnic ties support business with rotating credit; building business based on social ties first and then gradually expanding to other business ties via co-ethnic networks. – The early generation of Jewish entrepreneurs in Europe: e.g. good education foundation advantaged early generation of Jewish entrepreneurs in finance and cross-country trade; ethnic ties supported business with financial support; inter-ethnic business ties were fundamental for business success from the beginning.

Continued

Table 9.2 continued

Generations	Business contexts and entrepreneur's characteristics presented in this book
Later generations (e.g. second and third generations)	– Entrepreneurial capability-building via business experience and education as well as accumulated wealth enabled the second and third generations to choose either continuing family business or developing a different career beyond those parameters, many became professionals in other fields although they were the later generations of Italian and Vietnamese immigrants in Australia, or the Chinese and Jewish second and third generations in other parts of the world. Later generational entrepreneurs were well-educated with more technological knowledge and a global mind-set. These characteristics enabled them to develop business with cutting edge technology and target international markets rather than local markets.
Current generation	The current generation of entrepreneurs are those who have started new business in the current wave of globalization. Many of them were educated overseas with good knowledge, a global mind-set and cross-cultural capability. Many new born-global start-ups have been developed by this generation, while engaging in new patterns of transnationalism by building business ties and developing entrepreneurial activities between home country and other host countries. Ethnic identity and ethnic ties become less significant but new ideas and cutting edge technology are crucial for business success.

Conclusion

Research on the internationalization of entrepreneurship is still in its infancy with many unclear and uncertain issues and approaches as discussed in the preceding chapters. Therefore, further comprehensive research is required, with a holistic perspective by combining multiple areas, including philosophical, historical, cultural, social, political and economic domains in order to form and shape the area of internationalization of entrepreneurship. The research direction could focus on the similarities and differences among different ethnic entrepreneurial groups as well as between different generations. The focus should be on key elements of cultural mechanisms, individual characteristics and entrepreneur activities and behaviour embedded in the different contexts. A number of specific issues could be the key themes for future research:

1 To what extent does former work experience in general, and entrepreneurial experience in particular, help the development of sustainable business?
2 How do different ethnic entrepreneurial groups and different generations of entrepreneurs build social and business networks with different philosophical, cultural and social domains underpinnings?

3 How can innovative capabilities and proactive behaviours be developed in order to cope with risks and uncertainties effectively?
4 What kind of evidence-based research is required to illustrate particular internal and external factors determining effective decision-making?
5 How can entrepreneurs pursue opportunities beyond the currently controlled resources?
6 How do different schools of thought influence the antecedent to and outcomes of the above questions and other research questions that explore and examine entrepreneurship and internationalization?

Clearly, many issues could be developed as future research themes, and we have listed these key areas based on our observations and findings in this book. However, one important conclusion of this comparative analysis is that there is no single model that explains how to develop entrepreneurial internationalization effectively. The different examples identify certain similar but also different characteristics due to the different paths of development in economic, social, political and cultural realms. This heterogeneity once again establishes the importance of contextual contingencies at various levels (e.g. individual, local, national, international and transnational) and at different times. The implicit expectations of what an entrepreneur looks like and how an entrepreneur behaves are not always consistent with stereotypical entrepreneur-like traits and behaviours. The complexity is further exacerbated by the expansion of Western-derived best practices and management philosophies which often encounter challenges from indigenous ways of thinking and doing, making partial adoption and continuous modification a reality. We thus hope that this book can contribute to the dialogue and debate between the Eastern and Western ways of thinking and acting with regard to the internationalization of entrepreneurship and the future development of entrepreneurship globally.

References

Coviello, N., Kano, L. & Liesch, P. W. (2017) Adapting the Uppsala model to a modern world: Macro-context and microfoundations. *Journal of International Business Studies*, 48(9): 1151–1164.

Gomez, E. T. & Benton, G. (2003) Transnationalism and the essentializing of capitalism: Chinese enterprise, the state, and identity in Britain, Australia, and Southeast Asia. *East Asia*, Winter: 3–28.

Jones, M. V., Coviello, N. & Tang, Y. (2011) International entrepreneurship research (1989–2009): A domain ontology and thematic analysis. *Journal of Business Venturing*, 26(6): 632–659.

Levitt, P. (2001) *The Transnational Villagers.* Berkeley, CA: University of California Press.

Liu, Y. (2017) Born global firms' growth and collaborative entry mode: The role of transnational entrepreneurs. *Marketing Review*, 34(1): 46–67.

Mokyr, J. (2011) The economics of being Jewish, *Critical Review*, 23(1–2): 95–206.

Pascali, L (2016) Banks and development: Jewish communities in the Italian Renaissance and current economic performance, posted online 4 March 2016, www.mitpressjournals. org/doi/abs/10.1162/REST_a_00481 [accessed 20 August 2018].

Portes, A. & Guarnizo, L. E. (1991) Tropical capitalists: U.S.-bound immigration and small enterprise development in the Dominican Republic, in S. Diaz-Briquets & S. Weintraub (eds), *Migration, Remittances, and Small Business Development: Mexico and Caribbean Basin Countries*, Boulder, CO: Westview Press, pp. 101–131.

Razin, E. (2002) The economic context, embeddedness and immigrant entrepreneurs. *International Journal of Entrepreneurial Behaviour & Research*, 8(1/2): 162–167.

Waldinger, R., Aldrich, H. & Ward, R. (1990) *Ethnic Entrepreneurs: Immigrant Business in Industrial Societies*. London: Sage.

Wang, R. (2012) Chinese culture and its potential influence on entrepreneurship. *International Business Research*, 5(10): 76–90.

Yan, H., Wickramasekera, R. & Tan, A. (2018) Exploration of Chinese SMEs' export development: The role of managerial determinants based on an adapted innovation related internationalization model. *Thunderbird International Business Review*, 60(4): 633–646.

Yeung, H. W. C. (2002) Entrepreneurship in international business: An institutional perspective. *Asia Pacific Journal of Management*, 19(1): 29–61.

Zhou, M. (2004) Revisiting ethnic entrepreneurship: Convergences, controversies, and conceptual advancements. *International Migration Review*, 38(3): 1040–1074.

Zhu, Y., Webber, M. & Benson, J. (2010) *The Everyday Impact of Economic Reform in China: Management Change, Enterprise Performance and Daily Life.* London and New York: Routledge.

Index

Page numbers in **bold** denote tables, those in *italics* denote figures.

Printed in the United States
by Baker & Taylor Publisher Services